The IET Book Series on Advances in Distributed Computing and Blockchain Technologies

Call for authors' page.

The objective of this book series is to enlighten researchers with the current trends in the field of blockchain technology and its integration with distributed computing and systems. Blockchains show riveting features such as decentralization, verifiability, fault tolerance, transparency, and accountability. The technology enables more secure, transparent, and traceable scenarios to assist in distributed applications. We plan to bring forward the technological aspects of blockchain technology for Internet of Things (IoTs), cloud computing, edge computing, fog computing, wireless sensor networks (WSNs), peer-to-peer (P2P) networks, mobile edge computing, and other distributed network paradigms for real-world enhanced and evolving future applications of distributed computing and systems.

Topics to be covered include: distributed computing and its applications; distributed vs. decentralized systems; tools and platforms for distributed systems; performance evaluation of distributed applications; blockchain technologies; blockchains and application domains; blockchains vs. distributed systems; cryptocurrency and distributed ledger technology; blockchain and IoT; ubiquitous computing; pervasive computing; cloud, edge, and fog computing; Internet of Things (IoT) technology; security issues in IoT; software tools and platforms for implementing blockchains in IoT networks; performance optimization of blockchain technology for distributed systems; social and ethical impacts of blockchains in distributed applications; blockchain technology and sustainability.

Proposals for international coherently integrated multi-authored or edited books, handbooks, and research monographs will be considered for this book series. We do not endorse, however, call for chapter books. The chapter authors will be invited personally and individually by the book editors. Each proposal will be reviewed by the book series editors with additional peer reviews from independent reviewers. Please contact:

– Dr Brij B. Gupta, National Institute of Technology (NIT), India; e-mail: gupta.brij@ieee.org
– Prof. Gregorio Martinez Perez, University of Murcia (UMU), Spain; e-mail: gregorio@um.es
– Dr Tu N. Nguyen, Kennesaw State University of Georgia, USA; e-mail: tu.nguyen@kennesaw.edu

Blockchain Technology for Secure Social Media Computing

Edited by
Robin Singh Bhadoria, Neetesh Saxena and
Bharti Nagpal

The Institution of Engineering and Technology

Published by The Institution of Engineering and Technology, London, United Kingdom

The Institution of Engineering and Technology is registered as a Charity in England & Wales (no. 211014) and Scotland (no. SC038698).

The Institution of Engineering and Technology
Futures Place
Kings Way, Stevenage
Hertfordshire SG1 2UA, United Kingdom

www.theiet.org

British Library Cataloguing in Publication Data
A catalogue record for this product is available from the British Library

ISBN 978-1-83953-543-7 (hardback)
ISBN 978-1-83953-544-4 (PDF)

Typeset in India by MPS Limited

Cover Image: MF3d / E+ via Getty Images

Contents

6 Privacy provisioning on blockchain transactions of decentralized social media

Rohit Saxena, Deepak Arora, Vishal Nagar
and Brijesh Kumar Chaurasia

7 Blockchain-based knowledge graph for high-impact scientific collaboration networks

Yao Yao, Meghana Kshirsagar, Gauri Vaidya, Junying Liu,
Yongliang Zhang and Conor Ryan

Preface

Today's era of computation demands secure and trusted networks to keep information or data along distributed networks. The blockchain technology helps in moderating the solution for such demand. The blockchain can be referred as distributed ledger technology (DLT) and is stored to keep the history of transactions (digital records) in the form of blocks. It is kind of advanced database mechanism which allows information to be shared among multiple stakeholders in a transparent and distributed network.

This technology is able to secure social networks using distributed ledger and peer-to-peer cryptography. Its popularity has been increasing with the growth of social media and the Internet of Things (IoT). This edited book covers the following issues:

- Social media computing security in mobile and wireless communication, such as 5G over multimedia communication.
- Authentication of the legitimacy of content in online social media (OSM).
- Blockchain-based decentralized online social networking.
- Blockchain as secure mediation for central knowledge graph (KG) through artificial intelligence (AI) algorithms in Internet of Things (IoT).
- Next-generation computing of the era for better communication in social networks.

Chapter 1 discusses the ways of communicating with online social media (OSM) that have transformed and gained popularity in the life of users globally. Ever since their inception, OSMs have succeeded to infiltrate 4.48 billion people worldwide and there is an increased drift perennially highly influencing the privacy issues in OSMs. Even before the COVID-19 outbreak, OSMs were struggling to overcome issues such as censorship, privacy and user control. To resolve the significant issues in OSMs, decentralization of social services is considered a potential solution and blockchain technology at present is one of the most prominent techniques for the decentralization of online social platforms.

Chapter 2 discusses the use of distributed ledger-based payment infrastructure for fast processing, such as App payment security. This can help in the prevention of the data from any fraud or a security breach and improves payment security significantly. This chapter also argues the authenticating legitimacy of social network content. Blockchain technology helps in achieving transparency in the payment to enhance the overall systems. It also supports the role of an online business-to-business marketplace in trust formation using different policies and monitoring rules.

Chapter 3 provides the study focuses on the design, model and handling concerns associated with social networks. The study presents different types of social networks that have emerged due to the advancement of the Internet. This work also debates the challenges occurring in social networks with the increasing demand for their uses. It provided a list of different security threats and promising solutions for securing social media and the spread of fake news over a social environment. This chapter delivers different design factors for social networks according to user preferences, which will be quite interesting to the readers.

Chapter 4 examines the emerging trends in social networking platforms and mentioned the existing solutions to security risks that affect social networking platforms in today's social networks. Social networking platforms have become a hub for exchanging job searching, entertainment and educational information among people. These platforms offer a smooth flow of these services from one geographical border to another by allowing users to update their data, interact with each other and browse other users' profiles. However, sharing personal information over social networking platforms creates security and privacy issues for their users. This chapter provides a thorough examination of several security risks affecting Internet users along with the challenges social networking platforms face in numerous fields.

Chapter 5 provides insights into the development of the IoTs, virtual reality, artificial intelligence, and blockchain technologies in the world's rapid digital transition. The role of machine learning (ML) tools employ the data that users generate while using these technologies to make decisions. These choices support geotagging photographs, proposing music to users, boosting photobook authoring through extensive multimedia analysis and analyzing user preferences in games and brands. This chapter discusses how blockchain technology can be utilized to protect privacy in the decentralized social network's blockchain-based framework.

Chapter 6 demonstrates the privacy provisioning in blockchain for transactions of decentralized social media as well as the privacy of the identities of the members. This chapter provides a comprehensive study of privacy provisioning on blockchain. In the existing literature, there are a variety of scalability, security, and privacy concerns with Blockchain, including key management for recovery, on-chain privacy protection, transaction linkability, and adherence to privacy laws. These solutions allow users to anonymize themselves in all types of electronic transfer ledgers and regain control of their personal information.

Chapter 7 discusses a framework that leverages the intelligence of the crowd to improve the quality, credibility, inclusiveness, long-term impact, and adoption of research, particularly in the academic space. This integrated platform revolves around a central knowledge graph (KG) which interacts through AI algorithms with the community. In combination with IoT and blockchain technologies, a highly productive environment including liquid governance and arbitration is created to fairly acknowledge and attractively incentivize contributions of valuable intellectual property (IP) to this knowledge base.

Chapter 8 provides the integration of blockchain (BC) technology with 5G networks which is a newly emerging area. Driven by the dramatically increased capacity of 5G networks and recent breakthroughs in BC technology. Multimedia communication can potentially reach a wide range of areas and touch people's lives in profound and different ways. In recent years, great progress has been made in defining approaches, architectures, standards, and solutions. 5G applications have evolved significantly, including voice, video, wireless, information access, and social interaction networks. More interestingly, BC helps establish secure multimedia communication among users and potentially reduces communication latency, transaction costs, and provides global accessibility for all users.

Chapter 9 reflects with the purpose to investigate different trends in the adoption of blockchain-related approaches and advancements in an IoT environment and platform. It also introduces blockchain benefits along with the underlying concerns that the examination network has with the seamless integration of Blockchain and IoT. It also highlights the key unresolved problems and directions for future research. This chapter provides the design of an IoT and blockchain-based framework to secure intellectual property.

Chapter 10 provides insight into the existing vote-cast system using Blockchain technology. The current state-of-art of blockchain architecture for voting-cast systems is presented. The blockchain architecture fundamental concepts and its characteristics are discussed with respect to the social opinion vote-cast system.

Chapter 11 delivers a survey and analysis of one of the fast-evolving technologies called blockchain technology. It also covers all essential information required for a beginner to venture into this complicated field while also covering necessary concepts that can be useful for next-generation computing of the era. This chapter ends with a discussion on the most notable subset of innovative blockchain applications – smart contracts, decentralized autonomous organizations (DAOs), and super safe networks – and their future implications.

Chapter 12 demonstrates the social media computing aspects of healthcare that is fairly important and equally beneficial to a large extent. This chapter also addresses the adoption of blockchain technology in healthcare security and prevents fraud activities. Blockchain technology is transparent, ensures confidentiality and secure platform for social media computing related to personal and political aspects also supports the trends related to health issues.

Chapter 13 concludes all chapters with more on future perspectives and research directions in the field of security framework for social media computing using Blockchain technology.

Robin Singh Bhadoria
Neetesh Saxena
Bharti Nagpal

Foreword

The objective of this book series is to enlighten researchers with the current trends in the field of blockchain technology and its integration with distributed computing and systems. Blockchains show riveting features such as decentralization, verifiability, fault tolerance, transparency, and accountability. The technology enables more secure, transparent, and traceable scenarios to assist in distributed applications. We plan to bring forward the technological aspects of blockchain technology for Internet of Things (IoTs), cloud computing, edge computing, fog computing, wireless sensor networks (WSNs), peer-to-peer (P2P) networks, mobile edge computing, and other distributed network paradigms for real-world enhanced and evolving future applications of distributed computing and systems.

We are honored to write the foreword of this first book in our book series. This valuable contribution to the field of blockchain technology and social media computing will serve as a useful reference for those seeking to deepen their understanding of this rapidly evolving field and inspire further research and innovation. The authors have provided insightful and thought-provoking perspectives on the current state and future potential of blockchain technology in social media computing, and we are confident that this book will be a valuable resource for years to come.

As the world becomes more interconnected and reliant on technology, social media has emerged as a ubiquitous tool for communication, entertainment, and commerce. However, the centralized nature of many social media platforms has led to concerns about data privacy, security, and content moderation. With the rise of fake news, privacy breaches, and centralized control, the need for a more secure and decentralized social media platform has never been greater. In recent years, blockchain technology has emerged as a potential solution to many of these challenges, offering a decentralized and secure platform for social media computing.

The book *Blockchain Technology for Secure Social Media Computing* provides a comprehensive overview of blockchain technology's use in social media computing. With contributions from experts in the field, the book covers a wide range of topics, from the basics of blockchain technology to its applications in social media computing and emerging trends in the field. In addition, this book provides a comprehensive overview of the latest technologies, and applications of blockchain in online social media. From blockchain-based security for social media computing to emerging trends in social networking design, models, and handling, the authors cover a broad range of topics to address the challenges and opportunities of blockchain technology in the social media sphere.

The chapters are written by leading researchers and academics who share their experience and knowledge to provide readers with a practical understanding of how blockchain technology can be leveraged to build a more secure, transparent, and decentralized social media platform. It is an essential guide for researchers, practitioners, and students who are interested in learning more about blockchain technology and its potential to transform social media computing.

Prof. Brij B. Gupta, Director, CCRI & Professor, Department of Computer Science and Information Engineering, Asia University, Taichung, Taiwan

Prof. Gregorio Martinez Perez, Department of Information and Communication Engineering, University of Murcia, Spain.

Dr Tu N. Nguyen, Department of Computer Science, Kennesaw State University, Georgia, USA.

About the editors

Dr. Robin Singh Bhadoria is currently working as an associate professor in the Department of Computer Engineering & Applications at GLA University, Mathura, Uttar Pradesh, India. His current areas of interest cover the fields of big data analytics, service-oriented architecture, Internet of Things, wireless sensor networks, biometric computing and blockchain technology. He has authored or edited several research books on emerging technologies. He is an active member of IEEE (USA), IE (India), IAENG (HK), Internet Society (USA), and IETE (India).

Dr. Neetesh Saxena is currently working as an assistant professor in the School of Computer Science and Informatics at Cardiff University, UK. His areas of interest are cyber security and critical infrastructure security, including cyber-physical system security, IoT security, blockchain and cellular networks. He is a European Initiative Expert Visitor to Singapore by EPIC – European Pacific Partnership for ICT and is collaborating with Thales and Toshiba on industrial control cybersecurity.

Bharti Nagpal is working as an assistant professor in the Department of Computer Science and Engineering at Netaji Subhas University of Technology, New Delhi, India. She has more than 20 years of teaching experience. Her areas of interest are in information security, web technologies, big data analytics, data mining, social media computing, Internet of Things, machine learning and image processing. She has contributed to several book chapters.

Chapter 1

The blockchain technologies in online social media: insights, technologies, and applications

Mitali Chugh[1] and Neeraj Chugh[2]

Abstract

Online social media (OSMs) have transformed the way of communication and have gained popularity in the life of users globally. Ever since their inception in 1996, OSMs have succeeded to infiltrate 4.48 billion people worldwide and there is an increased drift perennially highly influencing the privacy issues in OSMs. For example, the distribution of misleading information on OSMs as the platform is incapable to moderate the content successfully. It has been witnessed in recent times of the COVID-19 epidemic that OSNs have permitted individuals to spread fake news on diverse social media platforms. Even before the COVID-19 outbreak, OSMs were struggling to overcome issues such as censorship, privacy, and user control. To solve the significant issues in OSMs decentralization of social services is considered a potential solution and blockchain technology at present is the most prominent technique for decentralization of online social platforms. However, a dearth of studies extensively discussing the merits of blockchain technology for OSMs. This chapter presents an overview of concerns related to traditional OSMs and explores what happens when blockchain is incorporated in OSMs emphasizing the prominent services and features of a few trending OSM platforms based on blockchain technology.

Keywords: Blockchain; Online social media platforms; Decentralized social media

1.1 Introduction

Online social media (OSMs) are a significant part of everyone's life and have transformed the way of communication. It provides a platform to share personal

[1]Cybernetics Cluster, School of Computer Science, University of Petroleum and Energy Studies (UPES), India
[2]Systemics Cluster, School of Computer Science, University of Petroleum and Energy Studies (UPES), India

information as a routine affair. Internet and social media users have grown exponentially giving importance to the management of privacy issues. For example, spreading deception on social media as there is a lack of content moderation effectively. This has been witnessed in recent times in the COVID-19 epidemic that social media has permitted individuals and groups to spread fabricated news broadcast on diverse social media platforms. The present centralized OSMs have a server that stores information about all the users which may lead to loss of data due to theft or crash of the server.

Cambridge Analytica, the Scandal on Facebook involved 87 million users who used an application distributed on Facebook, and the profiles of users along with friends were gathered. The gathered data was provided to Cambridge Analytica to analyze it for a political goal that is a privacy disclosure. Similar scenarios have steered social services toward decentralization. A Distributed Online Social Network (DOSN) [1] is a distributed platform based on P2P systems and trusted servers. Many other such DOSNs have been proposed in the last decade [2,3]. Although decentralized systems have been drastically transformed in the preceding years, specifically when incorporating blockchain technology to overcome issues relating to centralization.

As blockchain professionals endure to contemplate technological advancement, commercial models, and freedom of speech, blockchain has developed as a sustainable solution for resolving various problems, together with social media. Social media at all times has been a way to establish social communications for large masses, and in present-day, blockchain technology-based platforms are fascinating billions of people worldwide. Social media based on blockchain technology are decentralized platforms facilitating smart contracts and application development that provide end-to-end encryption to each communication enabling users to have information control and confidentiality. These platforms also offer to crowdfund, and in-platform transactions, and the users have access to special offers. A chain of blocks or public distributed ledger of records that the communicating individuals or groups share is a blockchain. The dearth of success and the surge of glitches regarding OSMs, such as data disclosure or forged news have been the prime inspiration to integrate blockchain into social media platforms. However, the actual advantage of bringing together blockchain and social media platforms is yet blurred, for the reason that the performance of these platforms is indefinite owing to the deficiency of a real investigation.

In this chapter, we intend to present an overview of the blockchain-based OSMs and their features. The research questions that the present work addresses are:

1. What are the issues related to traditional social media?
2. How blockchain does facilitate social media?
3. What are the benefits of decentralized social platforms?

In addition, we mention the leading blockchain social networks, and finally, we conclude the chapter by providing open problems, conclusions, and future works.

1.2 Blockchain-based social media: insights from literature

Various studies in the literature have discussed the significance of Blockchain in social media taking into account the various perspectives. Tee *et al.* (2019) suggest in their work that blockchain technology with advanced AI in social media platforms can efficiently validate news content for its trustworthiness [4]. Paul *et al.* have proposed a method to detect fake news on social media platforms. The system performs the calculations based on blockchain, BFS, and smart contract concepts and provides the ranking to the news on a scale of 1 to 5 [5]. Choi *et al.* in their study have provided insights on the use of social media analytics for supply chain operations management. They have compared the traditional social media platforms to blockchain-based platforms for accuracy, security, user privacy, etc., and have concluded that blockchain-based OSM platforms offer a more sophisticated environment that can enhance social media analytics for supply chain operations management [6]. Grover *et al.* concluded from the academic literature and social media based on their classification of industries into five stages of the innovation-decision process, namely, knowledge, persuasion, decision, implementation, and confirmation that actual applications of blockchain technology are yet in its early stages for most of the businesses [7]. Ochoa *et al.* proposed a framework that incorporates a blockchain for the fake news detection process. The main attribute of the framework is data mining usage as a consensus algorithm to validate the facts available on social networks. Using the proposed framework, it is possible to ascertain fake news, intimate readers, punish those who float fake information, and provide an incentive to those who publish true information on the network [8]. Mnif *et al.* focus on the acceptance drivers mapping for the blockchain technology by envisioning the users' insights constructs through blockchain hashtags. The findings reveal that users have more concerned about shareability, security, and decentralization attributes [9].

1.3 Blockchain: a facilitator for social media

Privacy and security issues have always been highlighted in the traditional social media platforms that have been predominantly used by billions of people and have transformed the method of communication. The traditional social media platforms namely Twitter, Facebook, etc. have entire control over users, groups, or business data. Also, a complete track of users' activity is maintained due to centralized social networking. The aggregated user profile and activity data are sold to the top bidder which is then used for marketing and advertising drives. As all platforms such as Twitter and Facebook are centralized, they exploit the user's content to a large extent. Blockchain facilitates overcoming the security and privacy issues of OSM platforms in the following ways.

1.3.1   *Freedom of expression and information privacy*

The privacy and security of user data is a big concern on OSM platforms due to its centralized technique to store it. Additionally, content mailed or forwarded on such platforms is employed often for political advantages and to restrain conflict. For an instance in 2020, there was a crypto-related scam in which Twitter accounts of some influential people were hacked including Joe Biden, Elon Musk, and Warren Buffet.

Blockchain-based social media platforms safeguard better confidentiality and let users express themselves at will. The transaction contents are in private shared between sender and receiver using distributed ledger technology.

1.3.2   *Permanency of saving user content*

In the centralized environment offered by traditional OSM platforms, shared data of users can be modified and deleted by anyone without the user's approval. Blockchain offers a decentralized social media platform "Minds" that uses an immutable ledger NS that enables users to have complete control over their shared content permanently, confirming that no one can remove it after it is published. However, the users have the right to delete all the earlier activities if they decide to do so.

1.3.3   *Content producers to acquire money for generating and sharing owned content*

Blockchain-based social media platforms let users have thorough control over their content in the aspect that where and how it can be shared. The distribution know-how offers them the enhanced capability to get the return from the production of passive income.

As discussed, blockchain OSMs offer the solutions to the challenges in traditional social media platforms. The fundamental concepts that are to be incorporated to develop an improved social media network are open-source code that helps to inspect data algorithms, decentralized control, democratic decision capability, and explainable AI for digital transformation to describe the whys and wherefores behind every decision.

1.4   Blockchain-based OSM proposals

At the present day, there are diverse research fields in which blockchain technology finds its applications, one of them is blockchain-based social media. Various blockchain-based social media platforms have been suggested [10,11] and many platforms are in the developing phase. However, a few such as SteemIt have exceeded even one million users [12]. The following four points characterize the main features of these platforms:

- *Lack of censorship*: The decentralization assists to eliminate censorship although users can be tracked using IP address, location, etc.
- *Lack of single-point of failure*: Traditional platforms for social media have centralized control that increases their vulnerability to attacks namely hacks,

and data breaches, on the other hand, blockchain-based social media have distributed control i.e. there is no single point of failure and data tampering is also avoided as each of the transactions is traced.

• *Valuable content rewards*: A user or generator on social media who creates valuable content can get cryptocurrencies in form of rewards. This process of rewarding blockchain facilitates by providing the process through which transactions are tracked and reviewed. This is among the salient features of blockchain-based OSM as rewarding is the successful way to assign value to the content, construct an economy model, etc.

• *Content authenticity*: In present OSMs, there is no authenticity check, and users are unprotected from fake news. As a replacement, blockchain technology usage is beneficial to deal with this issue through economic incentive to individually reward and rank content.

The blockchain OSMs platforms are built on the above-stated four concepts. The features that overcome each of the issues are: decentralization facilitates avoiding a single point of failure, immutability in blockchain platforms eliminates no censorship problem. The rewarding system enhances the content authenticity and mechanisms to ensure the same is in place.

The following section is about the main blockchain-based OSM platforms (BOSMs) that cover their salient features and their ways of overcoming the drawbacks of present online social networks.

In the past few years, several BOSMs [13] have been proposed that comprise a robust rewarding system. One of the primary features of BOSMs includes addressing privacy issues and detecting fake news.

1.4.1   SteemIt

SteemIt (Figure 1.1) [14] is an OSM platform that offers the Steem cryptocurrency [15] as a reward to the content creators and has more than one million users [16]. SteemIt offers Steem, Steem Power, and Steem Dollars as its currency units. Out of the three, Steem is the prime cryptocurrency and Steem Power and Steem Dollar are based on it. The users having Steem Power are bound to keep it for not less than 2 years and hold the network ownership. Steem Dollars is steady i.e. its value remains the same and offers flexibility to users who can sell it at any time. The three governing principles of SteemIt are stated in a white paper by Scott and Larimer (2017) [17] that states the chief governing principle is that the content creators receive the payment of dues from the venture. In addition, the principles talk about the value of capital which is considered valuable in all forms. SteemIt is a completely distributed platform for social media applications that do not have a single point of failure issue. Graphene [18] is the building block of Steem that can withstand 1,000 transactions/second in a test network.

1.4.2   SocialX

SocialX (Figure 1.2) [15] is decentralized and permits users to provide feedback on the content and earn tokens as rewards. SocialX has 10 features that are lacking in traditional social networks.

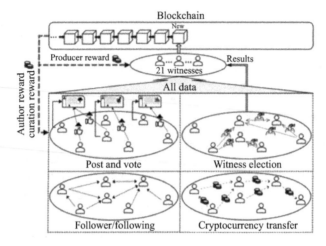

Figure 1.1   SteemIt blockchain overview [14]

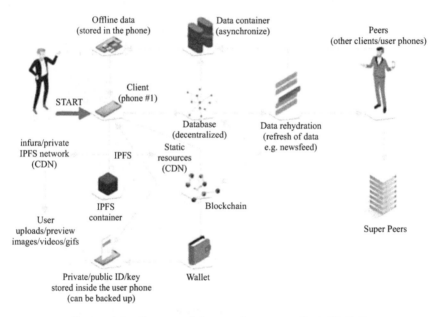

Figure 1.2   Process of decentralization in SocialX [16]

- It has the provision to separate fake likes, fake accounts, and fake followers. The community chooses the value of the content.
- It can influence and generate a large portion of high-quality content very fast.
- The significance of the platform is handled by the users.
- Accomplishes trustworthiness of data with blockchain technology with lesser budgets.

- It supports decentralized photos and videos.
- Each video or photo is assigned a monetized worth.
- It has a mechanism for managing rights and licenses of videos/photos.
- A reward system exists that provides SocialX tokens to the community.
- Form a huge community about what people like the most videos/photos.
- The valuable content is rewarded unbiased.

1.4.3   Sapien

It is a decentralized social news platform based on the Ethereum blockchain. Users have the authority for information control that they obtain by adapting to received news with their interest. Interesting characteristics of the platform comprise customization support and reward for the creators of content without the involvement of any central authorities. Moreover, the cryptocurrency for the Sapien platform is called SPN token which is built on a proof of value consensus mechanism for differentiating good network contents.

Content authenticity is one of the distinctive attributes of Sapien. The users who are found to have been found guilty of unauthorized content disclosure have their account proscribed, tokens 100% frozen and IP addresses permanently outlawed. The proof of value rewarding system facilitates the prevention of fake news. The user contributions are assessed based on which users accrue a score that reveals their repute. The SPN tokens characterize the reputation score that has an initial value of one and keeps on adding as the score grows. The reward distribution process is called charges that are based on voting. The greater number of charges denote the post as significant or valuable [17].

1.4.4   Hyperspace

Hyperspace is an ecosystem based on the attention economy as its rewarding model. There are community-owned spaces that are designed for letting users share their valuable content. The attention economy is a subcategory of the information economy in which customers accept services in exchange for their attention. The attention is based on both the quality and the quantity of the information [18]. Hyperspace uses AMP as its cryptocurrency although it does not describe an exhaustive rewarding system. When a user learns interesting online content, the Attention Economy Layer assists to spend a definite quantity of AMPs and share it with other users on the platform. Amplification is the process in which users share the content with other users and those who receive the link click on the link can see the content. As a result, one-third of the payment goes to the curator and another one-third goes to the user who has shared the content, the rest is kept in fractal reverse i.e. a common pool [13]. The data is stored in Interplanetary File System (IPFS), the decentralized cloud space, and the most active users are identified using the "User Power" that increases every time the user is involved in the event and decays over time. The main shortcoming of the system is its limitation to decentralization where at the beginning the content is uploaded to a server and then distributed to the other IPFS servers. The latest version of Hyperspace that was introduced in 2019 is based on the bitcoin blockchain on which an Omnilayer has been built and the transactions carried out are the bitcoin transactions.

1.5   Summary and open problems

Unlike the blockchain applications such as Bit Congress (Voting System) and Ethereum, Bitcoin blockchain-based OSMs do not involve the loss of hardware or money for making a profit. The key idea is to provide thought-provoking and meaningful content with the tokens that are making an impact in the network. In this section the main concerns that are related to blockchain-based OSMs platforms are listed:

- Identity testing is one of the most significant problems for blockchain-based OSMs where a user can register any number of times without any check for the identity and it has now become a serious concern in this domain. For instance, to elude Sybil attacks SteemIt offered a solution at inception where people having more tokens dictate trending feed damaged the system's ability to find out the best content. Hence, the resolution of the misuse issue but delivering good content to the users is so far to be established and implemented.
- *Content visibility*: The content visibility is public for blockchain-based OSM proposals. This is an advantage for the monetization of the content, however, it is not good for the socialization of users that need support for both public and private communications.
- *Decentralization of content*: The issue of blockchain usage as storage is that the content to be stored could be quite large and thus the blockchain-based OSMs support distributed storage. This is analogous to the preceding methodologies suggested in DOSNs [1], in which Distributed Hash Tables are used to store or index content. The issue of data control is however not addressed in this scenario as the users have to rely on other users who store data.
- *Scalability*: The user activity occurs at a very high frequency in OSMs and thus blockchain social platforms must consider the voluminous content generation by acknowledging the issue of discovering a scalable blockchain technology.
- *Blockchain technology*: The blockchain-based OSM proposals have Ethereum as their component, however, it has drawbacks when selected. The solution is yet to be identified to select the best blockchain technology and consensus algorithm for catering to the needs of the users that require a longer session [19,20].
- *No censorship*: The content that is available on the blockchain-based OSMs has no check-in legal aspect. Although it does not require centralized control, as the involvement of the user can assist in retrieving the illegitimate content. The published content is stored in a blockchain that is immutable and hence content deletion is not possible. There is a possibility that a bar is put on users; however, the content is still accessible. This is a great concern that has to be sorted out for no censorship implemented in those systems.

These open issues characterize problems in the real world and do not provide a strong impetus to the requirement of blockchain as storage or as backing to deliver a community vision of the content.

1.6 Conclusion

Blockchain technology is among the leading technology of the millennium. Several research arenas intend to employ it by developing its fundamental attributes. In this chapter, we have presented an account of blockchain-based OSMs presenting their key technical and social perspective. The studies in the literature have proposed models that propose the solution for the problems that have been discussed above in Section 1.4. Fu and Fang (2016) have proposed an algorithm for a decentralized personal data management system at MIT media labs to implement the "decentralizing privacy" and develop the existing system [21]. In the same aspect of privacy of sensitive data, Zang *et al.* have developed a blockchain-based privacy-preserving framework that uses public-key cryptography along with blockchain to facilitate secure data accessibility, sharing, and retrieving with fairmindedness and without perturbing possible loss to users' interest [22]. Rahman *et al.* have proposed a solution in a different dimension of access control management for blockchain-based OSMs [23].

Future work in this domain needs to explore the solutions to evaluate various privacy policy approaches and evaluate in-depth blockchain-based OSMs. This will enhance the platforms by implementing the proposed models for access control, privacy preservation, and rewards for content creation.

References

[1] B. Guidi, M. Conti, A. Passarella, and L. Ricci, "Managing social contents in decentralized online social networks: a survey," *Online Soc. Networks Media*, vol. 7, pp. 12–29, 2018, DOI: 10.1016/j.osnem.2018.07.001.

[2] R. Narendula, T. G. Papaioannou, and K. Aberer, "A decentralized online social network with efficient user-driven replication," in *2012 International Conference on Privacy, Security, Risk and Trust and 2012 International Conference on Social Computing*, 2012, no. September, pp. 166–175.

[3] L. A. Cutillo, R. Molva, and M. Önen, "Safebook: privacy preserving online social network," *IEEE Commun. Mag.*, vol. 47, no. 12, pp. 94–101, 2009.

[4] T. W. Jing and R. K. Murugesan, *A Theoretical Framework to Build Trust and Prevent Fake News in Social Media Using Blockchain*. New York, NY: Springer International Publishing, 2019.

[5] M. Rashid, P. M. Clarke, and R. V. O. Connor, "A systematic examination of knowledge loss in open source software projects," *Int. J. Inf. Manage.*, vol. 46, pp. 104–123, 2019, doi: 10.1016/j.ijinfomgt.2018.11.015.

[6] T. M. Choi, S. Guo, and S. Luo, "When blockchain meets social-media: will the result benefit social media analytics for supply chain operations management?" *Transp. Res. Part E Logist. Transp. Rev.*, vol. 135, p. 101860, 2020, doi: 10.1016/j.tre.2020.101860.

[7] P. Grover, A. K. Kar, and M. Janssen, "Diffusion of blockchain technology: insights from academic literature and social media analytics," *J. Enterp. Inf. Manag.*, vol. 32, no. 5, pp. 735–757, 2019, doi: 10.1108/JEIM-06-2018-0132.

[8]   I. S. Ochoa, G. de Mello, L. A. Silva, *et al., FakeChain: A Blockchain Architecture to Ensure Trust in Social Media Networks*, vol. 1010, no. August. New York, NY: Springer International Publishing, 2019.

[9]   E. Mnif, K. Mouakhar, and A. Jarboui, "Blockchain technology awareness on social media: insights from twitter analytics," *J. High Technol. Manag. Res.*, vol. 32, no. 2, p. 100416, 2021, doi: 10.1016/j.hitech.2021.100416.

[10] L. Jiang and X. Zhang, "BCOSN: a blockchain-based decentralized," *IEEE Trans. Comput. Soc. Syst.*, vol. 6, no. 6, pp. 1454–1466, 2019, doi: 10.1109/TCSS.2019.2941650.

[11] C. Li and B. Palanisamy, "Incentivized blockchain-based social media platforms: a case study of SteemIt," in *ACM Conference on Web Science (WebSci'19)*, ACM, 2021, pp. 1–10.

[12] R. Chatterjee, "An overview of the emerging technology: blockchain," in *2017 International Conference on Computational Intelligence and Networks*, 2017, pp. 126–127, doi: 10.1109/CINE.2017.33.

[13] D. Konforty, Y. Adam, D. Estrada, and L. G. Meredith, "Synereo: The Decentralized and Distributed Social Network," 2015.

[14] C. Li and B. Palanisamy, "Incentivized blockchain-based social media platforms: a case study of Steemit," in *WebSci 2019 – Proceedings of the 11th ACM Conference on Web Science*, 2019, pp. 145–154, doi: 10.1145/3292522.3326041.

[15] S. P. Ltd., "SocialX," 2018. https://socialx.network/wp-content/uploads/2018/%0A09/Whitepaper-SocialX-v1.1.pdf.

[16] B. Guidi, "When blockchain meets online social networks," *Pervasive Mob. Comput.*, vol. 62, pp. 101–131, 2020, doi: 10.1016/j.pmcj.2020.101131.

[17] N. A. B. Ankit, G. Robert, "Sapien. Decentralized social news platform," 2018. https://www.sapien.network/static/pdf/SPNv1_4.pdf.

[18] H. A. Simon, "Designing organizations for an information-rich world," *Int. Libr. Crit. Writings Econ.*, vol. 70, pp. 187–202, 1996.

[19] F. Schneider and F. Schneider, "Understanding online social network usage from a network perspective," in *9th ACM SIGCOMM Conference on Internet Measurement*, 2009, no. March, pp. 35–48, doi: 10.1145/1644893.1644899.

[20] A. De Salve, M. Dondio, B. Guidi, and L. Ricci, "The impact of user's availability on on-line ego networks: a Facebook analysis," *Comput. Commun.*, vol. 73, pp. 211–218, 2016, doi: 10.1016/j.comcom.2015.09.001.

[21] D. Fu and L. Fang, "Blockchain-based trusted computing in social network," in *2016 2nd IEEE International Conference on Computer and Communications Blockchain-Based*, 2016, pp. 19–22.

[22] S. Zhang, T. Yao, V. Koe, A. Sandor, and T. Weng, "A novel blockchain-based privacy-preserving framework for online social networks," *Conn. Sci.*, vol. 33, no. 3, pp. 555–575, 2021, doi: 10.1080/09540091.2020.1854181.

[23] M. Rahman Ur, B. Guidi, and F. Baiardi, "Blockchain-based access control management for decentralized online social networks," *J. Parallel Distrib. Comput.*, vol. 144, pp. 41–54, 2020, doi: 10.1016/j.jpdc.2020.05.011.

Chapter 2

Blockchain-based security for social media computing

Dimple Tiwari[1], Bhaskar Kapoor[2], Bharti Nagpal[3] and Bhoopesh Singh Bhati[4,5]

Abstract

Social media is rapidly developing in many folds, but as its growth expands, many issues are also growing. Some severe issues in social media are data security and less privacy because of its centralized nature, which exploits user information. As these are some biggest problems in social media, technologists associated blockchain technology with social media to provide security and privacy in all transitions of social media networks, which have the property of decentralization and strong end-to-end encryption to avoid tracking the user from third-party attacks. We can use distributed ledger-based payment infrastructure for fast processing of payment in real time to prevent the data from any fraud or a security breach and improve payment security significantly. Blockchain provides transparent payment flow to enhance the payment systems but still has many concerns which can be quickly dealt with to get maximum benefits of this technology. In logging or registering a legitimate user in social networks, we use two-factor authentication principles, which reduce the risk of an account being compromised and prevent an expropriating of a legitimate account and posting malicious content. To avoid all these pitfalls, the identification process should be very strong, and it should be capable enough to validate history. This system should not encourage people to over-emphasize or lie about their history.

Keywords: Social media; Blockchain technology; Fake news detection; Secure app-payments; Legitimated social-network content; Speech recognition

[1]ABES Engineering College, India
[2]Maharaja Agrasen Institute of Technology, India
[3]Department of Computer Engineering, NSUT East Campus (Formerly Ambedkar Institute of Advanced Communication Technologies & Research), India
[4]Indian Institute of Information Technology – Sonepat, India
[5]Ambedkar Institute of Advanced Communication Technologies & Research, GGSIPU, India

2.1   Introduction

Social media is growing very rapidly as it has become very popular and global use of communication among the people using social media. The use of social media raises various issues such as censorship, fake news, and privacy, as data is publicly available and can be misused. Nowadays, these social media platforms are freely available, but user data will become the property of the platform owner. As this is the business model for the service providers, they used activities of the users to make a profit out of it without concern of its users who are indirectly helping them to generate revenue by selling advertisements. Recent development in emerging technologies such as blockchain technology, artificial intelligence, and image processing provides a new direction to researchers in the field of security and privacy issues of users in this area. As blockchain technology is concerned, it mainly focuses on the privacy of the data produced by users stored on servers of centralized social networks, which helps find the habits, liking and disliking, preferences of the contents, or providing targeted advertisements. The nature of blockchain technology is decentralized (such as decentralized online social networks (DOSNs) based on P2P networks) [1,2] and having the characteristic of immutability (i.e. each activity is irreversibly stored and secured by end-to-end encryption), reliable, trustable, and verifiable [3]. So when blockchain technology is introduced in social media and the new term is popularized as blockchain online social media (BOSMs) [4], which is used for decentralized control on social data, competence in tracking the contribution participation level of specific creators or users, reward content creators for valuable content [5]. In this chapter, we study the use of blockchain in social media to understand the main challenges faced by platforms such as Facebook or YouTube in the real scenario from a technical point of view and provide a comparative analysis of different blockchain that should be used and study of new features which will be helpful in blockchain technology for future usages.

2.1.1   Basics of blockchain

We can represent blockchain as an emerging decentralized architecture like a ledger that records all transactions. Blockchain has a different layer [3] as shown in Figure 2.1, which can be named as:

- *Data layer*: it encapsulates the data block of layers below it using relevant asymmetric encryption. The node in the data layer used Merkle Tree Data Structure, Hash Function, Rivest Shamir Adleman (RSA), Secure Hash Algorithm (SHA) to encapsulate each transaction and code, which converts it into a new block with its received timestamp and connected as a new block in blockchain.
- *Network layer*: this layer is based on a contraption of distributed networks, data transmission, and data verification. The network layer makes sure that every node completes the recording of each transaction and verification process, and it is marked verified only if it verifies most of the nodes in the network.
- *Consensus layer*: enables blockchain to be more reliable and sensible in the distributed network by running consensus algorithms in all nodes [6]. It mainly

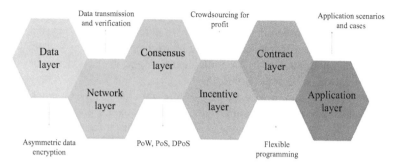

Figure 2.1   The layered architecture of blockchain

consists of PoW (Proof-of-Work), PoS (Proof-of-Stake), and DPoS (Delegated Proof-of-Stake).

- *Incentive layer*: this layer mainly focuses on issues related to crowdsourcing in nodes distributed in the networks and provides the mechanism for crowdsourcing to provide the highest profit to individuals in a guaranteed manner with real security of blockchain system [7]. So we can say that this layer merges currency issues with currency distribution to encourage bitcoin miners.
- *Contract layer*: some code and algorithms as part of flexible programming generate related scripts and intelligent contracts for data operation in blockchain.
- *Application layer*: this layer makes blockchain technical as well as creative by using (i) chain structure with timestamp; (ii) agreement between distributed nodes; (iii) PoW-based economy-intensive; (iv) smart contract, which is flexible and programmable applied in different application scenarios and cases [8].

2.1.2   Blockchain in social media

The core item in social media is content writing, which can be optimized by controlling the content and improvising the level of security using blockchain, which monitors the flow of events continuously and highlights the popular posts to control the fake entities and verify the entities by doing so proper checking—development of blockchain-based on user control mechanism, maximizing P2P sales and crowdfunding.

Social networks have many issues, and challenges like content censorship, data harvesting, privacy, and blockchain provides the solutions for these issues in these conventional networks. Other challenges are like: (a) no control over floating contents in social networks because owners of the social network have all the control over the content that is visible or not visible to its users. (b) Social media has centralized nature, and its users are receptive to various attacks, which can lead to leakage of personal information of them. Blockchain provides a solution to all these problems as it is decentralized in nature to remove all the intermediaries and duplication of content, and unauthorized parties cannot access erased content. It also gives control to the users, which enables them to see or not to see the unwanted or irrelevant content in their specified platform. Blockchain is distributed in nature to easily track each transaction and catch any tempered data. In last, we can say that there are two important factors that involve blockchain technology in social media are: verification and validation of online identities, and restriction can be implied on fake content by using smart contracts.

As the security part is concerned, we are familiar with some well-known attacks like malware attacks, spam attacks, phishing attacks, and cross-site scripting, but these days many other treats like de-anonymization attacks, cyber stalking, click jacking, and user profiling are also involved in security issues of social media networks. So, deploying blockchain system mechanisms in social media stop sending false information to peers such as double transactions and denial of service (DoS).

Rumors spreading have a high impact on e-social platforms and e-economics. They should be dealt with an effective mechanism like blockchain-driven social media, which is equipped with decentralized contracts and motivates trusted networks to secure information exchange. Blockchain-driven sequential algorithms work on the concept of credit-based virtual information exchange for peer-to-peer in social media to minimize the pair-wise rumor spreading style with proper validation. Blockchain technology is successful in the financial area because of its trusted contracts and security. This design concept of the smart contract can also be applied in information exchange with virtual gathered credits distributed to all social media members and collected further to decide the credibility of corresponding information in the social media and authenticity of the individual. This approach effectively minimizes the social and economic damage that occurs because of the propagation and exchange of fake information on social media. The diagram of information exchange in blockchain is depicted in Figure 2.2.

This chapter is organized as follows: Section 2.1 is dedicated to the social media issues and challenges with an overview of the role of blockchain technology in social media. Section 2.2 provides an overview of expanding and protecting freedom of speech. In Section 2.3, we describe the verification of the online user

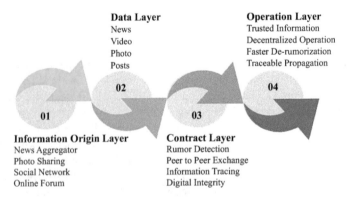

Figure 2.2   The architecture of blockchain-based information exchange

identification process. Section 2.4 focused on securities issues in-app payment using blockchain technology. Section 2.5 emphasizes the authenticity legitimacy for contents in social networks. Section 2.6 focused on finding a verified online shopping marketplace. Finally, Section 2.7 concludes the chapter.

2.2   Expanding and protecting freedom of speech

Social media is a mobile or web-based platform used by any individual or agency to exchange user-created content. Kaplan and Haenlein [9] describe web-based social media as a set of applications based on the technological and ideological foundation of Web 2.0 (Internet platform for interactive user participation) used for trafficking of user-generated contents [10]. Organization for Economic Cooperation and Development (OECD) classified user-generated content into three categories: (1) content available on the public website of social networking; (2) involve less creative effort; and (3) content that is not developed as a part of professional routines and practices. When social media is used on some devices like mobile phones, it is called mobile social media with added features like location-sensitivity (the current location of the user) and time-sensitivity (time delay between sending and receiving messages).

- *Freedom of speech*: These terms have existed since ancient times, dating back more than 2000 years ago. These two terms can be understood as a notation which everybody used to express without fear of reprisal through any media i.e., threats, persecution, and without other interference i.e. Censorship. Article 19 (1) (a) [CoI] confers on the right "to freedom of speech and expression," which means the one can express one's opinions and convictions openly by writing, or printing, by taking pictures or using any other mode and also has the right to publish or to propagate the views of others individuals. In reference of John Milton's arguments [10], we can represent "freedom of speech" as a multifarious right with the right to disseminate or express ideas and information.
- *Freedom of speech in social media*: Wide range of the Internet and rapid development of social media has become the modern tool of communication through which individuals can exchange information and idea using their legislative rights on freedom of expression. Internet and social media enable people to exchange information by fostering a feeling of community and connecting them instantly [10]. Thus, we can recognize freedom of speech as one's fundamental right that is exercised in any medium in all international documents.
- *Limitations in freedom of speech*: Freedom of speech does not negotiate on an individual's rights to publish/to speak without answerability. Freedom of Speech cannot be treated as a free license to use any informal speech and prevent punishment for those who exploit this freedom [10]. Restrictions can be imposed on the following ground: (i) contempt of court, (ii) defamation, (iii) morality or decency, (iv) public order, or (v) incitement to an offense.

2.3   Verifying the online user's identity

In conventional media, users have to register themselves using verification of the physical document, which is a tedious task and always risks identity theft by unauthorized access to these documents to avoid data breaches [11]. When blockchain technology is incorporated with social media to design the decentralized system for the registration process and for accessing the personal records by three consumers such as user, authority, and requester (i.e. third party) [12]. So, blockchain identity can help the society to have control on their details by the process of digitization for it, and when the entire system is owned and verified by the individual, it increases the reliability of the data.

In 2017, Javelin Strategy and Research [13] found that out of 15, there is only one whose identity is hacked in the United States because consumers cannot monitor the unauthorized access of private data. Jamal *et al.* proposed an Identity Verification System based on blockchain for storing personal records of individuals and allowing them to check who viewed or accessed their personal information or data. In this method, the authority uploads the user's personal records on blockchain after verification. The user can see the list of requesters and allows the third party to access their data. Blockchain as an emerging decentralized architecture which is something like ledger [12] which record all transactions and updated after continuous verification if altered by some partied involved. There is always a risk of safety in a traditional identity verification system because it has bulky storage of physical records [14]. Because this is stored in a distributed database, they might be misused by a third party as the user has no control on their personal information. Online user identity verification system using blockchain is depicted in Figure 2.3.

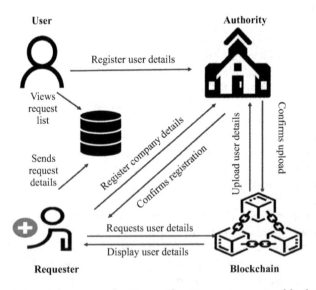

Figure 2.3   Online user identity verification system using blockchain

This system is just like a storage system of personal information of individuals and can be accessed for identity verification and authentication at the time of the registration process [15,16]. The main advantage of blockchain in online identity verification is to prevent data breaches of users' personal information by putting it in decentralized systems. An online identity verification system, which has complete control by its user, makes sure that the data content is correct and reliable and the system is transparent. Finally, the main objective of designing such a system is to make a decentralized blockchain to store personal records with maximum availability and make registration and verification easier for others who need to access this record.

2.4   Security with blockchain in app-payments

E-commerce became the most popular industry that evolved online over the world. All the online activities like bill payments, online shopping, virtual education, and e-bookings have required an online payment portal [17,18]. The emergence of the digital world and smart appliances has increased the need for various online payment applications. Due to wide adoption and online mode, these are more exploitable by financial frauds. The e-commerce industry has experienced a disruption in online transactions. Blockchain technology with biometric authentication has reinvented online payment mode and provided a reliable app-payment mechanism. The authenticity of blockchain technology relies on four fundamental perspectives: speed, cost, reliability, and convenience. Figure 2.4 depicts the flow of secure app payment with blockchain technology. Blockchain is a functional innovation that was first introduced in 2009. It facilitates digital information distribution with the restriction of content being copied. First, blockchain was introduced for cryptocurrency only, but since widely adopted for security in different applications. Blockchain technology maintains transparency, which means that

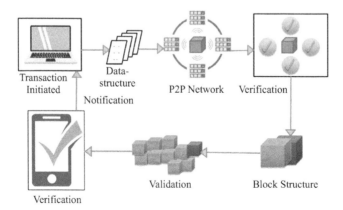

Figure 2.4   Secure app payment with blockchain technology

everyone is liable for their own actions and transactions. It follows the principle of cryptography for securing the blocks of information [19].

The network followed by blockchain is decentralized that supports effective online payment transactions. The information stored in different locations promotes the accessibility and verifiability of the transactions [19]. Blockchain architecture supports both public and private options. In the public option, everyone has permission to join and perform actions. In contrast, the private option enhances the security in blockchain architecture by restricting the entry of unauthentic users in the communication. These options help the blockchain for adjusting in various industries based on different requirements [20].

2.4.1   Blockchain advantages for app-payment security

Blockchain secured app payment has several benefits over traditional payment modes that make it widely adopted by different industries for their secure transactions. A few of them are listed in further subsections.

2.4.1.1   Decentralized architecture

Unlike other banks' architecture, blockchain supports a decentralized architecture that regulates the flow of transactions without the interference of intermediates. Therefore, the different–different parties can perform secure and verified online transactions without the need of a trusted third party sitting between them. Substantially, the absence of intervening parties reduces the complexity and the cost of blockchain technology and increases the flexibility of online app payments with no additional cost [21].

2.4.1.2   Distributed database

The distributed architecture of the database ensures synchronous and uniform information traversal. In this approach, data is continuously updated, promoting the instant clearing and settlement of the transactions [22]. Therefore, the online payments are very fast without the limitation of physical boundaries over the world. It also minimizes the risk of the market and capital prerequisites of third-party participants.

2.4.1.3   Cryptographic hash

The blockchain architecture uses the cryptographic hash function to secure transactions and payments. Every block of the transaction is recognized by its hash key, and a specific message digest is generated for it. Multiple key securities are applied to the crypto hash function for each block that enhances the complexity and prevents it from getting hacked [23]. Additionally, the decentralized nature and complex hash function decrease blockchain secured payments' probability by matting any fraud.

2.4.1.4   Distributed ledger

Blockchain technology maintains distributed ledger for the customers instead of handling the account holders' different accounts for their own ingoing and outgoing transactions. It ensures that the blockchain-based transactions are concurrent, pre-venient, terminal, and persistent, like payment asset transfers. For this reason, there is not any requirement of reconciliation in the blockchain secured transactions [24].

2.4.2 Blockchain disadvantages for app-payment security

Alongside the advantage of blockchain technology for secure app payments, it also has various disadvantages, generating the hurdle for adopting this mechanism.

2.4.2.1 Anonymity

Blockchain advances anonymity in online transactions due to its decentralized nature. Hence, it attracted fraud and made online-payment applications vulnerable to cyber-attacks. Anonymity in financial transactions increases the risk of fraud as anyone does not aware of the identity of each other, which promote the malicious intensity of human being for raising any kind of fraud and failure [25]. The anomalous user has more freedom to strike the attack on the system that can break the confidentiality, integrity, and authenticity of the transaction.

2.4.2.2 Complexity

The complex nature of cryptographic algorithms and hash functions increases the complications in simpler app payments. Thus, it is not handy for less computer friendly people. The people who have a fear of technology try to neglect this method for the transaction. It is globally known that cryptographic hash functions need the extra capacity of the machines to perform the calculations, which slow down the processing of transactions and increase delays [26]. A large bit's calculation is per-formed to perform the hash functions and generate the message digest. This requires the high storage and extra computational capacity of the system.

2.4.2.3 Massive resource

The underlying cost of applying blockchain technology for app payments is very high due to the hiring of developers, high computing technology, licensing cost, and many more. The enterprise cost of implementing blockchain technology sometimes goes over a billion dollars. So, the industries that want to adopt the idea of blockchain but do not have the budgets and funds skip the option and choose different mechanisms for securing the applications [27]. Expertise knowledge is required for implementing blockchain technology, which also needs massive finance and budget.

2.5 Authenticating legitimacy of social network content

Social media communications are more secure in current years than in the time when it was initially started. Numerous researchers are working on securing social network communications, and blockchain has emerged as the powerful technology that is widely applicable for securing social platforms. Several community detec-tion approaches have been available. One of them is analyzing user interests and preferences for categorizing into the different communities [28]. As social networks are becoming too complicated, therefore communication detection is difficult to calculate by simple rules. Hence, the reconsideration of different features, influence, relation, and interaction detection among the people is required for effective community identification. The authenticity and legitimacy of social network content and be checked by identifying the community that belongs to it [29].

Figure 2.5 presents the Sophos threat report. Here, Facebook has on high security risk among Twitter, LinkedIn, and Myspace. Figure 2.6 shows the analysis report of how social network is increasingly impacting the kid's life. The parents are worried about their children as they are more vulnerable to the harmful effect of social platforms [30]. Unauthenticated social content increases the crimes and spreads fake news, which can mislead the youth. Authentication and legitimacy of the social network content can identify using fake news detection techniques. Fake news is social news content that malicious users intentionally spread. There are four major fake news detection methods exist that are used to check the legitimacy of social network content.

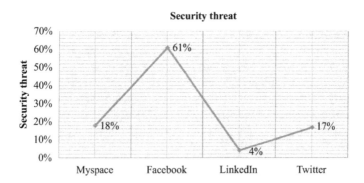

Figure 2.5   Social networks associated Sophos threat report

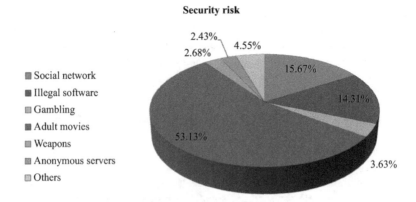

Figure 2.6   Security risk analysis of parental control

2.5.1   Fake news detection by knowledge-based approach

The knowledge-based system applies the fact-checking method to detect the authenticity of the social content. The objective of this method is to check the authenticity of the news by comparing the knowledge acquired from verified news content and prior known facts. The fact-checking method is divided into manual fact-checking and automatic fact-checking. First, manual fact-checking is further categorized into expert-based and crowd sourcing-based fact-checking. Expert-based fact-checking prefers the knowledge of domain experts to verify the news content. This method is simple to manage and usually provides reliable results [31]. Crowd sourcing-based fact-checking uses the opinion of a large population for analyzing the truth behind the news and concluding the facts based on maximum opinions. Second, automatic fact-checking reduces the limitation of manual fact-checking; it is capable of handling a large volume of content and newly generated information. This method employs the potential of natural language processing (NLP), network graphs, and machine learning for automatic fact calculation. In this method, first the facts are extracted and fed into the knowledge base, and after that knowledge is compared by the facts to check the facts.

2.5.2   Fake news detection by style-based approach

The style-based approach relies on the news's intention, and is there any intention to misguide the people or not? Malicious entities usually prefer to write the content in a provoking way so that the public is influenced and tries to attempt crime [32]. The performance of the style-based fake news detection method depends on two major factors.

- How effectively the style of content and image is captured.
- How well the classification techniques perform for presenting the different news facts and information.

The styling factor of the content is grouped into two sections, namely textual features and visual features. The textual feature of the content is mainly handled by the syntax, lexicon, semantic, and discourse language levels. On the other hand, visual features of news content are identified by the neural networks and hand-crafted features.

2.5.3   Fake news detection by propagation-based approach

Propagation-based method of fake news detection is worked based on analyzing the spread of fake news [33]. The input of the propagation-based method can be fed by either a news cascade or by a self-defined graph.

- News-cascade is the tree-based structure, which directly calculates online social network contents propagation. The tree's root node represents the first person who initiated the news, and further nodes of the tree depict subsequent sources and destinations where the news spreads. The propagation of the tree can be calculated by the number of steps the news travelled and by the time it was posted.

- Self-defined graph generates flexible and scalable networks to calculate the propagation of the news. These graphs use the homogeneous, hierarchical, and heterogeneous pattern for the network. Heterogeneous graphs construct the different nodes of edges for tweets, events, and users. In contrast, homogeneous graphs only contain a single type of node in the whole network. In contrast, hierarchical graphs have multiple nodes that share different relationships.

2.5.4 *Fake news detection by source-based approach*

Identifying the credibility of the news source is a very popular approach for identifying the authenticity of the social news content. The fake news cycle has three phases: (1) news creation, (2) news publishing, and (3) news propagation on social platforms. For checking the authenticity of the source, a score value has been assigned to the sources, and it is dynamically changed according to the periodic evaluation and the trustful servers. A higher score value depicts the more trustworthiness of the news source [34].

2.6 Finding verified online shopping marketplace

Online marketplaces are very popular in today's digital world. Many are well established and offer a different range of products in simple buying mode. Various online shopping sites like Amazon, Expedia, ShopClues, Myntra, and Flipkart are designed with different objectives and provide numerous facilities to their customers for easy access. The increasing demand for online shopping marketplace is attracting the fraudulent to develop a fake online website to cheat people and steal their money. For accepting the digital marketplace in future purchases, security is a major concern. For securing the online marketplace, a negotiation protocol is available, and it holds the various specified rules that every online marketplace agent should follow. If an agent does not follow the negotiation rules, then critical issues can occur.

2.6.1 *Verification steps for online marketplace*

It is essential to check the authenticity of the online shopping sites before investing and purchasing – the product from there [35]. Figure 2.7 presents a few standard steps to check the authenticity of the online marketplace.

1. • Scrutinize the URL
2. • Check Padlock option in address bar
3. • Rely on browser
4. • Look on trust seal
5. • Use website checker
6. • Focus on reviews

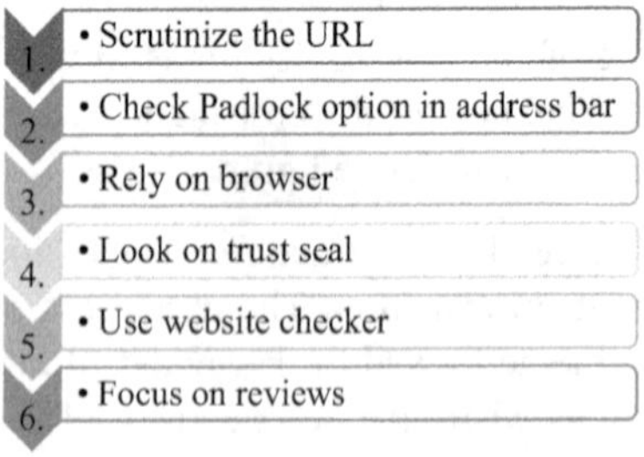

Figure 2.7   Online marketplace verification

- *Scrutinize the URL*: Few fraudulent websites crated the copy write URL of the Original websites. So before entering the bank credential to any shopping website, examine the URL first. Most of the time, cybercriminals just skip one word from the original website name.
- *Check Padlock*: Additionally, a padlock icon on the address bar is also providing authenticity information about the site. Just go and click the padlock option in the URL.
- *Rely on browsers*: It should require keeping updated the web browsers. If the web browser is updated and antivirus is installed in the system, it automatically suggests the website is secure or not.
- *Look on trust seal*: Trust seals are available in secure payment portals like Google Pay and PayPal, which tell users secure transactions.
- *Website checker*: The "UVoid.com" and "Google Transparency Report" are two popular websites, where you can type the URL of your website and check the authenticity details of the selected online marketplace.
- *Focus on reviews*: It is a very trustful and secure method to know about the details of the online shopping marketplace. Before purchasing the product from any online store, it should be required to analyze the people's reviews regarding that store.

2.6.2   *Cryptographic negotiation protocol modelling criteria for online marketplace*

Failures can arise due to poorly designed protocols. Therefore, a few criteria are listed to correctly develop the cryptographic protocol of the online shopping marketplace [36].

- *Customer type*: It affects whether a broker or significant service provider is associated with the negotiation protocol.
- *Type of session call*: Session is incoming or outgoing decides the negotiation protocol. Incoming session calls extra such as paging service to communicate with a registered agent. At the same time, an outgoing call is initiated from the customer terminal.
- *Negotiation mechanism type*: It is divided into two categories, complicated multiple negotiation and sealed-bid auction. The sealed-bid auction can easily expose the fraudulent. Rather complex bid strategy has more control over information flow.

2.6.3   *Verifying intermediates policies*

Searching engines and Internet service providers are empowering e-commerce and new web communities. They are employing harassment, infringement, market stealth, and a higher level of surveillance. This is the reason that individuals are losing control to maintain their own image on the market web. Intermediaries govern online life. Online intermediaries control and organize digitized content. Unfortunately, these are bound by weak customer protection enforcement [37].

2.6.4   Role of online business-to-business marketplace in trust formation

Due to unreliability in online transactions, institutional structures came into the picture to control and assure reliability in inter-organizational online transactions. Trust in Inter-organizations, gaining considerable attention in the literature. Here, institutional trust creation is the most favorable method to develop a trustworthy online environment without similarity and familiarity. Zucker categorized institutional trust into two parts [38]:

- *Certification by third-party*: It includes laws, licenses, protocols, and policies for regulation.
- *Escrows*: It guarantees the final results of the transactions.

Zucker's view for institutional trust is widely adopted by the researchers of e-commerce. Possibly, because the e-commerce get closer to the number of parties that have no familiarities and similarities. The inter-organizational trust provides two general beliefs:

- *Predictably in a trustor's expectations*: It is related to the party's credibility towards honesty, reliability, predictability, and expertise.
- *Confidence in Party's Goodwill*: It is associated with the expectation that the party will behave fairly and do not take benefit and unfair advantage.

It is required to remove the fraudulent entities [39] from the online marketplace by perceived monitoring, accreditation, and legal bonds [40].

- *Perceived monitoring*: It represents the group of activities to assure the transaction flow is running according to the predefined rules and policies. The major objective of the monitoring is to ascertain that all the transactions are being processed by well-established standards for good performance, quality, and delivery.
- *Perceived accreditation*: It is used to check the capacity of the organization to perform based on predefined standards. Accreditation is taken as the surrogate reputation of the online marketplace, which is provided by the accreditation authorities.
- *Perceived legal bonds*: These are the legitimated contracts to govern financial activities. It reduces random behavior and promotes trust in online transactions.
- *Perceived feedbacks*: This accumulates information about the past trading flow of the organization. Feedbacks depict the structural assurance that reduces the random behaviors and encourages credibility in the online marketplace, but these are effective only when the firms focus on it and make the decisions accordingly.
- *Perceived cooperative rules*: These are defined as the principles, standards, and values that should follow by the organizations. It increases the cooperation and joint regulation between several online marketplaces. Cooperative norms employ flexibility, credibility, and information sharing between online sellers. Extensive incorporation of the norms represents the good faith and trust of the organization.

2.7   Conclusion

E-commerce and online social communication are growing together. Here, blockchain technology emerged to secure both terminologies. This chapter presents the different aspects of social media computing, e-commerce, and blockchain security, as it is known that online platforms provide the freedom to share opinions and emotions towards different topics and situations. So, the various aspects related to freedom of speech have been discussed with the protection mechanism of blockchain as people communicate and share their opinions on social platforms. It is required to identify whether the information propagates on the online networks is trustful, to which extent. Therefore, various techniques have been discussed to reveal the identity of online users. Online shopping has increased day by day, which enhances the need for online payment. This chapter discussed the basics of social media and its issues and challenges in detail and how blockchain technology can be applied to social media to stop spreading rumors, solve the problem of content censorship, and protect individuals on the social media platform. We also illustrate the use of virtual credits base blockchain for peer-to-peer trustworthy information exchange to avoid large-scale rumors in social media. As we know that usage of social media is growing very rapidly, so there will be a hike in e-commerce transactions and crowd-funding transactions. Social media is very popular, and global use of communication among people using social media results in making a large infrastructure that is better in privacy and which can have actions with smart contracts and apps.

Social media is a very strong media to exercise the freedom of speech of individuals, but misuse or illegal acts at this platform also leads to legal censorship, but sometimes inevitable consequence of censorship violates the individual's civil rights. To overcome that problem, social media should be regularized with technologies like blockchain with security without obstructing the civil rights of individuals. Several fraudulent are taking advantage and stealing the money between the online transactions. This motivates us to present the advantages and disadvantages of blockchain technology for secure app payment. Fake news on online social platforms promotes crime and online vandalism. Consequently, different fake news detection techniques have been discussed, such as knowledge-based, propagation-based, style-based, and source-based. Finally, verification and validation of the online marketplace have been discussed to conduct reliable online shopping.

References

[1]   Datta, A., Buchegger, S., Vu, L. H., Strufe, T., and Rzadca, K. (2010). Decentralized online social networks. In: Furht B. (ed.), *Handbook of Social Network Technologies and Applications*. Springer, Boston, MA, pp. 349–378, https://doi.org/10.1007/978-1-4419-7142-5_17.

[2]   Guidi, B., Conti, M., Passarella, A., and Ricci, L. (2018). Managing social contents in decentralized online social networks: a survey. *Online Social*

Networks and Media, 7, 12–29, doi:https://doi.org/10.1016/j.osnem.
2018.07.001, ISSN 2468-6964.

[3]   Yong, Y. and Fei-Yue, W. (2016). Blockchain: the state of the art and future trends. *Acta Automatica Sinica*, 42(4), 481–494, doi:10.16383/j.aas.2016.c160158.

[4]   Guidi, B. (2020). When blockchain meets online social networks. *Pervasive and Mobile Computing*, 62(C), 101131, doi:https://doi.org/10.1016/j.pmcj.2020.101131.

[5]   Chen, Y., Li, Q., and Wang, H. (2018). Towards Trusted Social Networks with Blockchain Technology. *ArXiv, abs/1801.02796*.

[6]   Guidi, B., Michienzi, A., and Ricci, L. (2021). A graph-based socioeconomic analysis of Steemit. *IEEE Transactions on Computational Social Systems*, 8 (2), 365–376, doi:10.1109/TCSS.2020.3042745.

[7]   Guidi, B., Michienzi, A., and Ricci, L. (2020), Steem blockchain: mining the inner structure of the graph. *IEEE Access*, 8, 210251–210266, doi:10.1109/ACCESS.2020.3038550.

[8]   Fu, D. and Fang, L., Blockchain-based trusted computing in social network. In *2016 2nd IEEE International Conference on Computer and Communications (ICCC)*, 2016, pp. 19–22, doi:10.1109/CompComm.2016.7924656.

[9]   Kaplan, A. M. and Haenlein, M. (2010), Users of the world, unite! The challenges and opportunities of social media. *Business Horizons*, 53(1), 59–68, doi: https://doi.org/10.1016/j.bushor.2009.09.003, ISSN 0007-6813.

[10] Pradhan, N., Constitution of India-Freedom of speech and expression, https://www.legalserviceindia.com/legal/article-572-constitution-of-india-freedom-of-speech-and-expression.html. Accessed on 10/2/2022.

[11] Pascual, A., Marchini, K., and Miller, S. (2018). 2018 Identity Fraud: Fraud Enters a New Era of Complexity, https://www.javelinstrategy.com/cover-age-area/2018-identity-fraudfraud-enters-new-era-complexity.

[12] Jamal, A., Helmi, R. A. A., Syahirah, A. S. N., and Fatima, M.-A., Blockchain-based identity verification system. In *2019 IEEE 9th International Conference on System Engineering and Technology (ICSET)*, 2019, pp. 253–257, doi:10.1109/ICSEngT.2019.8906403.

[13] Zyskind, G., Nathan, O., and Pentland, A. (2015). Decentralizing privacy: using blockchain to protect personal data. In *2015 IEEE Security and Privacy Workshops*, pp. 180–184, doi: https://doi.org/10.1109/SPW.2015.27.

[14] Azaria, A., Ekblaw, A., Vieira, T., and Lippman, A. (2016). MedRec: using blockchain for medical data access and permission management. In *2016 2nd International Conference on Open and Big Data (OBD)*, pp. 25–30, doi: https://doi.org/10.1109/OBD.2016.11.

[15] Chen, Z. and Zhu, Y. (2017), Personal archive service system using block-chain technology: case study, promising and challenging, in *2017 IEEE International Conference on AI & Mobile Services (AIMS)*, Honolulu, HI, pp. 93–99, doi: 10.1109/AIMS.2017.31.

[16] Do, H. G. and Ng, W. K. (2017). Blockchain-based system for secure data storage with private keyword search. In *2017 IEEE World Congress on Services (SERVICES)*, pp. 90–93, doi: 10.1109/SERVICES.2017.23.

[17] Kungpisdan, S. (2005). Modelling, design, and analysis of secure mobile payment systems (Doctoral dissertation, Monash University).

[18] Isaac, J. T. and Sherali, Z. (2014). Secure mobile payment systems. *IT Professional*, 16(3), 36–43.

[19] Pryanikov, M. M. and Chugunov, A. V. (2017). Blockchain as the communication basis for the digital economy development: advantages and problems. *International Journal of Open Information Technologies*, 5(6), 49–55.

[20] Miraz, M. H. and Ali, M. (2018). Applications of blockchain technology beyond cryptocurrency. arXiv preprint arXiv:1801.03528.

[21] De Filippi, P. (2016). The interplay between decentralization and privacy: the case of blockchain technologies. *Journal of Peer Production*, Issue, (7).

[22] Muzammal, M., Qu, Q., and Nasrulin, B. (2019). Renovating blockchain with distributed databases: an open source system. *Future Generation Computer Systems*, 90, 105–117.

[23] Sheth, H. and Dattani, J. (2019). Overview of blockchain technology. *Asian Journal For Convergence in Technology (AJCT)*, ISSN-2350-1146.

[24] Deshpande, A., Stewart, K., Lepetit, L., and Gunashekar, S. (2017). Distributed ledger technologies/blockchain: challenges, opportunities and the prospects for standards. *Overview report The British Standards Institution (BSI)*, 40, 40.

[25] Niranjanamurthy, M., Nithya, B. N., and Jagannatha, S. J. C. C. (2019). Analysis of blockchain technology: pros, cons and SWOT. *Cluster Computing*, 22(6), 14743–14757.

[26] Zheng, W., Zheng, Z., Chen, X., Dai, K., Li, P., and Chen, R. (2019). NutbaaS: a blockchain-as-a-service platform. *IEEE Access*, 7, 134422–134433.

[27] Shin, E. J., Kang, H. G., and Bae, K. (2020). A study on the sustainable development of NPOs with blockchain technology. *Sustainability*, 12(15), 6158.

[28] Zhao, Z., Feng, S., Wang, Q., Huang, J. Z., Williams, G. J., and Fan, J. (2012). Topic oriented community detection through social objects and link analysis in social networks. *Knowledge-Based Systems*, 26, 164–173.

[29] Yu, R., Wang, J., Xu, T., *et al.* (2017). Authentication with blockchain algorithm and text encryption protocol in calculation of social network. *IEEE Access*, 5, 24944–24951.

[30] Rathore, S., Sharma, P. K., Loia, V., Jeong, Y. S., and Park, J. H. (2017). Social network security: issues, challenges, threats, and solutions. *Information Sciences*, 421, 43–69.

[31] Hassan, N., Arslan, F., Li, C., and Tremayne, M. (2017, August). Toward automated fact-checking: detecting check-worthy factual claims by ClaimBuster. In *Proceedings of the 23rd ACM SIGKDD International Conference on Knowledge Discovery and Data Mining*, pp. 1803–1812.

[32] Przybyla, P. (2020, April). Capturing the style of fake news. In *Proceedings of the AAAI Conference on Artificial Intelligence*, vol. 34, no. 01, pp. 490–497.

[33]   Meyers, M., Weiss, G., and Spanakis, G. (2020, October). Fake news detection on Twitter using propagation structures. In *Multidisciplinary International Symposium on Disinformation in Open Online Media,* pp. 138–158. Springer, Cham.

[34]   Figueira, Á. and Oliveira, L. (2017). The current state of fake news: challenges and opportunities. *Procedia Computer Science*, 121, 817–825.

[35]   Goo, S. K., Irvine, J. M., Tomlinson, A., and Schwiderski-Grosche, S. (2005, September). Designing and verifying secure protocols of the digital marketplace. In *2005 2nd International Symposium on Wireless Communication Systems*, pp. 86–90. IEEE.

[36]   Verification of online marketplace: https://clark.com/scams-rip-offs/how-to-spot-a-fake-online-store/. Accessed: 11/02/2022.

[37]   Pasquale, F. A. (2010). Trusting (and Verifying) Online Intermediaries' Policing. The Next Digital Decade, Essays on the Future of the Internet, 347.

[38]   Zucker, L. G. (1986). Production of trust: institutional sources of economic structure, 1840–1920. *Research in Organizational Behavior*, 8, 53–111.

[39]   Ba, S. and Pavlou, P. A. (2002). Evidence of the effect of trust building technology in electronic markets: price premiums and buyer behavior. *MIS Quarterly*, 26, 243–268.

[40]   Pavlou, P. A. (2002). Institution-based trust in interorganizational exchange relationships: the role of online B2B marketplaces on trust formation. *The Journal of Strategic Information Systems*, 11(3–4), 215–243.

Chapter 3

Emerging trends with social network – design, models and handling

Dimple Tiwari¹ and Bharti Nagpal²

Abstract

Social networking sites experiencing tremendous growth along with the advancement of web 2.0 in the past few decades. Online social sites offer alluring services for making relationships and for smooth communication among people. It became a fundamental need of human life and used for almost all area of lifelike entertainment, medical, shopping, education, legitimated activities, and business. Unfortunately, these become the target for intruders who attempt unlawful activities and harm social users' prestige and financial health. This study focuses on various concerns associated with social networking. This chapter presents the different types of social networks (SNs) that emerged due to the advancement of the Internet. Several challenges occur in SNs with the increasing demand for their uses. So, here we discussed some research and open challenges associated with SNs. However, SNs have gained popularity over the years, but users do not trust these platforms due to the increasing cyber-crimes. We provided a list of different security threats and promising solutions for securing social media and discussed the various SN security perspectives.

Keywords: Social networking; Machine-learning; Opportunistic network; Social threats; Multimedia threats

3.1 Introduction

Social networks (SNs) build with people that have the same behavior, interests, knowledge, activities, and backgrounds over online platform. Social communication can happen in different ways and on several platforms such as Twitter, Facebook, and Instagram. Users can share their posts in the form of text, images,

¹ABES Engineering College, India
²Department of Computer Engineering, NSUT East Campus (Ambedkar Institute of Advanced Communication Technologies & Research), India

and videos. Social networking also increased proportionally with the supplementary growth in wireless network communication techniques such as laptops, mobiles, tablets, and gaming tools [1]. The previous decade witnessed the substantial thunder of online SNs due to the enactment of internet support and web 2.0. The social platforms provide an adaptable and convenient environment for easy interaction regardless of geographical location. Hence, it received immense attention from academic and industrial researchers. The receptiveness of the social sites permits the users to collect a massive amount of knowledge about other users. Distressingly, SNs' vast information and easy accessibility attract malicious users to perform anomalous activities in these networks [2]. Social media becomes a handy tool as a vital communication channel to comment on global events, reform information discovery, and promote social communication.

Additionally, SNs facilitate connections between friends and families; it also connects professional and industrial groups for advertisement and marketing purposes. A person can join SN groups, creates their profile, connects with people, keeps in touch, and shares standard information in different forms. Most SNs platforms have some common features, and one of the fundamental properties of these sites is that they permit their users to make their profiles. Employing this feature, SNs users represent themselves for connecting with other people. They can share blogs, content, pictures, and videos in their profile, which all or only the selected friends can see in the network [3]. A SN is a dynamic architecture whose nodes represent the objects and edges represent the connection. Over time, they grow and revise hurriedly, as the nodes and edges can be added and deleted according to network connectivity.

Figure 3.1 depicts the online architecture of SNs connectivity. Several users like a particular person, industry, professional group, forum, and shopping sites can connect through different social platforms like Twitter, Facebook, Instagram,

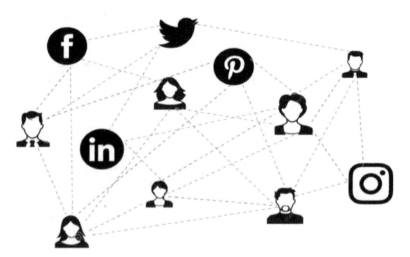

Figure 3.1   The online architecture of SNs

LinkedIn, and Pinterest. The analysis of these SNs helps in determining the people's social activities and behavior that may promote the future of social business and developments based on social sites communities. Different users can choose different social media platforms to fulfill their purposes.

The variety of services provided by the SN makes it exciting and attracts the companies to establish business and government to encourage public affirmations. For example, companies promote their brands on social platforms and get the users' opinions on their products [4]. The government launched its policies online and got feedbacks for further amendments.

3.1.1   Types of SNs

Online SNs (OSNs) are categorized into five major networks; cellular SNs, opportunistic SNs, mobile sensor SNs, community SNs, and vehicular SNs. Further subsections provide detailed information about the different kinds of SNs currently working in the online social environments.

3.1.1.1   Cellular SN

A cellular network is a radio network that spreads over a vast land area connected with several cells. Through cellular networks, organizations and researchers can extract the personal information of individuals like SMS records, call records, movement records, and so on [5]. This information is helpful for academic and professional researchers for a deep understanding of the social behavior and relationship of the people on cellular networks. Cellular networks are overgrowing due to the increasing demand for IoT-based environments [6]. Figure 3.2 depicts the

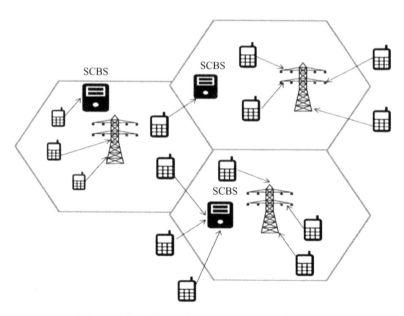

Figure 3.2   The architecture of the cellular SN

architecture of the cellular network. The intense need for social media using mobile phones increases the congestion on the wireless cellular networks in crowded areas.

Zang *et al.* [7] proposed an optimal device-to-device communication social approach that reduces the load of cellular networks with the resistance of SNs. Yuanjie *et al.* [8] presented a software tool to extract runtime operational information from the cellular networks, capable of providing internal analysis of device and functional logic inferences.

3.1.1.2 Opportunistic SN

In current years, opportunistic SNs emerged as an excellent mechanism in wireless communication networks. Unlike the mobile ad-hoc network, it does not require an end-to-end connectivity path for social communication. Instead, they establish the connection based on opportunistic contacts between mobile nodes. Therefore, opportunistic networks build more trustworthy SN schemes. Due to the enhancement of mobile social networking capabilities, opportunistic mobile SNs (MSNs) will become the most potent mechanism for future generation mobile communication [9]. Xiao *et al.* [10] presented an adaptive message allocation and spray routing strategy (MDASRS) algorithm for removing the barrier related to symmetry problems in opportunistic networks that measure the strength of connection among nodes by social pressure. Yu *et al.* [11] proposed a node social features relationship evaluation (NSFRE) algorithm to establish a fuzzy feature similarity matrix based on different features of the user's nodes. It provides the solution regarding the integrity, dynamic adaptive, and transitivity between social connectivity of the nodes. NSFRE algorithm improves the reliable transmission success rate and reduces the transmission delay with insufficient buffer space and less computing capacity.

Figure 3.3 depicts the layered architecture of the opportunistic SNs, where the lower physical layer is responsible for movements and encounters of the nodes in a network, and the upper social layer constructs the social relationships among the user nodes [12].

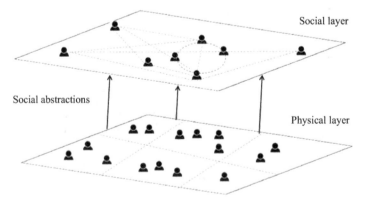

Figure 3.3   The layered architecture of the opportunistic SN

3.1.1.3 Mobile sensor SN

It employs conventional SNs, mainly for infrastructure and environmental monitoring. With the enhancement of mobile uses, mobile sensors SNs replaced the classical SNs. Now, smartphones and other intelligent devices are loaded with advanced sensors such as microphones, accelerometers, cameras, and digital compasses to explore the SNs. These networks increased with the expansion of mobile facilities and wireless communication networks with global functioning and Internet connectivity. It combined the property of mobile SNs (MSNs) and online SNs (OSNs) and emerged as a new field for researchers [13]. Dorffer *et al.* proposed a revisit blind sensor calibration as informed Nonnegative Matrix Factorization problem with missing entries. One matrix of this framework holds the calibration structure of the sensors, and another one contains the parameters of the entire sensor network. The experiments investigated more than 5,000 simulations, and the proposed model produced accurate results for all the considered applications [14]. Gu *et al.* [15] deployed the optimized model for mobile sensor networks using a chemical reaction optimization (CRO) mechanism. Experiments show that CRO provides reliable results with rapid deployment and enhances network performance effectively. It has been stated that CRO plays a significant role in the mobile sensor environment than classical particle swarm optimization (PSO).

3.1.1.4 Community SN

Community networks inherit wireless mesh networks (WMS) properties such as quick deployment, self-organization, easy maintenance, self-healing, high scalability, low cost, and reliable services [16]. Local communities deployed and managed with two significant properties: supporting local services and sharing internet connectivity. Examples of community networks are Dillon, Buffalo Free-Net, Big Sky Telegraph, Illinois, Montana, Ottawa, etc. The community has two main aspects: people who are linked together with their locality and geographical space; and people who share the same behavior or interest. Social media supports both kinds of aspects for making the relationship between people on social platforms.

3.1.1.5 Vehicular SN

A vehicular SN (VSN) is an emerging communication area that combines vehicular ad-hoc networks and mobile SNs for advancement in social media. This new paradigm introduced many research fields such as delivery services, data dissemination, and content sharing. VSNs are advantageous for nodes' social mobility and behavior to build novel route planning and recommendation systems [17].

Figure 3.4 presents the combined property of vehicular ad-hoc network and SN as a VSN. Vehicular communication can be called a virtual SN in automobiles. Each driver can share the information with their neighbors in case of heavy traffic or congestion in every type of transport, either land, air, or water [18]. They all can also be connected without the barrier of enormous distance. This advancement immense the social media popularity in the current digital world, and it will be dramatically increased in the upcoming years.

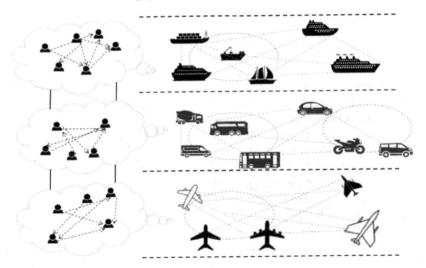

*Figure 3.4   A combined architecture of vehicular ad-hoc network and mobile SN
(vehicular SN)*

3.1.2   SN analysis

Social network analysis (SNA) is a mechanism used to investigate the behavior and
connection of an individual or a group within a SN. Due to the incremental growth
of SNs and e-commerce, many consumers prefer online shopping and online
feedback transactions. For deploying the macro policies to corporate promotions,
government and private organizations are promoting together. With the expansion
of different social media outlets, several consumers are always willing to post their
comments about the product after online shopping. It leads to social marketing and
brand monitoring through online platforms [19].

3.1.2.1   Sentiment analysis

Sentiment analysis (SA) plays a vital role in SNA; it is contextual mining that
extracts the subjective and objective information of content available on online
social platforms and helping the organizations to recognize the social sentiment of
their product, brand, or services. User modeling is an essential part of social
monitoring to identify user's opinions, preferences, and intent towards a product or
service. Gong *et al.* [20] proposed a probabilistic generative model that integrates
SN structure modeling and opinionated content modeling to extract the user's
intent. Extensive experiments were conducted on large Amazon and Yelp online
reviews to check the efficiency of the proposed model. The proposed model is more
interpretable and predictive than previous baseline models. SA is a calculative
approach that calculates the subjectivity, opinion, emotions, and polarity from text,
images, and videos available on social networks.

Figure 3.5 depicts the process of SA, which starts from the data acquisition
from social platforms. Next, data cleaning is required to prepare the data in the

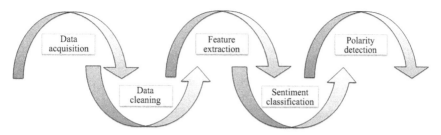

Figure 3.5   The process of the SA from data acquisition to polarity detection

machine-understandable form; after the data cleaning, essential features are extracted from numeric vectors that reduce the dataset's dimensionality and present only required features for sentiment classification. After that, the different classification techniques such as supervised, unsupervised, or ensemble learning are applied. Polarity detection is a final step that expresses the text as positive, negative, or neutral [21]. Basiri *et al.* [22] proposed an attention-based bidirectional CNN-RNN deep model (ABCDM) for SA by considering two different gated recurrent units (GRU) and independent LSTM layers. ABCDM is capable of extracting past and future contexts using temporal information of both directions. Carosia *et al.* [23] proposed SA based investment strategy for Brazilian stock market financial reviews. Results conclude: (1) convolutional neural network (CNN) is the most appropriate model for SA; (2) there is serious predominant of daily news sentiment for stock marketing, and (3) social network-based SA strategy can bring profitability for both long- and short-term investments. Tiwari *et al.* [24] proposed a bagging-based linear discriminant analysis model (BLDA) for sentiment extraction of restaurant services-related reviews. The proposed solution focuses on enhancement, pre-processing, standardization, and performance of SA with topic modeling and ensemble learning. Comparative results show that the proposed BLDA model outperformed over conventional Gaussian Naïve Bayes (GNB) and K-Nearest Neighbor (KNN) approaches.

3.1.2.2   Link analysis

Link analysis is used to identify the connection between nodes in social networks. The longitudinal data and shared affiliation are required for understanding the formation of nodes [25]. Link mining is associated with text mining and can be helpful in clustering, classification, prediction, and association-rules mining discovery. It is used in several applications such as recommendation systems and page ranking to identify friends and their interests [26]. Tang *et al.* [27] proposed a link analysis approach to place a new composition relationship between web services. This approach explores the known composition relations and similarity references among web services. Two heuristic rule methods have been combined to measure the degree of similarities between nodes. Experiments validate the authenticity of the proposed approach for social link predictions.

Further subsections of this work are organized as follows: Section 3.2 describes the various challenging aspects that affect the social networking sites;

Section 3.3 presents the static and dynamic models of social networking; Section 3.4 discusses the fake news detection and prevention mechanisms in social networks; Section 3.5 shows the factors that affect the design of social networks; Section 3.6 presents the several security challenges and promising solutions in social networking; Section 3.7 discusses the various security perspectives required in social networking, and Section 3.8 concludes the whole work.

3.2   Social networking challenges

With the advancement in SN technologies, several open challenges have also increased altogether. Numerous researchers are working in this field and facing many challenging issues for analyzing the social network properties and relationships. Atif *et al.* [28] presented various research-related social networking issues, and said that SN perceived challenges might hinder the further expansion of social networks to meet upcoming opportunities. Wang *et al.* [29] discussed various open challenges related to SNA and predictions.

Figure 3.6 classifies the social networking challenges into two parts: open social networking challenges and research-related challenges. Further subsections describe all the difficulties presented in detail.

3.2.1   SN open challenges

Social networking faces many open challenges to perform smooth actions, which will generate the hurdle for the upcoming growth of SNs in businesses and organizations.

3.2.1.1   Mobility

Mobility means the member of SN platforms may navigate at different locations during the usage of the connected environment. The corresponding node can move out of the range of the network and is disconnected completely. At the same time,

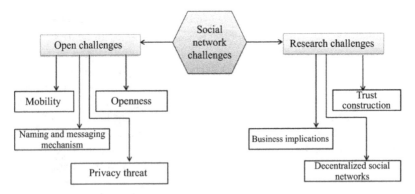

Figure 3.6   The open and research-related challenging aspects of SNs

another node cane comes into the network scope and tries to connect the network. Ad-hoc systems should handle these constraints with high bandwidth and extra power supply. On the other hand, the application level should provide the changing addressing services and network technologies (Wi-Fi and Bluetooth) in a mobile environment. An opportunistic network relies on human forwarding-based mobility, directly associated with human social practices that do not provide robust solutions. An intelligent contribution such as optimal routing and multi-link transformation services are required in wireless technologies [30].

3.2.1.2   Openness

A major ambiguity of the SN is its openness. When one tries to promote the sharing of knowledge, another never actually wants to meet and tightly closes itself, which leads to the hurdle in front of organizations and governments to advance their strategies and brands. Google+, LinkedIn, and Facebook allow users to create their profile on a centrally managed service, where each scrap of information passes through, a so-called monopoly [29]. For users, open means that they should have complete control of their knowledge and social network. At the developer site, it should eliminate the trust and provide an independent way to create their web services. The openness of social media promotes businesses and online services, but it also simultaneously stimulates the threats of cyber-crime and cyber-attacks.

3.2.1.3   Naming and messaging mechanism

Discriminant networking environments and applications employ different addressing modes. They may vary based on the different connection types, such as local networks or global networks. For example, a local network or intranet uses Bluetooth or 802.3 MAC address for connecting the neighbor nodes. In contrast, a worldwide network or Internet uses Wi-Fi or 802.11 wireless environments for connecting the nodes. Therefore, the interaction between the different levels of the network, leads to the address translation issues and naming-messaging problems. One central problem is how these high-level names get to translate into lower-level addresses for physical layer transmissions. So, the addresses mapping mechanism is required for smooth communication between different layers of the network. The fundamental topology of SN is highly dynamic. So the establishment of an end-to-end path between the nodes is infeasible, and the opportunistic network relies on people's social behavior forwarding mechanism. Accordingly, numerous forwarding approaches rely on social information for accurate forwarding decisions.

3.2.1.4   Privacy threat

Security of SNs is the biggest issue in social platforms, where one can easily track all the possible movements and working of individuals. In an ad-hoc wireless network, users do not even know from which specific device they connect. The measurement of privacy and security risk is a challenging task while surfing on social media sites, which initiates an efficient framework for detecting the risks and privacy threats in SNs [31]. Mamonov *et al.* [32] drawn an information processing framework that propounds the threat mitigation, commonly performed before the complete cognitive threat assessment. Continuous integration of virtual life with physical life exposes and increases privacy risks. According to the survey of PricewaterhouseCoopers, 42.8 million security breaches were detected in 2016, while it increased around 48% in 2017.

3.2.2 Research-related challenges

The employment of SN on a vast level, introduced new research challenges. A comprehensive analysis of these issues is required to promote research in this field. Here, this section presented a detailed discussion of the research-related challenges in SN.

3.2.2.1 Trust construction

Trust is mandate for the association between strangers in SNs. Usually, people have degraded their trust in SNs due to privacy and security issues. There is a need to employ stimulus trust construction into virtual SNs like physical social environments. Holcomb *et al.* [33] presented a way of creating a trustable digital domain using unique identifier, XML signatures, and trusted signers. Rathee *et al.* [34] proposed a trust-based hypothetical-mathematical model for ensuring secure communication among social network devices. The proposed trusted model has validated against several cyber threats such as DDoS attacks and falsification threats and proven authenticated. Trust works as a tool for the agent to select the right partner to achieve their own goals. Other potential partners can choose an agent to establish collaboration from the accumulated trust [35].

3.2.2.2 Business implications

Numerous business models have been deployed in SNs. Some sites gain money by posting advertisements on social platforms, while others facilitate the premium content on sites and charge subscription fees to access the content. Most of the business models just focusing on expanding the network instead of creating a robust business model. Researchers introduced some models of easy money sharing such as PayPal, Google Pay, and many more [36].

3.2.2.3 Centralized SNs

Current social platforms support the strategy of a centralized networks, where the user needs to register in every social site they are interested in joining. This process emerges inconvenience for users due to the dynamic nature of SNs. They do not have enough control over the information they show in their profiles. They can decide who can show their information but cannot filter the part of that information. Moreover, they do not know that how social sites will use their information later on. Many social sites use this information to target advertisements and gaining revenues from it. On the other hand, due to the centralized nature of SNs, challenges occur to identify same user on several social platforms. The prescribed issues generate the need for decentralized SNs, where no specific authority.

3.3   Social networking models

The SN is an emerging technology that has gained very much popularity in past decades. Here, people can interact and communicate together without the limitation of geographical distance. With the increasing popularity of SN, the need for dynamite and continuous change is also increasing in the SN environment. Therefore, the SN is categorized into two different networks: static and dynamic. The dynamic SN is newly introduced with the integration of advanced features. A minor variation between a static and dynamic SN creates a lot of confusion in the literature. It is needed to draw a critical boundary between them. So, this section presents the comparative discussion on both networks based on different parameters.

3.3.1   Static SN model

In a static SN, interactions occur at a particular time instance, and once the communication is complete, all the information has been deleted. These SN's contain only the static information regarding the network, which do not represent any change in the users' relationship [37]. The static network needs less security protection than dynamic SN as its information does not change rapidly and is deleted after a communication stops. Figure 3.7 depicts the static SN that follows the simple graph where nodes (V) define the individual users and edges (E) represent the communication link between them in a particular instance of time.

$$\log it(p_{ij}) = \beta_0 + \beta_s(s_i + r_j) + \delta X_{ij} - |z_i - z_j| \tag{3.1}$$

Here β_0 represents the basic probability of the relationship, s_i shows the sender's random effect, r_j shows the receiver's random effect, X_{ij} is the observable

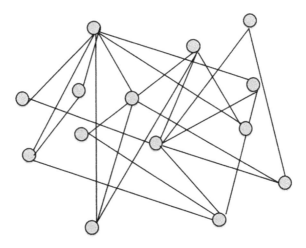

Figure 3.7   The architecture of the static SN

vector covariance, and z_i shows to unobservable social space [38]. The static network follows the terminology of waterholes that are significantly stronger within groups and weaker outside the groups. The static networks contain various edges that are not necessarily presented during actual communication but are required during the estimation of the transmission rate. These networks perform better for the average population while poorly perform for a large population.

3.3.2   Dynamic SN model

A dynamic SN is a connected network of people where interaction and communication occur over time, and all the information is considered during the connection. In such a scenario, chatting between users is dynamic. A dynamic SN is a newly emerging and challenging research field for researchers. It is a kind of network that dynamically evolves and rapidly changes over time. All the information generated in the dynamic network continuously changes the relationship of users at all-time stamps. In an active SN, people are connected worldwide over time and must preserve connection information. So, these networks require extra security and are more vulnerable to threats. Figure 3.8 depicts the architecture of dynamic SNs, which brings traditional SNA, multi-agent systems, link analysis (LA), and social simulation together within network theory. Dynamic analysis of SNs involves short segments of data. It applied to series of smaller intervals of data collected over the period, to examine the change in the interaction between the users [39].

Dynamic networks are different from the traditional static networks as they involve more extensive data, multi-mode, dynamics, multiplex networks, and varying levels of uncertainty. The dynamic SN contains large-scale network information, and it analyses them simultaneously. Dynamic SNA involves two advanced features: meta-network and agent-based modeling.

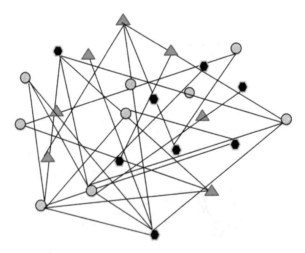

Figure 3.8   The architecture of the dynamic SN

Table 3.1   The comparison between static and dynamic SN models

Parameter	Static SN	Dynamic SN
Information	All the information removed that occurs during social communication	All the information preserved that occurs during the connection
Time	Interaction and communication among multiple people occur for a particular period	Interaction and communication among multiple people are not bounded, it occurs over a time
Community	Static SNs are capable of connecting with very short-distance communities	The dynamic SN provides long-distance communication and covers large community groups over the world
Accuracy	The static mode of connectivity provides inaccurate patterns of the network that leads to less accuracy	The dynamic model of the network generates exact patterns of the data, which leads to higher accuracy
Size	The size of the nodes and links remains the same during the whole period of connection	Nodes and links randomly change over time
Relationship	Changing the relationship between actors is restricted	It does not impose any restrictions for changing relationships between users
Instance	Security preserving mechanism considered as single instance to the same network	Security preserving mechanism considered as multiple instances to the same network
Security	Security issues are significantly less due to the single instance of the same network	Security concern is grave due to multiple instances of the same network
Features	Static characteristics are socio-economic, socio-demographic, and socio-cultural	Dynamic characteristics are interests, values, and beliefs, which change rapidly according to actual events
Techniques	Visualization techniques are proliferating for static SNs	Visualization techniques for dynamic SNs are growing slowly
Structure	The structure of a static SN does not change rapidly and may know in advance	The structure of dynamic SNs is not known in advance and grows or shrinks rapidly

3.3.3   Static vs. dynamic SN

This section presents the difference between static and dynamic SNs based on different parameters. Drawing a critical boundary between static and dynamic SN is required to remove the confusion of researcher's mind [40].

3.4   Social media fraud information handling and detection

Fraud handling and detection had existed since before the emergence of the Internet. Now, it becomes one of the greatest threats to journalism, democracy, and privilege of expression. Social media platforms perform a crucial role in boosting the spreading of fake news. Social media has proven as a most potent origin for counterfeit news circulation. Although some emerging patterns for phony news detection are in the early stage of development, various challenges still exist in the area of fake news detection. The substantial spread of fake news negatively impacts society and individual lives. First, it breaks the authenticity steadiness of the news ecology. Second, it deliberately convinces individuals to accept biased and imprecise beliefs.

3.4.1   Fraud detection

The broadly adopted definition of fake news is "fictitious articles deliberately fabricated to deceive readers." SNs and news venues publish fake reports to increase readership or for psychological conflicts. The process of fake news detection is categorized into four major categories. Table 3.2 describes all four significant types of fake news detection from social platforms.

3.4.2   Fraud prevention

The phenomenon of fraud information is not new. Instead, the mode of spread is changing rapidly in both speed and extent. SN sites like Instagram, Facebook, LinkedIn, and Twitter are the fertile base for the spreading of fraud news. Now, this is a time for programmers and researchers to develop software that can prevent the spread of fraud news. There are lots of methods available to prevent the spread of fraud information at social platforms.

3.4.2.1   Authority check

Authority check is one of the mechanisms by which news can be classified in the category of fraud or legitimate. This mechanism checks the author and origin of the news, which helps in identifying the report's authenticity. The company and individuals have reviewed and searched for collecting the information about their biasness for a particular topic. The information regarding the organization's business helps in judging the legitimacy of the viral news.

3.4.2.2   Timeliness

The publishing time of the news also helps in identifying the truthfulness of the content. It is required to check the content is up-to-date and the site is regularly updating. The news which is published on time and updated periodically is considered legitimate news. Whereas, ancient and modified news are suspected as fraud information.

3.4.2.3   Fact-checking tools

Nowadays, several tools are available to check news correctness that filters and segregates the fraud information from the original word. Software like Yandex, Google Image, and TinEye are some software that can detect the duplicity of images by which we can notice the repetition of the fake images. The CIVIX software provides a quick strategy to investigate the information from multimedia content like images, text, and videos. Snopes is software that offers evidence-based fact-checking. It extracts the urban myths, rumors, conspiracies, and general misinformation from the content. This software checks the truthfulness of the content priory and helps to prevent the spreading of fraud information.

Table 3.2 *The different categories of fake news detection*

No.	Detection category	Description		Sub-category
1.	Knowledge-based detection	Since fake news fabricates the false myths in news content, the most effective detection approach is to examine the truthfulness of the major claims provided by the news. A knowledge-based detection mechanism uses external sources to check the facts related to news content. Due to limited research in knowledge-based fake news detection, external graphs are required to check the facts and patterns. These graphs may introduce the extra burden as: they are very usual for entities, and relationship description and new facts are also may miss in external knowledge graphs. Hence, Han *et al.* [41] investigated knowledge-based fake news detection without using an external knowledge graph. They transformed the problem of fake news detection into a sub-graph classification task and had calculated the relationships between the facts to form an individual knowledge graph. The fact-checking techniques of knowledge-based detection are categorized into three parts: computational-oriented, expert-oriented, and crowdsourcing-oriented	1.	**Computational-oriented:** fact-checking provides an automatic and robust system to classify the facts into true and false claims. This technique mainly relies on machine-learning (ML), information retrieval (IR), natural language processing (NLP), and network-graph theory
			2.	**Expert-oriented:** recently, various social platforms employed expert-based fact-checking. This fact-checking is conducted by highly credible experts, which is simple to manage and produces tremendous trustworthy results
			3.	**Crowdsourcing-oriented:** fact-checking methods rely on a big population and collect the crowd's thoughts, then aggregates the ideas to generate the final assessment of news truthfulness. Comparatively, it is difficult to manage than expert-oriented fact-checking and exploits by the biased fact-checkers
2.	Source-based detection	Source-based fake news detection relies on the facts of the different news sources and offers an excellent base to believe. The source of news contains two types of stance, implicit and explicit. An explicit perspective holds direct expressions as "Thumb up" for good and "Thumb down" for bad. Where implicated stance automatically extracts from social media posts [42]. The spread of false news generates a massive amount of data from different perspectives, and this data is further fruitful for advanced levels of fake news detection.	1.	**Accessing a source as authors and publishers:** this technique relies on the credibility of unreliable authors and publishers. It explores the relationships of unknown authors and publishers to other publishers and authors. Various websites and resources have also been validated to extract the ground truth about the credibility of the publishers
			2.	**Accessing a source as social media users:** are emerging sources for news stories. Instinctively, low credibility users

(*Continues*)

Table 3.2 (Continued)

No.	Detection – category	Description	Sub-category
		Karimi et al. [43] studied different degrees of fake news by investigating multiple news sources. They proposed a multi-source multi-class fake news detection (MMFD) framework that combines an automated degree of falseness, automatic feature extraction, and multi-source fusion to detect fake news	are more likely to spread fake news over social platforms than trustworthy users. So, here users are classified into two categories: malicious users and normal users
3.	Style-based detection	This method also relies on news content, similar to knowledge-based detection. However, it assesses the intention of content rather than checking the authenticity of content like knowledge-based detection. It strictly focuses on the writing style of the content to identify the forgery of news. The style-based method employs manipulation in the content to differentiating between the fake-style and true-style news writing. Jiang et al. [44] find that microblog rumor contains some frequent keywords in their writing styles. They studied the syntactical structure of the text and introduced a more straightforward way of fake news detection	1. **Objectivity-oriented:** captures the style signal of content; the decrement of the objectivity such as yellow-journalism and hyper-partisan represents the misleading content 2. **Deception-oriented:** captures the claims and illusory statements from content. Deep syntax and rhetorical structure-based advanced NLP tools are available to spot the illusory phase detection from the content. Wang et al. [45] implemented the CNN to extract fake news fidelity from the content
4.	Propagation-based detection	The propagation-based method predicts the credibility of the news content. The basic assumption is that the credibility of news events is highly related to credible posts. It can use homogeneous or heterogeneous credibility networks to propagate the fake news detection process. Homogeneous networks contain the same types of entities, either posts or events. In contrast, heterogeneous networks include multiple entities such as events, posts, sub-events, or newsgroups. It can be of two types: self-defines graphs or news cascades	1. **Self-defined:** presents the indirect links and captures the additional information about the report propagation 2. **News-cascades:** presents the direct information about the report propagation. It provides the tree structure that directly propagates the definite report article on SNs. The root node of the cascade tree presents the origin of the news, and other nodes represent the users who further spread the fake news [46]

3.5   SNs design factors

These days, people spend most of their time on internet platforms. They perform different activities like gaming, shopping, digital payments, and many more. The increment in the usage of the Internet leads to the popularity of smart and portable devices. The design of the SN is very much affected by the user's preferences. As much, the design of the SN is intractable and straightforward that will attract the users to join. There are many users' preferences available that are in the users' minds for preferring the design of the SNs. Bartosik-Purgat *et al*. [47] conducted a study that presented the ratio of few factors to influence the users' choice for choosing a particular social platform. Table 3.3 shows few factors that affect the user's preference for designing social networking sites.

Figure 3.9 presents the percentage of the factors affecting the SNs design according to the users' preferences. Bartosik-Purgat *et al*. [47] conducted a

Table 3.3   The factors affecting the design of social networking according to the user preferences

Factor no.	Factor	Description
F1.	Activation of SN account	The easy process of account activation in SN attracts the users to that platform
F2.	Way of using SN platform	The interactive and communal interface of the social sites promotes the popularity of the social platform
F3.	A number of people connected	As much as the people connected with the particular SN attract more users for joining that specific social platform
F4.	The attractiveness of the SN platform	Attractive social platforms are more capable of joining multiple users in comparison to non-attractive social media
F5.	Compatibility with gaming applications	The handy support of the social platforms with gaming applications increases the popularity of the network
F6.	Compatibility with mobile applications	Most of the people access social platforms through their mobiles. Therefore, easy compatibility with mobile applications is required in the design of SNs
F7.	Amount of fees for accessing the SN platform	People prefer free social platforms instead of paid media over the world. Even the minute charges of social platforms decrease the popularity of SNs. Users do not want to pay anything for social connections
F8.	A number of service functions	The number of services provided by the social platforms increases the interest of users to join them
F9.	The name of the SN platform	The name of the social platform has also attracted the public
F10.	Advertisement pop-ups on the SN platform	The advertisement pop-ups irritate the users. So, the minimum release of the advertisement, get more attracted to the users

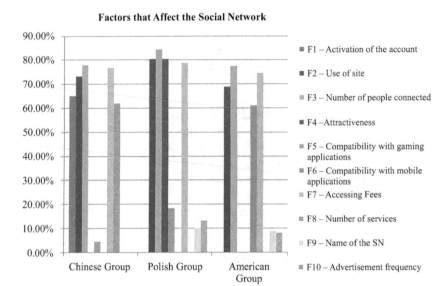

Figure 3.9   The ratio of the factors that affect the design of social networking according to the user's preferences

cross-cultural survey of the Chinese groups, Polish groups, and American groups to find the users' preferences for joining any social platform. According to their survey, all the (Chinese, Polish, and American) group users prefer the Factor-3 (number of people connected with SN). It is the preferable choice of the users in all the groups to join any SN. It has been stated that the interactive design of the SN attracts more people. Once a few people connect, many more also get connected due to the popularity of that particular SN.

3.6   SN threats and challenges

People share private information on SNs, permitting their personal information to their friends and families, which lead to privacy and security-related threats in SNs; malicious users can steal their knowledge and use it for their benefit. Therefore, SNs do not provide a trustworthy environment. Therefore, people do not believe in these platforms and, it may hinder the popularity of SNs in upcoming years.

3.6.1   Security challenges

Social platforms like Facebook, Twitter, LinkedIn, and Instagram permit a billion users to connect and share their private information worldwide. User's information, including images, texts, and videos, can illegally capture malicious users and companies to enhance their revenues. Many threats can put the risk on social media datasets, classified into three major categories: social threats, traditional threats, and multimedia threats. Figure 3.9 depicts the classification of social networking security threats [48].

3.6.1.1 Social threats

The social threat is the fastest growing threat from the past few years, where attackers break the relationship of the users, communities, and groups and interact with them in different ways such as a minor, an employee of a bank corporation, or as organization. Here, attackers attract minors by expressing love, sympathy and offering online gifts to them. Their motive is blackmailing, harassing, sharing pornography, and spying. This section presents a brief description of different social threats that break the security of social relationships. Figure 3.10 depicts the classification of social networking threats.

(A) *Cyberstalking*

It is defined as monotonous and undesirable communication directed by the electronic or digital media to harass individuals. It is a crime in which a stalker harasses the victims using digital media such as instant messaging, e-mails, or messages posted on social media forums or groups. Stalkers take the benefit of anonymity offered by the internet to persecute the victims. Excessive use of social media for personal and private transactions leads to the incidence of cyber-stalking [49]. Cyber-stalker can monitor the victims online or some time offline, track the victim's location, exasperate, intimidate, or blackmail.

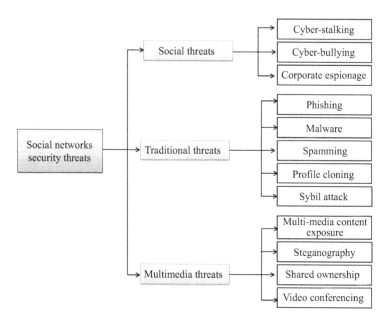

Figure 3.10 The classification of social networking security threats

(B) *Cyber-bullying and cyber-grooming*
   Cyberbullying is a deliberate act of harassing individuals using electronic means. Cyber-grooming is the task of befriending individuals online to build an emotional angle to facilitate sexual abuse. Minors are highly prone to these kinds of attacks due to their weak age growth [50]. The anonymity of digital platforms promotes the groomers to simultaneously address multiple minors and leads to exponential growth in the cases of cyber grooming.

(C) *Corporate espionage*
   This attack is conducted for corporate or financial frauds, which also known as corporate spying, economic espionage, and industrial espionage. It is conducted in two forms: in the first form, the attackers acquire the firm's intellectual property information, manufacturing techniques, policies, pricing, or sale. In the second form, the attackers steal the trade secrets of corporations by launching different types of malware.

3.6.1.2   Traditional threats

Traditional threats affect the social environment in different and unique ways. It includes phishing, malware, virus, and information theft in an online social environment.

(A) *Phishing*
   It is a practice of sending fraudulent messages in a repetitive nature; e-mail is the primary source of these attacks. Here, the attacker may use the fake website and email addresses to expose individual's private information. They attempt to make an identical clone of original websites for their wrong intentions. Phishing aims to acquire individual's personal and sensitive information like username, password, debit, or credit card numbers by impersonating a legitimate entity that generally occurs by sending a forged email, bogus messages, or mimicking an online bank [51].

(B) *Malware*
   It is a nasty program that holds viruses, worms, and Trojan horses to damage the victim's system or applications. The SN is totally based on connecting and sharing, where these can easily be transmitted from one location to another. Cybercriminals use malware to steal or corrupt the information of banks, financial, or government organizations to increase their revenues.

(C) *Spamming*
   It is an unsolicited digital communication typically done by sending multiple spam e-mails, phone calls, or social media posts to large numbers of receivers for advertisement, phishing, spreading malware, and many more. Fake accounts play a crucial role in social spamming to distribute malicious content over SNs. Most social sites like Facebook and Twitter allow bots to be used that promote spamming over SNs [52].

(D) *Profile cloning*
   In this type of attack, the attacker makes the clone profile of existing users on the same or another social platform and starts sending the friend request to the

contacts of the original user for their benefit. The SN has considered one of the most popular platforms that attract billions of people to make social relationships and promoting profile cloning on SNs. Intruder inherits the unique features of the victim such as personal page, the home page, messaging list, friend list, and friend request list to pretend himself as an actual user [53].

(E) *Sybil attack*

Here, attackers create fake identities in huge volumes that help them get significant advantages in distributed and peer-to-peer networks. SNs contain a vast amount of users and their profiles. Therefore, social platforms are promoted as the major source for Sybil attacks. A Sybil attack can spoil individuals or corporation's reputations and corrupt important information from their accounts [48].

3.6.1.3 Multimedia threats

Data sharing plays a vital role in social networking sites, where people can share their photos, text messages, activities, videos, interests, etc. Nevertheless, the advancement in multimedia sharing techniques such as face recognition, location tracking, re-tagging, and web searching increases the threat of illegal utilization of these multimedia facilities.

(A) *Multimedia content exposure*

This is an attack in which intruders steal the information from the content posted by the users. For example, users posted the picture of their house; in that case, the intruder can find their house's address. Some other case users tag that "he is far away from his place," in that scenario attacker can know that no one is there in his home, and it is open for an intruder. Talukder *et al.* [54] introduced a Privometer tool for reducing the content exposure on Facebook by quantifying their sex fondness and political perspective from their posts.

(B) *Steganography*

It is a technique of hiding private information within ordinary files or messages. It is a prevalent technique in the current security perspective, but attackers increasingly use it to cover their malicious activities. These types of tasks endanger the popularity of social networking sites. Additionally, it can affect admissible users and connect them with crimes they do not commit.

(C) *Shared ownership*

Shared multimedia content can be related to multiple persons. For example, two friends might capture the picture together, and one of them posted that picture through his account. It may espouse the privacy of another person who may never want to reveal that.

(D) *Video conferencing*

It is supported by the various social sites that increase the more interaction between the people. However, this leads to more cyber-attacks on social platforms, where a malicious user can easily intercept the video connection by exploiting the possible vulnerabilities. Furthermore, one user can record the whole video conferencing for blackmailing the other user.

3.6.2   Promising security solutions

With the growing popularity of social networking, various threats are also increased in this field. Therefore, extreme protection is needed to maintain the popularity of SNs in upcoming years. Many developers and researchers are working for securing the social sites. The researchers have introduced a variety of solutions to deal with the SN threats mentioned above.

3.6.2.1   Steganalysis

The SN supports users to post huge multimedia content, which attracts the intruders to cover their malicious information in legitimated posted content. Therefore, it is required to use steganalysis mechanisms to find this negative information from acceptable content. Ye *et al.* [55] proposed the architecture of digital images steganalysis using deep residual networks. The key invention of the proposed solution is to expand the first portion of the detector to compute the noise residual. Chaumont *et al.* [56] presented the structure of deep neural techniques for the different scenarios of steganalysis.

3.6.2.2   Digital watermarking

Digital watermarking is used to embed a stamp with authorized content with the motive of proving co-authorship. This method can be visible or invisible. This technique protects the copyright of multimedia content and not affects the usage of the content. Nagai *et al.* [57] proposed a digital watermarking scheme for ownership authorization of digital content using deep neural networks. First, they formulated the novel challenges associated with digital watermarking and defined its requirements, then proposed a general framework for embedding watermarking parameters for multimedia content.

3.6.2.3   Storage encryption

Various social platforms are still available that do not have their own data centers, and they use third-party data centers to store user's private information. These data are vulnerable to leak, or a third party can utilize that information for malicious purposes. Therefore, the data should be stored in an encrypted format to protect it from other organizations and attackers. The researchers have proposed several cryptographic techniques to offer the facility of secure storage and recovery in SNs.

3.6.2.4   Biometric tools

Biometrics is used to secure various applications like forensic and for identifying the people using different traits. Due to the tremendous growth of cyber-attacks on SNs, it is mandatory to use biometrics to restrict web access. Biometric techniques can be divided into two parts: identification and verification, based on the security requirements. Identification means to compare the person with all the previously exist templates on different parameters for identifying the person. Verification is a one-to-one comparison technique in which the particular person's information is compared with his template in the database [58]. Social platforms like Facebook,

Amazon, Google, and Apple encourage biometrics as a service in their products and applications.

3.7 Security perspectives in social networking

SNs are facing the challenges of ethical affairs regarding the user's information's privacy and security. The threat of information leakage has increased nowadays due to the advancement in cyber-attacks. There are different concerns available for securing social media platforms. Here, we studied the perspective of various researchers about SNs security. Figure 3.11 presents all the SN security perspectives discussed here.

3.7.1 Risk perspective

Security issues raise the risk perspective in social networking. Schaik *et al.* [59] presented a study to examine privacy and security settings of SNs. These settings concern with the information sharing and the account access of the users. It has concluded that precautionary behavior is the most recurrent risk for the regulation of information sharing.

3.7.2 Student perspective

Social networking is more popular among youngsters rather than other age groups. It plays a vital role in student life for gathering the study materials and searching for the best online classes. Lawler *et al.* [60] presented a study to evaluate the student's perception about the information systems security. The survey finds that the students are less knowledgeable regarding the privacy of information gathering and sharing on SNs. Results of the study show that the students are not aware of the privacy of their

Figure 3.11 The security perspectives of the social networking

data storage on SNs, and they do not even read the SN sites' privacy policies. They do not know that how their personal information is gathered and misused by the attackers.

3.7.3   Company perspective

Internet systems have gained attention in companies; most of them adopt social technologies and transfer their advantages in their organizations. Almeida *et al.* [61] presented the most frequent security risks enabled in the social applications and provided the best solutions for the corporate infrastructure perspectives. They concluded that viruses, malware, information overexposure, spyware, exposed data points, spam values, and data leaks are the most common risk factors that exploit enterprise's social applications. Security perspective hinders the adoption of SNs in companies. Some best practices like browser settings, application control list, anti-malware software, avoid clickjacking, data loss protection, and traffic shaping can protect the social platforms and increase the interest of the companies in adopting the social networking facilities.

3.7.4   Trust perspective

Social platforms do not provide trustworthy interaction among the users. People feel insecure while maintaining the relationship over there. Trust construction is the most important issue faced by social networking sites. People are showing distrust in online SNs, which decreasing their popularity. Shin *et al.* [62] examine the SN's trust, security, and privacy through reliable measures. They proposed a new trust model for greater acceptance of the social applications. They first theorized the user's perceived privacy and security measures for the acceptance of SNs before building the trusted SN model.

3.7.5   Information sharing perspective

Information sharing service is the most vulnerable point in the SN. The multimedia content shared by the users can deliberately expose by intruders. Hajli *et al.* [63] explore the security perspective of information sharing on social sites. SN users are always worried about information sharing through social sites. This study demonstrates the perceived security controls required by the users for information sharing behavior. Additionally, it suggested that gender has shown to be a critical factor that influences the security perspective of information sharing on social platforms.

3.7.6   Cyber-crime perspective

Social platforms have become a significant source for performing criminal activities nowadays. Most of the cyber-crimes and frauds are accomplished on social sites. Cybercrime may harm someone's security and financial health. Cybercrimes like phishing, cyber-bullying, spamming, and profile cloning have originated from social networking sites. Therefore, it is required to protect the SN from these kinds of threats to build the user's trust. Saridakis *et al.* [64] suggested that users with extensive risk tendencies are more susceptible to victimizing cyber-crimes, and those who apply extra protective measures on their social activities are less prone to cyber-attacks.

3.8   Conclusion

Social platforms are highly preferred as a communication medium by millions of users nowadays and have attracted various researchers for their studies. Although the significant research contributions have focused only on this field's positive outcomes, the negative aspects of the social platforms gaining a lack of attention and the implications of their solution have rarely been discussed. This study spotlights all crucial elements of the social networking platforms. It contributes to the literature by formulating the different practices of SN, including types of SNs, types of SNA, and different perspectives of SN securities.

Additionally, we discussed static and dynamic SN models and provided a clear difference line between both the models. With the advancement of social networking, the threat of social protection has also increased. Intruder exploits most of the activities performed on SNs, such as multimedia content sharing, connecting, blogging, and tagging. Therefore, we classified the different types of threats and attacks that exploit the vulnerability of the SNs. Moreover, promising solutions have also been talked over for the implication in industry and research. Furthermore, our finding recommends that SN has generated new research directions with various opportunities like developing a trustworthy model for securing the social platforms, investigating a novel security breaches and threats, detecting and preventing the advance cyber-crimes, and enhancing the services of SNs. Future studies will present the advance and emerging trends associated with SNs.

References

[1]   Qiu, T., Chen, B., Sangaiah, A. K., Ma, J., and Huang, R. (2017). A survey of mobile social networks: applications, social characteristics, and challenges. *IEEE Systems Journal*, 12(4), 3932–3947.

[2]   Bindu, P. V. and P. Santhi Thilagam (2016). Mining social networks for anomalies: methods and challenges. *Journal of Network and Computer Applications*, 68, 213–229.

[3]   Persia, F. and D'Auria, D. (2017, August). A survey of online social networks: challenges and opportunities. In *2017 IEEE International Conference on Information Reuse and Integration (IRI)* (pp. 614–620). IEEE.

[4]   Al Falahi, K., Atif, Y., and Elnaffar, S. (2010, December). Social networks: challenges and new opportunities. In *2010 IEEE/ACM International Conference on Green Computing and Communications & International Conference on Cyber*, Physical and Social Computing (pp. 804–808). IEEE.

[5]   Roy, A., De, P., and Saxena, N. (2015). Location-based social video sharing over next generation cellular networks. *IEEE Communications Magazine*, 53 (10), 136–143.

[6]   Chinchali, S., Hu, P., Chu, T., *et al.* (2018, April). Cellular network traffic scheduling with deep reinforcement learning. In *Thirty-Second AAAI Conference on Artificial Intelligence*.

[7]   Zhang, Y., Pan, E., Song, L., Saad, W., Dawy, Z., and Han, Z. (2013, August). Social network enhanced device-to-device communication underlaying cellular networks. In *2013 IEEE/CIC International Conference on Communications in China-Workshops (CIC/ICCC)* (pp. 182–186). IEEE.

[8]   Li, Y., Peng, C., Yuan, Z., Li, J., Deng, H., and Wang, T. (2016, October). Mobile insight: extracting and analyzing cellular network information on smartphones. In *Proceedings of the 22nd Annual International Conference on Mobile Computing and Networking* (pp. 202–215).

[9]   Wu, J. and Wang, Y. (eds.). (2014). *Opportunistic Mobile Social Networks*. London: CRC Press.

[10]   Xiao, Y. and Wu, J. (2020). Data transmission and management based on node communication in opportunistic social networks. *Symmetry*, 12(8), 1288.

[11]   Yu, G., Chen, Z. G., Wu, J., and Wu, J. (2019). Quantitative social relations based on trust routing algorithm in opportunistic social network. *EURASIP Journal on Wireless Communications and Networking*, 10(1), 1–18.

[12]   Zhu, K., Li, W., Fu, X., and Zhang, L. (2015). Data routing strategies in opportunistic mobile social networks: taxonomy and open challenges. *Computer Networks*, 93, 183–198.

[13]   Zhang, S., Wang, G., Liu, Q., and Abawajy, J. H. (2018). A trajectory privacy-preserving scheme based on query exchange in mobile social networks. *Soft Computing*, 22(18), 6121–6133.

[14]   Dorffer, C., Puigt, M., Delmaire, G., and Roussel, G. (2018). Informed nonnegative matrix factorization methods for mobile sensor network calibration. *IEEE Transactions on Signal and Information Processing over Networks*, 4(4), 667–682.

[15]   Gu, M., Gao, C., Lyu, J., Fan, W., and You, L. (2021). Study of node distribution and density optimization in mobile sensor network 3D space. *Wireless Communications and Mobile Computing*, 2021, 1–7.

[16]   Chen, Z., Zhou, J., Chen, Y., Chen, X., and Gao, X. (2009, September). Deploying a social community network in rural areas based on wireless mesh networks. In *2009 IEEE Youth Conference on Information, Computing and Telecommunication* (pp. 443–446). IEEE.

[17]   Rahim, A., Kong, X., Xia, F., *et al.* (2018). Vehicular social networks: a survey. *Pervasive and Mobile Computing*, 43, 96–113.

[18]   Vegni, A. M. and Loscri, V. (2015). A survey on vehicular social networks. *IEEE Communications Surveys & Tutorials*, 17(4), 2397–2419.

[19]   Zhou, Q., Xu, Z., and Yen, N. Y. (2019). User sentiment analysis based on social network information and its application in consumer reconstruction intention. *Computers in Human Behavior*, 100, 177–183.

[20]   Gong, L. and Wang, H. (2018, July). When sentiment analysis meets social network: a holistic user behavior modeling in opinionated data. In *Proceedings of the 24th ACM SIGKDD International Conference on Knowledge Discovery & Data Mining* (pp. 1455–1464).

[21] Tiwari, D. and Nagpal, B. (2020, March). Ensemble methods of sentiment analysis: a survey. In *2020 7th International Conference on Computing for Sustainable Global Development (INDIACom)* (pp. 150–155). IEEE.

[22] Basiri, M. E., Nemati, S., Abdar, M., Cambria, E., and Acharya, U. R. (2021). ABCDM: an attention-based bidirectional CNN-RNN deep model for sentiment analysis. *Future Generation Computer Systems*, 115, 279–294.

[23] de Oliveira Carosia, A. E., Coelho, G. P., and da Silva, A. E. A. (2021). Investment strategies applied to the Brazilian stock market: a methodology based on sentiment analysis with deep learning. *Expert Systems with Applications*, 184, 115470.

[24] Tiwari, D. and Nagpal, B. (2021, March). Ensemble sentiment model: bagging with Linear Discriminant Analysis (BLDA). In *2021 8th International Conference on Computing for Sustainable Global Development (INDIACom)* (pp. 474–480). IEEE.

[25] Kossinets, G. and Watts, D. J. (2006). Empirical analysis of an evolving social network. *Science (80)*, 311(5757), 88–90.

[26] Metz, C. (2016). AI is Transforming Google Search. The Rest of the Web Is Next| WIRED.

[27] Tang, M., Xie, F., Liang, W., Xia, Y., and Li, K. C. (2019). Predicting new composition relations between web services via link analysis. *International Journal of Computational Science and Engineering*, 20(1), 88–101.

[28] Al Falahi, K., Atif, Y., and Elnaffar, S. (2010, December). Social networks: challenges and new opportunities. In *2010 IEEE/ACM International Conference on Green Computing and Communications & International Conference on Cyber, Physical and Social Computing* (pp. 804–808). IEEE.

[29] Wang, Y., Vasilakos, A. V., Jin, Q., and Ma, J. (2014). Survey on mobile social networking in proximity (MSNP): approaches, challenges and architecture. *Wireless Networks*, 20(6), 1295–1311.

[30] Elwhishi, A., Ho, P. H., and Shihada, B. (2013). Contention aware mobility prediction routing for intermittently connected mobile networks. *Wireless Networks*, 19(8), 2093–2108.

[31] Kamoru, B. A., Jaafar, A., Jabar, M. A., Murad, M. A. A., and Babangida, M. (2019). Risk measurement of IT privacy and security threat in social networking sites on users perspective. *Risk*, 28(2), 251–257.

[32] Abawajy, J. H., Ninggal, M. I. H., Al Aghbari, Z., Darem, A. B., and Alhashmi, A. (2017, October). Privacy threat analysis of mobile social network data publishing. In *International Conference on Security and Privacy in Communication Systems* (pp. 60–68). Cham: Springer.

[33] Holcomb, W. (2009). World peace using social networks. In *W3C Workshop on the Future of Social Networking Position Papers*.

[34] Rathee, G., Garg, S., Kaddoum, G., Jayakody, D. N. K., Piran, M. J., and Muhammad, G. (2020). A trusted social network using hypothetical mathematical model and decision-based scheme. *IEEE Access*, 9, 4223–4232.

[35] Castelfranchi, C., Falcone, R., and Marzo, F. (2006, May). Being trusted in a social network: trust as relational capital. In *International Conference on Trust Management* (pp. 19–32). Berlin, Heidelberg: Springer.

[36] Anglade, T. P., Pekelman, O., and Montagne, L. (2008). The Social Web: Small Businesses/Big Solutions. https://www.w3.org/2008/09/msnws/papers/af83.pdf.

[37] Tai, C. H., Tseng, P. J., Philip, S. Y., and Chen, M. S. (2011, December). Identities anonymization in dynamic social networks. In *2011 IEEE 11th International Conference on Data Mining* (pp. 1224–1229). IEEE.

[38] Static Social Network: https://slideplayer.com/slide/14593622/. Accessed by: 06-09-2021.

[39] Braha, D. and Bar-Yam, Y. (2006). From centrality to temporary fame: dynamic centrality in complex networks. *Complexity*, 12(2), 59–63.

[40] Sonkar, S. K., Bhatnagar, V., and Challa, R. K. (2013). An analogy between static and dynamic social network based on critical parameters. *International Journal of Social Network Mining*, 1(3–4), 334–355.

[41] Han, Y., Silva, A., Luo, L., Karunasekera, S., and Leckie, C. (2021). Knowledge Enhanced Multi-modal Fake News Detection. arXiv preprint arXiv:2108.04418.

[42] Shu, K., Sliva, A., Wang, S., Tang, J., and Liu, H. (2017). Fake news detection on social media: a data mining perspective. *ACM SIGKDD Explorations Newsletter*, 19(1), 22–36.

[43] Karimi, H., Roy, P., Saba-Sadiya, S., and Tang, J. (2018, August). Multi-source multi-class fake news detection. In *Proceedings of the 27th International Conference on Computational Linguistics* (pp. 1546–1557).

[44] Jiang, Y., Liu, Y., and Yang, Y. (2017, February). Language Tool based university rumor detection on SinaWeibo. In *2017 IEEE International Conference on Big Data and Smart Computing (BigComp)* (pp. 453–454). IEEE.

[45] Wang, W. Y. (2017). "Liar, liar pants on fire": a new benchmark dataset for fake news detection. arXiv preprint arXiv:1705.00648.

[46] Zhou, X. and Zafarani, R. (2020). A survey of fake news: fundamental theories, detection methods, and opportunities. *ACM Computing Surveys (CSUR)*, 53(5), 1–40.

[47] Bartosik-Purgat, M. and Guzek, M. (2016). Factors influencing the choice of social network sites in the light of cross-cultural research. *China-USA Business Review*, 15(9), 438–452.

[48] Rathore, S., Sharma, P. K., Loia, V., Jeong, Y. S., and Park, J. H. (2017). Social network security: issues, challenges, threats, and solutions. *Information Sciences*, 421, 43–69.

[49] Kaur, P., Dhir, A., Tandon, A., Alzeiby, E. A., and Abohassan, A. A. (2020). A systematic literature review on cyberstalking. An analysis of past achievements and future promises. *Technological Forecasting and Social Change*, 163, 120426.

[50] Diomidous, M., Chardalias, K., Magita, A., Koutonias, P., Panagiotopoulou, P., and Mantas, J. (2016). Social and psychological effects of the internet use. *Acta Informatica Medica*, 24(1), 66.

[51] Aleroud, A. and Zhou, L. (2017). Phishing environments, techniques, and countermeasures: a survey. *Computers & Security*, 68, 160–196.

[52] Al-Rawi, A., Groshek, J., and Zhang, L. (2019). What the fake? Assessing the extent of networked political spamming and bots in the propagation of #fakenews on Twitter. *Online Information Review*.

[53] Meligy, A. M., Ibrahim, H. M., and Torky, M. F. (2015). A framework for detecting cloning attacks in OSN based on a novel social graph topology. *International Journal of Intelligent Systems and Applications*, 7(3), 13.

[54] Talukder, N., Ouzzani, M., Elmagarmid, A. K., Elmeleegy, H., and Yakout, M. (2010, March). Privometer: privacy protection in social networks. In *2010 IEEE 26th International Conference on Data Engineering Workshops (ICDEW 2010)* (pp. 266–269). IEEE.

[55] Ye, J., Ni, J., and Yi, Y. (2017). Deep learning hierarchical representations for image steganalysis. *IEEE Transactions on Information Forensics and Security*, 12(11), 2545–2557.

[56] Chaumont, M. (2020). Deep learning in steganography and steganalysis. In *Digital Media Steganography* (pp. 321–349). London: Academic Press.

[57] Nagai, Y., Uchida, Y., Sakazawa, S., and Satoh, S. I. (2018). Digital watermarking for deep neural networks. *International Journal of Multimedia Information Retrieval*, 7(1), 3–16.

[58] Arora, S. and Bhatia, M. P. S. (2020). Biometrics for forensic identification in web applications and social platforms using deep learning. In *Forensic Investigations and Risk Management in Mobile and Wireless Communications* (pp. 80–113). Hershey, PA: IGI Global.

[59] Van Schaik, P., Jansen, J., Onibokun, J., Camp, J., and Kusev, P. (2018). Security and privacy in online social networking: risk perceptions and precautionary behaviour. *Computers in Human Behavior*, 78, 283–297.

[60] Lawler, J. P. and Molluzzo, J. C. (2010). A study of the perceptions of students on privacy and security on social networking sites (SNS) on the internet. *Journal of Information Systems Applied Research*, 3(12), 3–18.

[61] Almeida, F. (2012). Web 2.0 technologies and social networking security fears in enterprises. arXiv preprint arXiv:1204.1824.

[62] Shin, D. H. (2010). The effects of trust, security and privacy in social networking: a security-based approach to understand the pattern of adoption. *Interacting with Computers*, 22(5), 428–438.

[63] Hajli, N. and Lin, X. (2016). Exploring the security of information sharing on social networking sites: the role of perceived control of information. *Journal of Business Ethics*, 133(1), 111–123.

[64] Saridakis, G., Benson, V., Ezingeard, J. N., and Tennakoon, H. (2016). Individual information security, user behaviour and cyber victimisation: an empirical study of social networking users. *Technological Forecasting and Social Change*, 102, 320–330.

Chapter 4

Social networking: challenges, security issues, and emerging trends

Neha Sharma[1], Rakesh Kumar[1] and Mayank Swarnkar[1]

Abstract

In today's society, social networks are becoming increasingly popular. Social networking platforms have paved the way for billions of users to build connections with their family, friends, and colleagues. In addition, these sites have become a hub for exchanging job searching, entertainment, and education information among people. These platforms provide the smooth flow of these services from one geographical border to another by allowing users to update their data, interact with each other, and browse other users' profiles. However, sharing personal information over social networking platforms creates security issues for their users. This chapter provides a thorough examination of several security risks affecting Internet users. We also offer challenges social networking platforms face in numerous fields. We then discuss the emerging trends in social networking platforms. Lastly, we also mentioned the existing solutions to security risks that affect the social networking platforms.

Keywords: Social networking; Security threats; Cyber security risks

4.1 Introduction

Social networking platforms have gained significant popularity in recent years. These platforms establish a virtual connection between individuals with similar interests and behaviors. The primary reason for these platforms' favor is the convenient exchange of data, photos, videos, and other information among billions of online users. The fundamental concept of social networking platforms is shown in Figure 4.1. These platforms provide a mechanism that enables users to build connections with their family, friends, and colleagues. These platforms have become successful and prominent because users can update their personal information, interact with each other, and browse other users' profiles [1]. In addition, these

[1]Department of Computer Science & Engineering, Indian Institute of Technology (BHU) – Varanasi, India

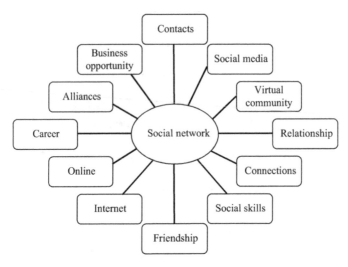

Figure 4.1   Fundamental concepts of social networking platforms

platforms can be beneficial for users who belong to different geographical borders. These platforms provide an outlet for every online user to exchange information about job searching, entertainment, and education. However, sharing data on these platforms at a massive rate has invited risks for their users. The data exchanged on these online platforms is a desirable target for attackers to carry out invasions such as spam, malware, phishing, social bots, identity theft, and many more. Moreover, attackers can commit serious Internet crimes such as account hijacking, impersonation, and bank fraud by gaining unauthorized access to users' data. Social networking platforms such as Facebook produce and share multimedia content among their users. The sharing of such content has increased security risks for authentic users. An attacker can conceal malicious information with multimedia content and share it in the network. It gives an easy path for attackers to steal users' personal information, such as their identity and location. Many researchers have discussed solutions such as watermarking, steganalysis, digital oblivion, and others for protecting users attacked by threats caused by multimedia data. On the other hand, solutions like spam, phishing, and other detections have been proposed to mitigate traditional threats. Besides studying these attacks, many security researchers studied security issues in social networking platforms that target minor and significant organizations [2]. All these motivations insist us to write this chapter. All these motivations insist on writing this chapter.

This chapter is organized as follows: Section 4.1 discusses challenging aspects of social networking. A brief study of network models provides in Section 4.2. Section 4.3 describes fake news detection and its prevention. Section 4.4 analyses the factors that affect the design of social networks. Security challenges and promising solutions in social networking are discussed in Section 4.5. Finally, Section 4.6 concludes the chapter and gives future directions.

4.2 Challenging aspects of social networking

Social networking platforms have many challenging aspects such as privacy, access for those with disabilities, cyber security, commercial advertising, terms of agreements, data protection, optimization transparency, fake profile detection, and understanding phishing risks.

4.2.1 Privacy

Online privacy is one of the main concerns for social networking platforms. The invention of social networking sites has enabled social profiling, which is a growing concern for Internet privacy. These platforms facilitate participatory information sharing and collaboration. People share information saved by these sites for later use through these platforms. Examples of problems include cyberstalking, location disclosure, third-party information disclosure, and government use of information in investigations without safeguarding a search warrant. These platforms have also been criticized for collecting personal data by companies to target ads at users. In contrast, these social platforms have taken steps to improve privacy for users. However, there is still a need for a significant change in the direction of cyber bullies, trolls, hate speech, etc. [3].

4.2.2 Access for those with disabilities

Social networking platforms are an excellent tool for sharing information directly with consumers. However, if these platforms' content is not accessible to people with disabilities, then access to critical information is missed. Access to these platforms for disabled people will inform them of real-time updates during an emergency. Despite widespread Internet services and social networking platforms across the globe, there are many accessibility barriers such as audio description, captioning, color contrast, poor design, and flashing images that have restricted people with disabilities such as hearing, sight, mobility impairment to access the Internet and these platforms. Thus, people with mental or physical disabilities require long-term support from family, digital society, and tech giants to "get online" and express their views [4].

4.2.3 Cyber security

Cybercrimes have increased since the adoption of social networking platforms for personal and business use among individuals. They occur due to the lack of knowledge about the risks involved with these platforms. They include tampering with computer source documents, loss or damage to computer resources, attempting hacking, accessing digital signature certificates by misrepresentation of facts, publishing false digital signature certificates, fraud digital signature certificates, breaking of confidentiality or privacy, and failure to aid in decrypting the information intercepted by a government agency. Thus cyber security plays a significant role in protecting users' personal and professional intake from attacks on the Internet [3].

4.2.4   Commercial advertising

Tech giants use social networking platforms to rank their products and services by processing users' private data. These favored the spread of advertisements that are based on sensitive data such as race or religion. Many companies are illegally collecting users' personal information without their knowledge and selling it to advertising companies [5]. Commercial advertising has several detrimental effects on these platforms, including deceptive advertising that gains consumers' trust by using false and misleading interpretations of their products and children-targeted advertising that portrays a cute and happy child to persuade parents to purchase the product. These advertisements undermine social or cultural traditions, and the repeated display of advertisements confuses consumers and others.

4.2.5   Terms of agreements

The terms of the agreement constitute a binding contract between the user and the social networking platforms, and the user must abide by them to utilize the platforms' services. The terms of an agreement are favorable to the user when payment is involved in the agreement. The user now has more significant rights as a result. The user must, however, give up some privacy in the absence of payment by enabling these platforms to follow the information through cookies. Almost all these platforms have a similar policy agreement that takes ownership and controls browsing habits and sells this information to third-party marketers [5].

4.2.6   Data protection

The recent rise in social networking platforms has invited attacks such as identity theft, cyberstalking, and unwanted screening of a user's profile through the personal information users post online [3]. Social networking sites suffer from the data protection issue because people have the right to free speech and flexible communication on these platforms. These platforms collect, store, and process information users share and use algorithms to give them personalized content.

4.2.7   Optimizing transparency

Social networking platforms demand new knowledge and skills from people. Dealing with these platforms in an informed way requires an understanding of new technologies and their legal implications to use these technologies. Many services of these platforms lack the transparency and trust of users and consumers [6]. Being transparent on social networking platforms does not mean that every detail has to be made public, but it involves some points. First, acknowledge the mistakes online and fix them. Second, these platforms allow direct connection between a user and a business. Responding publicly to their complaints, questions, good and bad comments will help a business to build trust among users. Third, being honest about products will build trust between clients and businesses.

4.2.8 Fake profile detection

Social networking platforms have become an essential part of every individual's life. Some people are continually active on these platforms to spread hate messages such as rumors, bullied text, and others through the creation of fake profiles. The primary purpose of fake accounts is to access personal information like name, phone number, credit card details, and other details to steal money [7]. Sometimes, messages of fancy offers and giveaways come directly from the brand, but both the account and the offers are fake. Imposters take pictures and details of the actual page and create a fraudulent page to reach out the customers of the original brand.

4.2.9 Understanding phishing risks

Social networking platforms have become a prominent tool for businesses to offer their latest product information and attract new business. It makes them an attractive platform for cyber-criminals to deceive their victim by creating phishing attacks, eavesdropping, and other attacks. These attacks begin when an attacker sends a link to a user purposely designed to entice the victim. Once the user clicks the link, he is taken to phishing (that looks genuine) site. Users must provide the authentication details and validate them through Google Drive, OneDrive, or others to see the content they entered. This is how an attacker can access the user's account through phony pages [8].

4.3 Network models: static and dynamic

Communication is essential in developing pleasant and healthy interpersonal connections. Since the beginning, it has been an integral part of our lives. Communication growth is a constant process. Communication has gotten more widespread as contemporary technology has advanced. People used to communicate through gatherings in the early days. People began engaging through technology by sending letters and conversing on the phone. After a few years, communication was established via electronic mail and chat. People are now communicating with one another via social networking platforms. These platforms have become a medium for quick and easy interaction among people. These provide benefits to people interested in establishing relationships with their friends, family, and relatives and business and professional relationships with their clients and colleagues. A social networking site is considered a graph of interaction between individuals who build social connections for sharing content based on similar interests and backgrounds. A graph of these platforms consists of people and interactions between them. A graph for any social networking platform can be represented as $G = (V, E)$, where G is a graph, V is a set of vertices or nodes, and E is a set of edges or links. Nodes in a chart represent people, and edges represent the relationship between people. Two network models are considered for these platforms: static model and dynamic model [9]. A static model describes people and interactions between them at a particular time such that all the information shared between people is removed. A dynamic model represents people and interactions that occur over time, and all the shared information is considered. Several critical parameters stated by various authors differentiate between the static model and dynamic model represented in Table 4.1.

Table 4.1   Difference between static model and dynamic model in SNSs

S. no.	Parameter	Static model	Dynamic model	References
1	Time	Interaction takes place at a particular instant in time.	Interaction takes place all over the time.	[10]
2	Relationship	Restrictions are imposed while changing the relation between actors.	Restrictions are not imposed while changing relation between actors.	[11]
3	Information	All the information during interaction is removed.	All the information during interaction is considered.	[12]
4	Effect	Inward change is observed.	Outward change is observed.	[10]
5	Accuracy	Inaccurate information can be given about patterns in the data.	Accurate information can be given about patterns in the data.	[12]
6	Size	Nodes and links cannot be updated.	Nodes and links can be updated.	[11,13,14]
7	Community	Individual roles and social status are unchanged.	Individual roles and social status are changed.	[15]
8	State	Network states are unchanged.	Network states are different with time.	[16]
9	Instance	Single instance of the same network is considered for privacy preserving techniques.	Multiple instances of the same network are considered for privacy preserving techniques.	[17]
10	Circle	People are not allowed to move in or move out of the network.	People are allowed to move in and move out of the network at any time.	[16]
11	Privacy	Publishing the single instance of the same network doesn't raise privacy risks.	Publishing the multiple instances of the same network can raise privacy risks.	[17]
12	Representation	A graph is represented as $G = (V, E)$ where V is a set of vertices and E is a set of edges that represents relationship between users.	A graph is represented in time stamp t as $G(t) = (V(t), E(t))$ where $V(t)$ is a set of vertices and $E(t)$ is a set of edges that represents relationship between users over time.	[17]
13	Features	Static characteristics are socio-demographics, socio-economic and socio-cultural characteristics.	Dynamic characteristics are belief, values, and interests which change based on event in real world.	[18]

(Continues)

Table 4.1   (Continued)

S. no.	Parameter	Static model	Dynamic model	References
14	Techniques	Visualization techniques for static network develop rapidly.	Visualization techniques for dynamic network develop slowly.	[19,20]
15	Clustering	Clustering algorithm approximately measurement-based and probability-based.	Clustering algorithm mostly measurement-based and probability-based.	[21]
16	Expansion	Network cannot be expanded once created.	Network can be changed and expanded over time.	[22]
17	Structure	Knowledge about structure is prior known.	Knowledge about structure may not know in advance.	[22]
18	Evolution	Changes are seen slowly.	Rapid changes are seen over time.	[23]
19	Rate	Spreading of worm is slow in static networks.	Spreading of worm is much faster in dynamic networks from one node to other.	[23]

4.4   Fake news detection and its prevention

According to Cambridge Dictionary, *Fake News* is defined as "fake stories manufactured and circulated on the Internet to affect public sentiment and look real" [24]. Fake news is not a new concept, but it has been a topic of discussion even before the emergence of the Internet as publishers used to spread misleading information among people through newspapers, magazines, and articles. The propagation of fake news has increased with the explosive use of social networking platforms. These platforms have become a fertile ground for fabricated stories without verifiable facts or sources. Different notions of misinformation, disinformation, and mal-information are interchangeably used to denote fake news. Misinformation is false or misleading information shared by a person who believes it is true. The spreading of misinformation is unintentional and often confused with deliberately deceptive disinformation. Disinformation is false information shared by a person intending to deceive people's opinions. Mal-information is information based on reality and facts but shared intending to cause harm to people, organizations, or countries. Social networking platforms have recently experienced an enormous influx of bogus information. Therefore, many researchers and tech giants automatically work together to detect fake news on these platforms. This section will discuss some approaches based on news content and social context. Fake news detection methods are illustrated in Figure 4.2.

4.4.1   Content based

This method analyzes the news article's content (either text or image or both). This approach is categorized into knowledge-based, style-based, and linguistic-based.

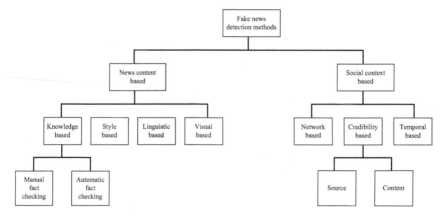

Figure 4.2   Fake news detection methods

4.4.1.1   Knowledge based

This approach is based on expert fact-checking manually or via tools (known as automatic fact-checking). Manual fact-checking is further divided into crowd-sourced and expert-based categories.

- Manual fact checking
  1. Expert based: In this method, experts check the authenticity of the facts presented in the news article by using their domain knowledge and making decisions. Some websites that use expert-based methods such as Snopes [25], PoltiFact [26], and GossipCop [27] are unsuitable for websites containing enormous amounts of data because they will consume a lot of time in decision-making. Some researchers use these fact-checking websites to create their datasets LIAR [28] and FakeNewsNet [29].
  2. Crowd sourced: In this method, the crowd uses "wisdom" to check the truth of the news article's facts. A similar approach is used by Fiskkit [30]. This website provides a platform for people to discuss important news articles and determine their accuracy. The crowd-sourced method has better scalability than the knowledge-based method but may have collisions between the opinions stated by different people on the fact that may distort the capability of making an accurate decision. Some popular datasets created using this method are CREDBANK [31] and AMT (Amazon Mechanical Turk) [32].
- Automatic fact checking
  This method is required because manual fact-checking approaches do not perform well with vast volumes of data generated from social networking sites. Manual fact-checking of a large amount of data is time-consuming and may lack accuracy. Therefore, automatic fact-checking methods heavily rely on natural language processing, machine learning, data mining, and network or graph theory approaches [33] for fact-checking tasks. This method is

further divided into (1) fact extraction, collecting facts, and constructing a knowledge base. And (2) fact-checking checks the authenticity of the truth by comparing it with the attributes present in the knowledge base. This method uses open web source to check whether the given claim is true or false. Automatic fact-checking is a complex method because it requires real-world datasets that are often incomplete, noisy, unstructured, and unlabeled.

4.4.1.2 Style based

This method is similar to the knowledge-based approach. However, this method does not evaluate the content of the news article but assesses the intention of the writer to mislead people's opinion. Many authors intend to influence people by using catch fake titles that contain capitalized words, proper nouns, and fewer stop words. The content style consists of two features: textual and visual elements that help distinguish between a legitimate author and a fake author. Textual features comprised types from at-least four language levels: lexicon, syntax, discourse, and semantic [34].

4.4.1.3 Linguistic based

Linguistic features have been popular for detecting fake news in articles. These features are mainly categorized into five primary types: (1) readability index quantifies reading difficulty based on word length, number of syllables, and sentence length. (2) Psycho-linguistic features describe the emotions and behavior of a person. (3) Stylistic features explain the style of a sentence. (4) User credibility features describe information about the user. (5) Quantity gives information about a sentence based on the number of words and number of sentences.

4.4.1.4 Visual based

Visual content usually has more power than text for captivating users' attention, and thus, publishers use the image as a tool to propagate false notions among people and mislead them. Images are trendy and have a substantial impact on microblogs news propagation [35], and it is easier to draw people's attention toward false content through image content.

4.4.2 Social context based

This method is categorized into three types such as network-based, temporal-based, and credibility.

4.4.2.1 Network based

People connect on social networking platforms based on their common interests and backgrounds and form a network. This network helps the smooth flow of information from one end to another. On the other hand, this network can also be used to detect fake news by identifying the person who shared the fake news, the relationship among spreaders, and how fake news propagates in the network.

4.4.2.2   Temporal based

News articles on social networking platforms are often not static but are constantly being updated with new additional information and twisted versions. This phenomenon is commonly observed in cases where rumors are circulated multiple times after the original article post.

4.4.2.3   Credibility based

In this method, credibility of the news is checked to detect its fakeness. The credibility of the source of the fake news is checked in quality and believability. There are two indicators: (1) source and (2) content for identifying the credibility of the news.

4.4.3   Fake news prevention

We are unable to stop fake news from appearing on social networking platforms. However, if we take ownership of our acts, we may try to prevent them from spreading. Here are a few things you can do to help with the problem rather than the solution.

1.   Before sharing an article, it is imperative to read the news article's title.
2.   Use fact-checking websites to identify fake news.
3.   Report option on social platforms can be used to flag posts that are spam, harmful, or inappropriate.
4.   If you are unsure about an article, do not share, like, or comment.

4.5   Factors that affect the design of social networks

The current study focuses on finding a complete model that predicts the usage of social networking sites rather than testing the universality of the acceptance model in the context of these sites. This acceptance model looks at how preferences toward these platforms impact usage. To create a more rigorous model that depicts the use of these platforms, one that incorporates various design factors related to security, such as the perception of these platforms' characteristics, the reasons that people use the Internet, their concerns about privacy, level of innovation, age, and gender.

4.5.1   The perception of social networking platform characteristics

The acceptance model incorporates more precise attitude components such as perceptions and user satisfaction as drivers of a new social networking platform's intention to use and actual use. The extent to which an individual feels that employing a given system will improve their job performance is described as user satisfaction. Furthermore, the ease of use refers to an individual's belief that utilizing a given technology requires no physical or mental effort. However, the acceptance model has been used effectively for Internet-related technologies and services, including software platforms, e-commerce, online banking, etc. The current study indicates that cognitive utility and user satisfaction are associated with the speed and magnitude of social networking platforms users based on analysis from prior studies [36].

4.5.2   The reasons that people use the Internet

According to research, Internet use can be motivated by five factors: social utility, leisure, informativeness, accessibility, and enjoyment. It is clear from the study that the majority of motivations are connected to interpersonal or social usefulness. This research also revealed the connections between other reasons for accessing the Internet and the frequency and duration of use of social networking platforms [37].

4.5.3   Concerns about privacy

The desired people have to maintain their private sphere, which is called privacy, free from intrusion by other people and institutions. The interested people have been able to control, or at least significantly influence, how information about them is handled, known as information privacy. Privacy is crucial on the Internet because it encourages customers' trust, leading to the increased usage of social networking platforms. However, sharing information among individuals on the community of social media is widespread, resulting in individuals' sensitivity to exposing personal data compared to other areas such as traveling, financial, computer, sports, and vehicle platforms. As a result, this study argues that there is a link between privacy concerns and the usage of social networking platforms [3].

4.5.4   Level of innovation

It is described as a person's inclination to think outside the box. It is determined by people and is regarded as crucial in technological acceptance. Associated with creativity is also incorporated into acceptance model studies to broaden the area of acceptance model application. It has been discovered that a user's creativeness is a favorable indicator of Internet use frequency. Hence, it has been shown that innovation is a significant indicator of the adoption of personal computers and social networking platforms [38].

4.5.5   Age

It is inversely related to Internet usage. The adoption of particular Internet-related technologies, including social networking and banking platforms, has been observed. As a result, the research suggests a negative correlation between age and social networking platforms used [38].

4.5.6   Gender

According to traditional literature, men are more inclined than women to accept new technologies related to social networking platforms and also found that men are more willing than women to take on new technologies earlier. The survey also found that female students use social networking more frequently and for extended periods each session than male students. The current study also suggests a gender difference in using social networking platforms when taken as a whole [38].

4.6   Security challenges and promising solutions in social networking

In the modern era, social networks are ubiquitous. Numerous social networks such as Twitter, Facebook, WhatsApp, Instagram, YouTube, and others are used by millions of people because they enable communication with loved ones and sharing of personal data through these social platforms. However, problems with protecting a user's privacy and safety might arise, mainly when the user's submitted material consists of multimedia, such as images, videos, audio, and other personal information. There are both good and bad consequences, causing risks as social networking grows in popularity. All of this relates to an increase in various social criminal acts as well as their promising solutions. These are categorized into four classes of threats such as multimedia social threats, traditional networking and information security threats, as shown in Figure 4.3.

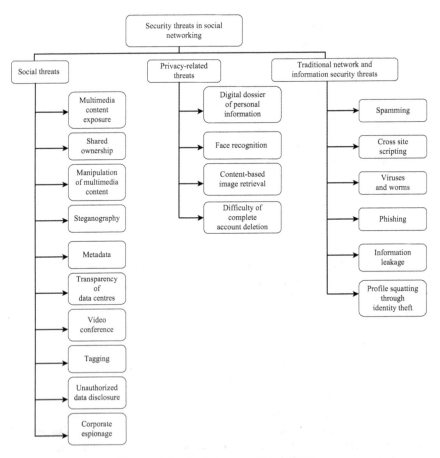

Figure 4.3   Social networking threats

4.6.1 Multimedia social threats

Social networking platforms that allow users to exchange multimedia content, such as movies, images, activities, and other information, fall under this category. Users of modern social networking platforms can exchange audiovisual content socially, which increases the likelihood of unauthorized usage of these contents. For example, photographs or videos uploaded by users on this platform might expose their position through geotagging as a social networking tool. This type contains a range of risks, including those covered in subsections: exposure to multimedia content, shared ownership, modification of multimedia content, steganography, metadata, and more [39], as shown in Figure 4.3.

4.6.1.1 Multimedia content exposure threat

This risk includes disclosing user personal multimedia textual information (i.e., user id, address, and other sensitive information) on social networking platforms. For instance, a user's uploaded photo from a recent activity may reveal the user's present position, and trespassers may use this private information to their advantage. Many social application platforms have been developed, such as face recognition systems, speech recognition systems, and other similar platforms that can divulge personal information without user consent. The solution to this threat is watermarking technique. It embeds data into media content to prove ownership of it. It can be visible or invisible. Visible watermarking is often clear text or a trademark incorporated in the picture and correctly identifies the source. The naked eye cannot see invisible watermarking, which comes in various strengths, semi-frail, and fragile forms. After a harmful assault or data processing, the data can be retrieved when watermarking is used [40].

4.6.1.2 Shared ownership

This issue covers the shared data related to multiple users across social networking platforms. For example, if a user uploads collective pics of considerable users without other users' consent on social networking platforms, that may reveal the privacy of other users. Even if it makes sense, the optimal privacy settings must not be determined by the convergence of each user's security settings. The solution to this type of threat is the co-ownership method. Multiple users can establish their privacy preferences for co-owned videos and photos thanks to the co-ownership paradigm [41].

4.6.1.3 Manipulation of multimedia content

The social networking site enables users to exchange private multimedia content, which poses a risk of being altered or manipulated by unethical individuals. Several media distortion technologies such as holo-matrix, twitch, and others are available to modify users' multimedia data on social networking sites. The solution for this type of threat is also watermarking, as discussed in Section 6.1.1 [42].

4.6.1.4 Steganography

This is the process of hiding a secret message within the multimedia data in order concealing from public users of the social networking platform. This technique has grown in popularity as technology and science have advanced, and many legitimate applications are now available on social networking sites. For instance, hackers may use a malicious script embedded in multimedia documents to initiate attacks. Unaware opening one of such documents causes the malicious script to be activated, which causes significant damage. The existing solution to this threat is steganalysis. Utilizing steganalysis tools or processes to locate adverse information inside multimedia data is essential [43].

4.6.1.5   Metadata

This is the data that offers information on the data but not the substance, such as a message's text or the image itself. The metadata on social networking sites contains essential information about other data, such as a user's location, ID, address, and additional relevant information. If it is revealed to intruders, attacks could be launched. The existing solution to this type of threat is metadata security. This method encodes media metadata and saves it in the file [40].

4.6.1.6   Transparency of data centers

This is also a significant problem on social networking platforms that can compromise user privacy since unencrypted data shared by many users might entice unwanted activity from an unauthorized user by offering a direct connection to this material. The service providers can see the shared data on these platforms. Large social networking sites with their data servers, like Facebook, LinkedIn, WhatsApp, etc., are reliable. However, we cannot rely on small platforms since they keep data on servers owned by other parties, which might be revealed to marketing merchants and divulge personal information. The existing solution for this threat is encrypting storage. Multiple cryptographic algorithms may save and recover data from social networking platforms without revealing it to a third-party service provider [40].

4.6.1.7   Video conference

The majority of social networking sites provide their members the option to engage via audio or video conferencing. Since hackers may intercept the broadcast video stream by taking advantage of any flaws, it can give out more information to them. They can access their webcams by exploiting protocol vulnerabilities and recording the video conferencing to extort users by modifying it. The solution for this type of threat is detecting malware in multimedia data. Many tracking approaches for detecting malware online propagation through the web have been presented. However, because malware has unique propagation pathways, these processes cannot be used to identify its proliferation on social networking platforms [40].

4.6.1.8   Tagging

The social networking sites include tagging functionality for multimedia data to improve user engagement and search functionality. Through this, users may tag images and videos that can be used to locate other users and connect to additional information that might put users' privacy at risk. For example, malicious users propagate their malicious content to numerous users by quickly tagging large audiences. The existing threat solutions are co-ownership, privacy settings, and report users, discussed in the previous sub-sections [44].

4.6.1.9 Unauthorized data disclosure

The social networking platforms include tagging functionality for multimedia data to improve user engagement and search functionality. Through this, users may tag images and videos that can be used to locate other users and connect to additional information that might put users' privacy at risk. For example, malicious users propagate their malicious content to numerous users by quickly tagging large audiences. The existing threat solutions are co-ownership, privacy settings, and report users, discussed in the previous sub-sections. The discussed remedy to this threat is watermarking, storage encryption, privacy settings, etc. [45].

4.6.1.10 Corporate espionage

Social networking site-based social engineering assaults are an increasing but sometimes underappreciated risk to a business's IT infrastructure. The damage to enterprise copyright law is the primary concern here. Still, access to insiders may also be necessary for a wide range of other crimes, including damaging malicious activities of enterprise networks, employee extortion for the disclosure of private client information, and even physical asset access. The current solutions for this threat are zero trust and modern desktop techniques. Zero Trust is an evaluation and implementation that believes individuals within and outside an enterprise can be infiltrated and spoofed. This strategy focuses on identity verification checks through innovations such as multi-factor authentication, physical equipment status, and encoding. Modern Desktop refers to using Microsoft office 365 in the data center with the Windows 11 operating system to run an organization's internal computer systems. It provides consumers with access to the newest, safest productivity tools [46].

4.6.2 Privacy-related threat

It is described as any risk or sequence of threats to illegally use or publicly expose sensitive information stolen from an insured to collect money, securities, or other valuable physical or intellectual property from the insured. It may include various threats such as digital dossiers of personal information, face recognition, content-based image retrieval, image tagging, and others, as shown in Figure 4.3.

4.6.2.1 Digital dossiers of personal information

It is a typical vulnerability associated with personal data access via profile browsing, as a digital dossier of personal data by a third party on a social networking site. It is a typical vulnerability associated with private data access via profile viewing, as a digital dossier of personal data by a third party on a social networking site. Information can be revealed on social platforms by intruders to blackmail or damage personal information so that users miss opportunities related to employment or others. For example, until permissions can be altered, users' personal information is searchable on social networking sites such as WhatsApp, Facebook, LinkedIn, and others. The solution to this threat is digital oblivion. It involves setting an expiration date on digital data so that no one may access it once that date has passed [47].

4.6.2.2   Face recognition

It can connect profiles on social networking platforms by liking images across them. For example, anonymous profiles on social media connect users with unknown photos that may be adversarial for getting personal information for alteration or damage. Different solutions for protection from facial recognition are limited data storage time, data sharing restriction, explicit notification in public areas, requiring opt-in for new applications, etc. [48].

4.6.2.3   Content-based image retrieval

It is a new technology that can correlate attributes, including identifying elements of a room (like a painting), in substantial image databases, increasing the likelihood that users will be able to locate anything. It makes it possible to infer location information from profiles, including pictures of people's residences that appear anonymous. Risks related to the unintentional revelation of location information, such as bullying, unsolicited marketing, blackmail, and others, might result from this. The solution to this threat is digital oblivion, as discussed earlier [42].

4.6.2.4   Difficulty of complete account deletion

It is typically more difficult for users of social networking sites to delete relevant sources than it is to delete their user accounts from any online social network. The user's private details may be compromised. The data cannot be erased and used to create a digital record. For example, public remarks published by a person utilizing their identity on other profiles will stay accessible even after they delete their profile. The solutions for this threat are multi-factor authentication, least privilege permissions, protecting your system administrator credentials safe and not using them for routine operations, etc. [42].

4.6.3   *Traditional network and information security threats*

These are the traditional security breaches for any organization with a complex network that does not maintain properly. It includes various types of traditional network and information security threats such as spamming, cross-site scripting, viruses and worms, phishing, and others, as shown in Figure 4.1.

4.6.3.1   Spamming

It is a process in which undesired, unsolicited digital communication is transmitted in large quantities. It is frequently delivered by e-mail, but it can also be delivered via text messages, phone calls, or social media. Spam on social networking sites can cause traffic congestion, loss of trust, difficulty using the underlying software, and phishing and referral to pornographic websites. Several remedies to this problem include steganalysis, virus identification, spammer detection, and so on.

4.6.3.2 Cross-site scripting, viruses, and worms

Cross-site scripting attacks, in which intruders insert malicious code to overcome control on the precise origin, make social networking systems susceptible. An attacker can use this flaw to hijack the profile on a social networking platform, launch a phishing attack, and disseminate unwanted information through email and instant messaging traffic. Furthermore, it may be used for service denial and resulting reputation loss. A network level firewall is a typical method of preventing cross-site scripting and virus infection. Because HTTP/HTTPS protocols have unrestricted access via standard firewall settings, these firewall obstacles are ineffective [47].

4.6.3.3 Phishing

Phishing is a social networking threat in which an intruder can send a fake communication to fool a user into disclosing sensitive information to the intruder or install harmful software, such as ransomware, on the victim's infrastructure. It can expose user credentials and credit card or bank account details, causing reputational and financial harm. The data is protected from threats such as digital oblivion, phishing detection, and spammer detection [47].

4.6.3.4 Information leakage

Information leakage occurs when a system is supposed to be impenetrable to an eavesdropper yet leaks some information to an unauthorized user. A few possible problems with this risk include data leakage, phishing for data, spamming, marketing activities, etc. Different solutions to this type of threat are selecting a role-based access management software, increasing the effectiveness of your strategy by using application control, employing a risk management framework for vulnerabilities, protecting your access points effectively, data encryption, etc. [46].

4.6.3.5 Profile squatting through identity theft

An attacker can create a malicious profile by using the user's personal information that impersonates them, thereby causing all sorts of problems for the victim. It may cause serious harm to a user's or a brand's reputation, which could result in social and financial disgrace. Many solutions to this type of threat are imposing restrictions on your credit, examining your economic statements regularly, avoiding accessing public WiFi, maintaining strong and unique credentials, etc. [46].

4.7 Conclusion

Social networking platforms are a well-liked method of communication for billions of Internet users since they allow users to share views, ideas, pictures, and videos with friends regardless of their location or financial situation. However, using these services might expose users to serious cyber security risks. This chapter discussed various challenges, security issues, and promising solutions in social networking. We also comprehensively studied static and dynamic models based on several critical parameters. We also described numerous methods for fake news detection and its prevention. We also examined factors that affect the design of social networks. We also illustrate the security issues of social networking with their existing solutions. In the future, we aim to contribute some experimental works to understand theoretical concepts better.

References

[1] Wang F, She J, Ohyama Y, *et al.* Maximizing positive influence in competitive social networks: a trust-based solution. *Information Sciences.* 2021; 546:559–572.

[2] Sapountzi A and Psannis KE. Social networking data analysis tools and challenges. *Future Generation Computer Systems.* 2018;86:893–913.

[3] Obar JA and Oeldorf-Hirsch A. The biggest lie on the Internet: ignoring the privacy policies and terms of service policies of social networking services. *Information, Communication & Society.* 2020;23:128–147.

[4] Voykinska V, Azenkot S, Wu S and Leshed G. How blind people interact with visual content on social networking services. In: *Proceedings of the 19th ACM Conference on Computer-Supported Cooperative Work & Social Computing (CSCW'16).* New York, NY: Association for Computing Machinery, ACM; 2016, p.1584–1595.

[5] Shareef MA, Mukerji B, Dwivedi YK, *et al.* Social media marketing: comparative effect of advertisement sources. *Journal of Retailing and Consumer Services.* 2019;46:58–69.

[6] Zhang Z and Gupta BB. Social media security and trustworthiness: overview and new direction. *Future Generation Computer Systems.* 2018;86:914–925.

[7] Shu K, Sliva A, Wang S, *et al.* Fake news detection on social media: a data mining perspective. *ACM SIGKDD Explorations Newsletter.* 2017;19:22–36.

[8] Lee NM. Fake news, phishing, and fraud: a call for research on digital media literacy education beyond the classroom. *Communication Education.* 2018; 67:460–466.

[9] Sonkar SK, Bhatnagar V, and Challa RK. An analogy between static and dynamic social network based on critical parameters. *International Journal of Social Network Mining.* 2013;1:334–355.

[10] Adler RM. A dynamic social network software platform for counter-terrorism decision support. In: White CC (ed.), *Proceeding of the 1st International Conference on IEEE Intelligence and Security Informatics (ISI'07).* New Brunswick, NJ: IEEE; 2007, p. 47–54.

[11] Safar M, Farahat H, and Mahdi K. Analysis of dynamic social network: E-mail messages exchange network. In: Gabriele Kotsis EP and David Taniar (eds.), *Proceedings of the 11th International Conference on Information Integration and Web-based Applications & Services (iiWAS'09).* New York, NY: Association for Computing Machinery, ACM; 2009, p. 41–48.

[12] Berger-Wolf TY and Saia J. A framework for analysis of dynamic social networks. In: Tina Eliassi-Rad MCDG, and Lyle Ungar (eds.), *Proceedings of the 12th ACM SIGKDD International Conference on Knowledge Discovery and Data Mining (KDD'06)*. New York, NY: Association for Computing Machinery, ACM; 2006, p. 523–528.

[13] Immorlica N, Lucier B, and Rogers B. Cooperation in anonymous dynamic social networks. In: David C, Parkes MT, and Dellarocas C (eds.), *Proceedings of the 11th ACM Conference on Electronic Commerce (EC'10)*. New York, NY: Association for Computing Machinery, ACM; 2010, p. 241–242.

[14] Yang T, Chi Y, Zhu S, *et al.* Detecting communities and their evolutions in dynamic social networks—a Bayesian approach. *Machine Learning.* 2011; 82:157–189.

[15] Lin YR, Chi Y, Zhu S, *et al.* Analyzing communities and their evolutions in dynamic social networks. *ACM Transactions on Knowledge Discovery from Data (TKDD).* 2009;3:1–31.

[16] Xu A and Zheng X. Dynamic social network analysis using latent space model and an integrated clustering algorithm. In: Bo Yang YDLTY, Zhu W, and Ma J (eds.), *Proceedings of the 8th IEEE International Conference on Dependable, Autonomic and Secure Computing (DASC'09)*. Chengdu, China: IEEE; 2009, p. 620–625.

[17] Bhagat S, Cormode G, Krishnamurthy B, *et al.* Privacy in dynamic social networks. In: Michael Rappa JFSC and Jones P (eds.), *Proceedings of the 19th International Conference on World Wide Web (WWW'10)*. New York, NY: Association for Computing Machinery; 2010, p. 1059–1060.

[18] Alt JK and Lieberman S. Representing dynamic social networks in discrete event social simulation. In: Björn Johansson JMT and Jain S (eds.), *Proceedings of the 42nd Conference on Winter Simulation (WSC'10)*. Baltimore, MD: Winter Simulation Conference; 2010, p. 1478–1489.

[19] Peterson E. Time spring layout for visualization of dynamic social networks. In: Cole J, (ed.) *Proceedings of the 1st IEEE Network Science Workshop (NSW'11)*. West Point, NY: IEEE; 2011, p. 98–104.

[20] Gove R, Gramsky N, Kirby R, *et al.* NetVisia: heat map and matrix visualization of dynamic social network statistics and content. In: Alex (Sandy) Pentland LS, and Clippinger J (eds.), *Proceedings of the 3rd IEEE International Conference on Privacy, Security, Risk and Trust/3rd IEEE International Conference on Social Computing (PASSAT'11)*. Boston, MA: IEEE; 2011, p. 19–26.

[21] Duan D, Li Y, Li R, *et al.* Incremental K-clique clustering in dynamic social networks. *Artificial Intelligence Review.* 2012;38:129–147.

[22] Kim K, McKay RI, and Moon BR. Multiobjective evolutionary algorithms for dynamic social network clustering. In: Pelikan M (ed.), *Proceedings of the 12th Annual Conference on Genetic and Evolutionary Computation (GECCO '10)*. New York, NY: Association for Computing Machinery, ACM; 2010, p. 1179–1186.

[23]   Nguyen NP, Xuan Y, and Thai MT. A novel method for worm containment on dynamic social networks. In: Dan Cuviello RS (ed.), *Proceedings of the 29th International Conference on Military Communications (MILCOM'10)*. San Jose, CA: IEEE; 2010, p. 2180–2185.

[24]   Fletcher R, Cornia A, Graves L, *et al.* Measuring the reach of "fake news" and online disinformation in Europe. *Australasian Policing.* 2018;10:25–33.

[25]   Snopes: Fact Checking [Webpage on the Internet]. Snopes Media Group Inc.; c1995-2022 [cited 2022 Jul 15]. https://www.snopes.com/fact-check/.

[26]   Punditfact [Webpage on the Internet]. Poynter Institute; 2020 [cited 2022 Jul 15]. https://www.politifact.com/punditfact/.

[27]   Gossip Cop [Webpage on the Internet]. Suggest; 2020 [cited 2022 Jul 15]. https://www.suggest.com/c/entertainment/gossip-cop/.

[28]   Wang WY. "Liar, liar pants on fire": A new benchmark dataset for fake news detection. arXiv preprint arXiv:170500648. 2017;2:422–426.

[29]   Shu K, Mahudeswaran D, Wang S, *et al.* Fakenewsnet: a data repository with news content, social context, and spatiotemporal information for studying fake news on social media. *Big Data.* 2020;8:171–188.

[30]   A better way to discuss the news [Webpage on the Internet]. fiskkit; 2000 [cited 2022 Jul 15]. https://fiskkit.com/.

[31]   Mitra T and Gilbert E. Credbank: a large-scale social media corpus with associated credibility annotations. In: Ceren Budak DQ and Cha M (eds.), *Proceedings of the 9th International AAAI Conference on Web and Social Media (ICWSM'15)*. Atlanta, GA: AAAI Press, Palo Alto; 2015, p. 258–267.

[32]   Amazon Mechanical Turk [Webpage on the Internet]. Amazon; 2000 [cited 2022 Jul 15]. https://www.mturk.com/.

[33]   Cohen S, Hamilton JT, and Turner F. Computational journalism. *Communications of the ACM.* 2011;54:66–71.

[34]   Conroy NK, Rubin VL, and Chen Y. Automatic deception detection: methods for finding fake news. *Proceedings of 78th Association for Information Science and Technology (ASIST '15).* 2015;52:1–4.

[35]   Jin Z, Cao J, Zhang Y, *et al.* Novel visual and statistical image features for microblogs news verification. *IEEE Transactions on Multimedia.* 2016;19: 598–608.

[36]   Alalwan AA. Investigating the impact of social media advertising features on customer purchase intention. *International Journal of Information Management.* 2018;42:65–77.

[37]   Siddiqui S and Singh T. Social media its impact with positive and negative aspects. *International Journal of Computer Applications Technology and Research.* 2016;5:71–75.

[38]   Warner-Søderholm G, Bertsch A, Sawe E, *et al.* Who trusts social media? *Computers in Human Behavior.* 2018;81:303–315.

[39]   Yadav US, Gupta BB, Peraković D, *et al.* Security and privacy of cloud-based online social media: a survey. In: Lucia Knapcikova MPMB and Peraković D (eds.), *Sustainable Management of Manufacturing Systems in Industry 4.0.* Switzerland, AG: Springer; 2022, p. 213–236.

[40]   Rathore S, Sharma PK, Loia V, *et al.* Social network security: issues, challenges, threats, and solutions. *Information Sciences.* 2017;421:43–69.

[41]   Xiong J, Zhang Y, Lin L, *et al.* ms-PoSW: a multi-server aided proof of shared ownership scheme for secure deduplication in cloud. *Concurrency and Computation: Practice and Experience.* 2020;32:e4252.

[42]   Boididou C, Middleton SE, Jin Z, *et al.* Verifying information with multimedia content on twitter. *Multimedia Tools and Applications.* 2018;77: 15545–15571.

[43]   Kadhim IJ, Premaratne P, Vial PJ, *et al.* Comprehensive survey of image steganography: techniques, evaluations, and trends in future research. *Neurocomputing.* 2019;335:299–326.

[44]   Walter N, Brooks JJ, Saucier CJ, *et al.* Evaluating the impact of attempts to correct health misinformation on social media: a meta-analysis. *Health Communication.* 2021;36:1776–1784.

[45]   Li K, Cheng L and Teng CI. Voluntary sharing and mandatory provision: private information disclosure on social networking sites. *Information Processing & Management.* 2020;57:102128.

[46]   Zeebaree S, Ameen S, and Sadeeq M. Social media networks security threats, risks and recommendation: a case study in the Kurdistan region. *International Journal of Innovation, Creativity and Change.* 2020;13:349–365.

[47]   Ayaburi EW and Treku DN. Effect of penitence on social media trust and privacy concerns: the case of Facebook. *International Journal of Information Management.* 2020;50:171–181.

[48]   Andrejevic M and Selwyn N. Facial recognition technology in schools: critical questions and concerns. *Learning, Media and Technology.* 2020;45: 115–128.

Chapter 5

Social media computing: tools and deployment platform for smart contract

Yuvraj Prakash[1], Antriksh Goswami[2] and Aditya Pratap Singh[1]

Abstract

With the development of the Internet of Things, virtual reality, artificial intelligence, and blockchain technologies, the world is currently experiencing a rapid digital transition. In order to give their customers an immersive experience, social media platforms are also developing through incorporating the internet of things and virtual reality. Machine learning (ML) tools employ the data that users generate while using these technologies to make decisions. These choices support geotagging photographs, proposing music to users, boosting photobook authoring through extensive multimedia analysis, and analyzing user preferences in games and brands. The users could be put in danger as a result of this data sharing. We will talk about how blockchain technology can be utilized in social media computing. We will also talk about the decentralized social network's blockchain-based framework. We will talk about the hands-on tools used for developing blockchain-based social media platforms towards the conclusion.

Keywords: Decentralized social media; Solidity; Smart contract; BCOSN; Hashing algorithm

5.1 Introduction

The simplest way to communicate with someone on the Internet is now through social media. You can post your ideas, films, images, and other content on social media. However, because of the rise in online crime, revealing personal information on social media has lost its trustworthiness. And managing the growing amount of data transmitted over the internet with centralized servers has become challenging [1]. The use of decentralized servers for data management is desirable.

[1]Department of Computer Engineering and Application, GLA University Mathura, India
[2]Department of Computer Science and Engineering, National Institute of Technology Patna, India

In comparison to centralized servers, blockchain provides a decentralized platform and higher security. We can create a decentralized framework using smart contracts that will dramatically change social media networking. A centralized social media server, such as Facebook, Instagram, or Twitter, can access all our data. While in a decentralized system, you have complete choice over what data you wish to access. Mastodon, Pixelfed, and Diaspora are three examples of decentralized social media which are alternatives to Twitter, Instagram, and Facebook. The primary benefit of moving away from a centralized server to a decentralized one is that your data will be owned by you only [2].

Today, there are several peer-to-peer networks, such as torrents [3]. The major purpose of these networks is file sharing. To connect and share user data in a decentralized online social network (DOSN), the same type of protocol might be used with a few privacy policy modifications [4]. Access control management is the key area of concern in a DOSN [5]. In a centralized online social network (OSN), the central server verifies that a user has permission to access another user's data. In a DOSN, distribution and encryption rules [6] are used to implement access control management. Users in a DOSN control who has access to their data. It is possible to configure the distribution policy at the node level or at the network level. All nodes must conform to the same policy if it is established at the network level. The data's availability is the only factor controlled by the distribution policy [5]. No matter whatever policy is selected, the privacy of the data is ensured [7].

In this chapter, we will discuss the blockchain in social media computing applications. Section 5.2 discusses about the blockchain architecture. Section 5.3 discusses the programming framework for blockchain. Section 5.4 discusses the blockchain-based online social network. Finally, we concluded the chapter in Section 5.5.

5.2   What is blockchain

Blockchain is a type of database which is immutable ledger, distributed and completely transparent [8].

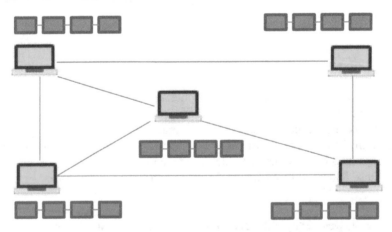

Figure 5.1   Blocks sharing in a distributed computer network

- *Distributed*: Block entries are distributed among the computers or peer-to-peer networks that are connected with each other. Therefore, even if a computer fails, there is no possibility of data loss. As you can see in Figure 5.1.
- *Immutable ledger*: A blockchain ledger refers to a block where data can be written. Data that has been written to a block cannot be changed once it has been written. Its immutability is what creates mutual trust between the parties.
- *Transparent*: All connected computers are able to see any changes made in the block.

Note: Not everyone can view a transaction, only the block owner can. All the data are encrypted by secret code using cryptography.

5.3 Hashing algorithm

Hash: Hash is the unique address of the block by which the block is identified. Each block is connected with the other using the previous hash as shown in Figure 5.2.

This hash is generated by using SHA256 (Secure Hash Algorithm) as shown in Figure 5.3. It was developed by the National Security Agency (NSA) in USA 2001. SHA256 is of 64 hexadecimal characters, and each character consists of 4 bits. Because of this, it is known as SHA256. Blockchain is a chain of blocks where each block points to its previous block using a previous hash as shown in Figure 5.4. Block no. 1 in the blockchain is called Genesis Block and its previous hash will be 0.

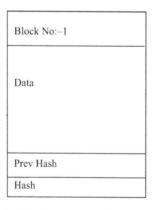

Figure 5.2   Fields contained by a single block

Figure 5.3   Working of SHA256

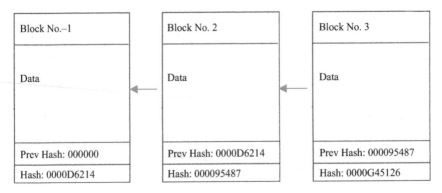

Figure 5.4   Blockchain formation

5.4   Solidity

Smart contract is the main component which is used for implementing various applications such as voting, crowdfunding, multi-signature wallets etc. These applications share a common smart contract with every connected computer in the network which consists of the main logic of the application as shown in Figure 5.5.

5.4.1   Smart contract

Smart contracts are similar to programs that run on the Ethereum blockchain. Ethereum blocks include executable smart contracts on all connected networks [9].

5.4.2   Compilation of smart contract

The environment is necessary for smart contract compilation on the Ethereum network. Remix-IDE, EthFiddle, Gitter, Visual Studio, etc. are a few IDEs that provide an execution environment for smart contracts.

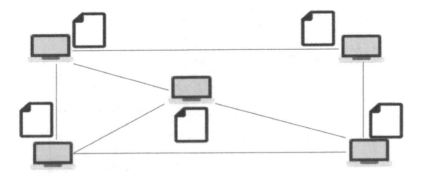

Figure 5.5   Sharing a common smart contract with every computer connected

The file extension for solidity is ".sol." When a ".sol" file is compiled using the solidity compiler, it splits into two parts.

- *Application binary interface* (ABI): ABI is used to communicate with smart contracts in the Ethereum network. Interaction between contracts or with parties outside the blockchain.
- *Byte code*: The Ethereum Virtual Machine (EVM) can only run bytes of smart contracts; the whole smart contract cannot be executed.

5.4.3   Mainnet vs. Testnet

When a contract is deployed on EVM, some ether or gas is deducted from your wallet during contract execution. Ether comes in two varieties: Mainnet and Testnet.

- Mainnet: When we do transactions with the real value of ether. Example: Ethereum Mainnet.
- Testnet: When we do the transaction with a fake value of ether. It is used for testing your contract. Example, Rinkeby Test Network, Ropsten Test Network, etc.

5.4.4   Variables

In solidity, there are two types of variables: the state variable and the local variable.

5.4.4.1   State variable

State variables are those that we assign in the contract at the contract level. There are three ways to initialize state variables:

1. uint public age = 45;
2. uint public age;
   constructor () public {age = 45;}
3. uint public age;
   function setage() public{age = 45;}

5.4.4.2   Local variable

Variable that declare inside the function. The variables are maintained in the stack rather than on storage. Initialization of local variable:

```
1. function store() pure public returns(uint){
   uint age = 45;
   return age;}
```
Note: Some datatypes, such as strings, Arrays, and Struct, cause errors when initialized in local variables. We use the memory keyword with the datatype to prevent errors, and you cannot use the memory keyword at the state level since it would result in errors.

```
function store() pure public returns(uint){
string memory name = "Ram";

uint age = 45;
return age;}
```

5.4.5   *Function*

In Solidity, to create any function, we use the function keyword and the name of the function.

function function_name()

- **View:** View keyword is used to restrict the function state. In this, we can read the state variable.

  contract level
  { uint public age = 45;
  function function_name() public view returns(uint) {
  return age; // reading age from state variable.
  } }

- **Pure:** Pure keyword is used to restrict the function state. In this we cannot read and write in the state variable.

  contract level
  { uint public age = 45;
  function function_name() public pure returns(uint) {
  uint roll = 99;
  return roll; } } // Not reading nor modifying the state variable.

5.4.6   *Constructor*

In Solidity, constructor keyword is used to create the constructor. The constructor's primary functions are to choose the contract's owner and initialize the state variable. Constructor will only run once.

Only one constructor can be created, and its optional. If no constructor is expressly specified, the compiler creates a default constructor.

5.4.6.1   **Without argument**

uint public age;
constructor ()
{age = 45;}

5.4.6.2   **With argument**

uint public age;
constructor(uint new_age) {
age = new_age; }
// You have to pass value of new_age at runtime.

5.4.7   *Arrays in Solidity*

The term "array" refers to a grouping of related data components in a single region in contiguous memory. Each data element can be retrieved simply by its index number. Arrays are of two types: static array and dynamic array.

5.4.7.1   Static array

It implies an array with a fixed size. The length of the array is known at compile time. The size of the array cannot be modified at runtime. Declaring and initializing an array in Solidity.

- uint[5] public arr = [1,2,3,4,5];

5.4.7.2   Dynamic array

The length of the array is not known by the compiler. The size of array can be modified at runtime. Syntax to initialize and declare a dynamic array.

- uint [] public arr; // Array has been created.

Some methods are defined in the dynamic array for push, pop, length, etc. The syntax for push, pop, and length are shown below.

- function pushElement(uint item) public {
    arr.push(item);
    }
- function length() public view returns(uint) {
    return arr. length;
    }
- function popElement() public {
    arr.pop();
    }

5.4.7.3   Bytes array

To increase data security, Solidity makes use of byte arrays. A byte's array is a non-changing data structure. It indicates you cannot modify any element of byte array at specified index. Syntax for byte array is:

- bytesN public datatype_name ; // where N lies between (1 and 32).
- 3 bytes or 24 bits or 6 hexadecimal size of array will be created.
    contract ByteArray
    {
    bytes3 public b;
    function setter() public
    {
    b = "abc";
    }}
    output will be: "0x616263"

The ASCII code is used to determine the bytes' array's output. If the value does not fit the whole array, padding is applied by inserting 0 to the end.
    Example:
    contract ByteArray {
    bytes3 public b;

```
function setter() public
{
b = 'ab';
}}
```
output will be: "0x616200"

Above we have discussed the fixed size bytes' array. Now we are going to look at how the dynamic size bytes' array is initialized and declared.

```
contract ByteArray
{
bytes public b = "xyz";
function pushElement() public {
b.push("a");
}
function length() public view returns(uint) {
return b. length;
}
function getElement(uint i) public view returns(bytes1) {
return b1[i]; // will return the value of ith position. And Bytes1 is used because
we are returning only single byte from bytes array.
}}
```

5.4.8   Loops in Solidity

In Solidity, there are three types of loop: While, For, and Do-While.

5.4.8.1   Syntax for While Loop

```
Contract WhileLoop {
uint[5] public arr ;
uint public count;
function loop() public{
while(count<arr.length)
{
arr[count] = count;
count++;
}}}
```

5.4.8.2   Syntax for For Loop

```
Contract ForLoop {
uint[5] public arr ;
uint public count;
function loop() public{
for(uint i = count;i<arr.length;i++)
```

```
{
arr[count] = count;
count++;
}}}
```

5.4.8.3   Syntax for Do-While Loop

```
Contract DoWhileLoop {
uint[5] public arr ;
uint public count;
function loop() public{
do
{
arr[count] = count;
count++;
}while(count<arr.length);
}}
```

5.4.9   IF-ELSE statement in Solidity

Syntax for If-Else

```
Contract IFElse {
function check(int a) public pure returns(string memory){
String memory value;
if(a>0) {
value = "Greater than zero";
}else if(a = = 0){
value = "Equal to zero";
}else{
value = "Less than zero";
}
return value;
}}
```

5.4.10   Visibility in Solidity

Using Solidity, you may determine who has access to your contract's functions and state variables, and how they interact with each other. The visibility of a function may be set to external, public, internal, or private depending on the application. The table shown below indicates which specifier can access the function Outside, Within, Derived, and other.

Public	Private	Internal	External
Outside	x	X	Outside
Within	Within	Within	x
Derived	x	Derived	Derived
Other	x	X	Other

5.5   BCOSN framework

Blockchain online social network (BCOSN) [2], is made up of three layers: the application layer, the storage layer, and the blockchain layer as shown in Figure 5.6. The application layer allows access for users to communicate with the storage layer and the blockchain layer.

5.5.1   Blockchain layer

The BCOSN's initial stage is the blockchain layer. The blockchain data may seem transparent in certain ways. Data must be encrypted in order to preserve its privacy before uploading to the blockchain. Those with authority are the only ones who can access the data. In order to restrict the quantity of data kept at the blockchain layer, the recommended design simply keeps the basic identification data necessary to execute social interaction features in the blockchain layer and maintains the details of the data supplied by users at the storage layer. We integrate the primary interactive OSN functions at the blockchain layer by integrating with smart contracts [10].

5.5.2   Application layer

The application layer is essentially client-oriented; users may take part in social activities online. The five primary components that make up the application layer are the blockchain manager (BM), user manager (UM), cache manager (CM), interaction manager (IM), and storage manager (SM). The BM is in responsible for supervising interactions with the blockchain layer. The Blockchain Module (BM) should be used for all interactions between users and the blockchain layer. The BM also distributes smart contract event alerts to other modules. We set up a unique SM for interacting with the storage layer so that consumers may choose from a variety of storage providers.

Users may register and maintain their information, including their contact information and that of their friends, with the help of the UM. Before using the social network, users must first register. The primary purposes of user registration are to establish new smart contracts, submit basic data, and get a set of identifying keys. With the aid of IM, a user may engage with the smart contract and take part in social activities like friend-adding and publishing in UM and IM, several network connections and encoding/decoding procedures are used. In order to speed up processing, we use the CM to cache information, such as key and texts, on local

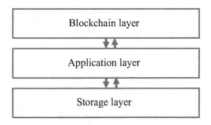

Figure 5.6   BCOSN framework

disks. Due to the ability to encrypt local data and preserve it in the storage layer at the appropriate moment, users may maintain their conversations in sync even while moving platforms or devices.

5.5.3   Storage layer

Storage layer is the third and last layer of the BCOSN. The storage service maintains data backups and guarantees data accessibility in addition to storing customers' data. Data integrity and authenticity may be confirmed using the hash value, which is used to encrypt the data recorded in the storage layer.

5.6   Limitations of BCOSN

1. The BCOSN integration with the existing blockchain systems is quite expensive.
2. The built-in effectiveness of current blockchain has an impact on the BCOSN as well.
3. The blockchain stores the encrypted user profiles indefinitely, which may not entirely abide to all requirements.

5.7   Conclusions

Decentralized online social media application based on blockchain network will be the new emerging applications. This provides better performance, privacy, and immutability of our data. However, this new framework also has certain issues, which has been discussed in this chapter. We have also discussed the solutions for BCOSN. Overall, in the literature, the solutions are experimentally verified and proved to have reasonable complexity. The future scope can be geotagging photographs, proposing music to users, boosting photobook authoring through extensive multimedia analysis, and analyzing user preferences in games and brands.

References

[1] Minin, E. D., Tenkanen, H., and Toivonen, T. (2015). Prospects and challenges for social media data in conservation science. *Frontiers in Environment Science*, 3, 63.
[2] Zhang, L. J. (2019). BCOSN: a blockchain-based decentralized. *IEEE Transactions on Computational Social Systems*, 99, 1–13.
[3] Cohen, B. (2001). BitTorrent. http://www. bittorrent.com/.
[4] Jahid, S., Nilizadeh, S., Mittal, P., *et al.* (2012). DECENT: a decentralized architecture for enforcing privacy in online social networks. In *2012 IEEE International Conference on Pervasive Computing and Communications Workshops*. IEEE.

[5]   Yeung, C.-M. A., Liccardi, I., Lu, K., *et al.* (2009). Decentralization: the future of online social networking. In *W3C Workshop on the Future of Social Networking Position Papers*, vol. 2.

[6]   Paul, T., Famulari, A., and Strufe, A. (2014). A survey on decentralized online social networks. *Computer Networks*, 75, 437–452.

[7]   Uvais Mon V. V. N., Sumukh, R., Vignesh, V., Zabiulla, S., and Yashpal Gupta. (2022). A review on decentralized online social network. *IJRES*, 10, 53–57.

[8]   Ali, O., Jaradat, A., Kulakli, A., and Abuhalimeh, A. (2021). A comparative study: blockchain technology. *IEEE Access*, 99, 1.

[9]   Buterin, V. (2014). Ethereum: a next-generation smart contract and decentralized application platform. *White Paper*, 3, 2.

[10] Rouhani, S. and Deters, R. (2019). Security, performance, and applications of smart contracts: a systematic survey. *IEEE Access,* 7, 50759–50779.

Chapter 6

Privacy provisioning on blockchain transactions of decentralized social media

Rohit Saxena[1], Deepak Arora[2], Vishal Nagar[1] and Brijesh Kumar Chaurasia[1]

Abstract

Blockchain is one of the most disruptive and emerging technology in the present era, due to its unique characteristics immutability and decentralization. The transactions in a blockchain are publicly available, thereby accessible to all users. So, the privacy provisioning in blockchain for transactions of decentralized social media as well as privacy of the identities of members is needful. The chapter provides a comprehensive study of privacy provisioning on the blockchain. In the existing literature, there are a variety of scalability, security, and privacy concerns with blockchain, including key management for recovery, on-chain privacy protection, transaction linkability, and adherence to privacy laws. Following the self-sovereign identity (SSI) model, new privacy-preserving blockchain solutions are emerging to address these issues. These solutions allow users to anonymize themselves in all types of electronics transfer ledgers and regain control of their personal information. This chapter provides a comprehensive study of privacy provisioning schemes along with their challenges in this fascinating and disruptive technology.

Keywords: Blockchain; Transactions; Privacy provisioning; Social media; Cryptography

6.1 Introduction

Beyond cryptocurrencies, a transformation is underway in a variety of disciplines, such as healthcare [1], smart cities [2], decentralized Internet of Things (IoT) [3], e-administration [4], or smart transport systems [5]. The transition to verifiability, democracy, and universal coverage of tokenized crypto assets of any form is evolving as an outcome of the decentralization that blockchain technology offers.

[1]Department of Computer Science and Engineering, Pranveer Singh Institute of Technology, India
[2]Department of Computer Science and Engineering, Amity University Uttar Pradesh, Lucknow Campus, India

Blockchain allows for decentralized, direct, and intermediary-free transfers of digital cryptographic assets using the ledger while permitting public certainty along with the origin for digital transactions and records. Users' anonymity, confidentiality, and control over privacy in their ledger transactions are all at risk due to the General Data Protection Regulation (GDPR) [6], response times and scalability [7], threats to security [8], or concerns related to privacy [9–11]. As an outcome, Blockchain solutions are prone to these problems. Due to these privacy concerns, people and companies are hesitant to adopt and use blockchain in their activities and enterprises because of the prospect of sharing personal records and transactions of decentralized social media in a globally accessible database. Despite the use of pseudonyms, users' movements are not entirely anonymous because all activities concealed by these aliases may be identified and linked, particularly when handling transactions with multiple entries involving several different addresses from a number of accounts pertaining to a single person [12]. In this regard, new privacy-preserving blockchain [13] ideas and platforms, such as uPort [14] or Sovrin [15], present improved decentralized ledgers that allow users to secure and protect their privacy in online transactions. In permissioned Blockchains, the governance of user-related data stands out for putting a strong emphasis on preserving user privacy. Once the blockchain has been introduced, the Identity Management (IdM) solutions have started the transition from the conventional web-centric strategy or identity federation technologies toward the self-sovereign identity (SSI) model [15]. Because of self-sovereign identities, the users can control their data at any time with any network setup. This strategy allows for the anonymization of data pertaining to user transactions and interactions inside services and the removal of user personal data from third-party services, including Identity Providers and Service Providers. In the worst scenario, it prevents third parties from leaking personal data and being a possible source for other, more significant hazards, such as identity-related cybercrimes (e.g., identity theft). Malignant smart contracts, malevolent trusted third parties (TTP), transaction linkability, privacy in blockchain peer-to-peer (P2P) networks, privacy-usability records, management and recovery of private keys, and adherence to privacy laws are some of the privacy issues that are required to be addressed by the deployments of Blockchain. These difficulties persist despite SSI's excellent features and benefits. In order to overcome these problems, several blockchain solutions, for example, mixer services [16,17], attempt to allocate a third party the responsibility of hiding the transaction within a substantial number of unassociated transactions of decentralized social media. Thus, crucial data like the payer, recipient, or price paid can be completely anonymized [18,19], but occasionally at the penalty in terms of excessive charges and transaction delays. Several solutions for privacy-provisioning in social media have been provided by [20–23]. The use of the Blockchain framework can provide better privacy to social media by recording it as a transaction on Blockchain. There are numerous privacy provisioning approaches that have been applied on Blockchain. This study explores the privacy vulnerabilities with blockchain technology, reviews the Blockchain's privacy-provisioning solutions, and analysis the privacy-provision solutions.

6.2   Blockchain concepts

Blockchain replaces the traditional centralized model of trustworthiness with a completely decentralized network of nodes. Based on synchronized distributed ledger technology (DLT), it maintains information replication and sharing among numerous nodes dispersed across numerous remote locations, acting as a decentralised database. Satoshi Nakamoto first presented the idea of blockchain in [24] as the technical underpinnings of a revolutionary e-cash system. There are other explanations of blockchain, for example, [13] or [25], which succinctly state that it is a globally accessed ledger dispersed over a network that records transactions. All transactions are verified by network nodes depending upon blockchain types using consensus before being appended to the blockchain. Each transaction's history can always be replicated, but recorded data cannot be changed or removed. The ledger transactions' origination, responsibility, traceability, and transparency are just a few benefits that blockchain offers. By eschewing central authorities, it offers a truly decentralised root of trust, fostering trust amongst stakeholders and users who were previously untrustworthy or unfamiliar. It is extremely challenging to alter transaction records due to the decentralized architecture. Additionally, blockchain transactions are replicated across a perfectly decentralized P2P network for stockpiling, eliminating the possibility of data loss. The core blockchain components and principles are shown in Figure 6.1 together with an illustration of blockchain.

   Transaction: Transactions are data structures that scramble the transfer of value between participants in the blockchain. A transaction may be characterized by sender and destination transactions also known as input and output, respectively.

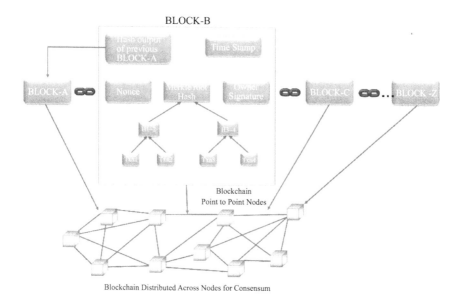

Figure 6.1   Architecture of blockchain

Block: It is a container data structure that collects transactions for insertion in the public ledger. A block additionally contains a hash pointer to the blockchain's prior block. The block contains a header, timestamp, nonce, metadata, transactions, etc.

Genesis block: It is the first block of any one of the blockchain. It establishes the origination of the connected linked list of hashed references.

Merkle root: A binary hash tree, in which every parent node is the hash of its child nodes and the leaves of the Merkle Tree are the hash pointers of the transactions in a block. As demonstrated in Figure 6.1, Merkle tree's root is a hash that ensures the integrity of each transaction in a block, including the order in which they occur. The hash of the root of tree (*aka* Merkle tree), along with the previous block's hash pointer and any consensus data necessary to validate the node. The Merkle tree enables computing the correct block hash for confirming the chain's integrity without needing to save all of the transaction data on storage.

Network: It is the collection of nodes that engage in P2P communication with one another, exchanging blockchain data, adding transactions followed by validating the transactions, and then determining which new blocks should be added to the chain's head.

Consensus: The mechanism used by network nodes to determine the blockchain's current state which is defined by all transactions which change with the addition of a new transaction. Due to potential delays in broadcasting the new transaction to all the connected nodes, it is impossible to predict the sequence in which the transactions are received at a given node. Because the central authority node is unavailable, the consensus method is maintained by the network to verify the transaction thereby, transferring the faith from the centralized authority to decentralized verification which is done using cryptographic techniques.

Fork: In accordance with the consensus mechanism, the network may accept more than one block at an instance in the chain. As a result, the chain splits in two. One of the forks may keep on adding blocks while the other is used by another portion of the network. The chains are not compatible because they utilize different hash references for each block, therefore the network must decide which fork to employ. The longest fork in Bitcoin is the one that is legitimate. The issue of malicious nodes forking the network before spending any money to recover it is resolved by this. The shorter fork is rejected during the consensus algorithm.

Script: It is a small piece of code, written in a restricted programming language that defines the requirements for validating a transaction. For instance, the Bitcoin script permits deferring payments until a specific date or until the chain has more signatures from other nodes.

Smart contract: Smart contract is an independent program designed in any scripting language. It automatically executes when specific conditions are met. Any transaction that is obtained by the successful execution of a smart contract can be confirmed by another node that has executed a similar smart contract on the same input. An Ethereum blockchain specifies the programming language named Solidity and the generated bytecode is run on Ethereum Virtual Machine (EVM) [26].

The architecture of the blockchain depends upon the permissions that are given to users for reading and writing on the ledger. Generally, blockchain architecture has been categorized into three types. Public or permissionless blockchain with no access restrictions, where everyone may read, publish, and take part in consensus. Although the participants use some form of anonymity or pseudo-anonymity, the transactions are transparent. It is beneficial for cryptocurrency, however, it typically has privacy problems, private or permissioned blockchain requires invitations or permissions from the network before engaging in consensus or performing operations on the distributed ledger. Existing participants may choose future entrants as part of the access control mechanism; alternatively, a regulatory body may provide participation licenses; or a consortium may make the selections [27]. The participating stakeholders' agreements allow the consensus to be carried out. This particular blockchain also permits the ledger to be updated solely by a selected group of people.

6.3 Privacy issues in blockchain

The development of alternative cryptocurrencies has been the largest implementation of blockchain technology thus far because it was developed to support the Bitcoin cryptocurrency. Absolute anonymity is not guaranteed in bitcoin as has been shown in the literature. Due to measures that enhance security and non-repudiation of transactions, blockchain technology is transforming not only the world of cryptocurrencies but also how businesses manage their data and business/operational procedures. Along with these enhancements, the utilization of blockchain technology in various fields also brings about a variety of privacy issues. The next subsections provide descriptions of these issues.

6.3.1 Transaction linkability

The freedom to autonomously create new public addresses is granted to users of the public blockchain. By associating the user's public key addresses with each unique address in a blockchain transaction, the ledger keeps a record of all of their previous transactions graphs [28–32]. In blockchains based on tokens, different addresses that belong to a particular user could be associated by:

(a) *Transactions with multiple entries*: These transactions call for the usage of various addresses associated with the same user, along with the information of all the relevant private keys to complete the transaction [9,12,33,34]. Each transaction of digital assets should have a distinctive, one-time address to minimize this linkability issue, thereby reducing the number of input addresses in a transaction. The transactions of the users can also be linked to wallets, allowing a malevolent user to access balances, destinations, or other private data.

(b) *Transactions involving change*: When a given user uses the same public address, it is possible to track him down and obtain resources that have changed. The user must be able to create a new public address for receiving the returns in order to increase the secrecy of these transactions.

(c) *Malignant mixing services*: Users can use the centralized and outsourced mixing services to increase their privacy by blending transactions from various issuers. However, since the service might be aware of both the input and output pairs, it could constitute a privacy concern. As a result, privacy depends on an honest middleman [35–37].

(d) *Payment through the web*: The service provider can associate the original identity with that of the customer's identity through cookies in the browser that performs the transaction using the cryptocurrency [38]. This further indicates that the assault is resistant to mixing techniques like CoinJoin [39].

(e) *Blockchain P2P network privacy*: Users who submit new transactions are identifiable across the entire network [10] via the IP addresses since the blockchain nodes interact with one another in a P2P overlay network across the Internet. Regardless of the alleged anonymity of newly generated, randomly generated addresses, another node in the blockchain network could connect to the address with a wallet and actual user by analyzing the public addresses employed in the blockchain [40]. In order to deploy a privacy layer between its clients and the P2P blockchain network, privacy-focused blockchains like Monero [41] must first establish a connection to an overlay network such as TOR (onion routing) [42] or I2P (garlic routing) [43]. However, the authors of [44] demonstrated that connecting to the blockchain network utilizing TOR as a network privacy layer opens up a new set of vector threats.

6.3.2   *Recovery and management of private-keys*

The private keys are crucial for privacy and security since every transaction needs to be signed by the user, and appropriate key management [45] mechanisms must be implemented. Identity theft may occur along with privacy leaks if the system is exploited. The blockchain keys are kept in users' devices using blockchain wallets, either online or (offline). Wallets can also be the target of theft attacks [46], in which the attacker could destroy or take the user's private keys. Due to the possibility of various Trojans and malware crashing key storage and accessing keys for encryption, this issue also impacts encrypted wallets. The user can either use a wallet to safeguard the keys stored on his own device or utilize cloud wallets to manage the private keys on his behalf. This technique relies on a third party for security and assumes that the party won't misuse the keys in any way. Traditional measures, namely, backup of the wallet file using copy backups, paper wallets that contains QR codes of the public and private keys [47]. Threshold cryptography [48], which partitions the private keys into shares kept in various locations to ensure that even if a portion is compromised or misplaced, the keys remain safe and could be restored by the user, is one defence against intrusion of malware that could compromise a user's device when the user controls his own wallet. Another option is to have super-wallets, which minimize loss or theft damage by having the user retain their primary wallet at a safer place, and after that create sub-wallets with smaller amounts for their smartphone wallet [49].

Because these wallets act as the entry point for massive sums of assets, making them tempting targets for attackers, additional risks emerge by hosting the secret private keys at the third-party centralized service. The key management service might be decentralized, as recommended by KMSChain or NyCypher [50], in order to bring down risk by enabling technology to collect their keys with a number of providers (proxies) that have backup copies of their master keys. Users are unable to conduct transactions with the assets linked to their private keys when they lose their private keys. Various other serious problems could be the impersonation of users and spending cryptocurrency which can be addressed by several blockchain solutions, such as Uport [14] and Sovrin [51], which offer procedures for the private keys' recovery and revocation. Consensus procedures are used to verify a user's legitimacy in relation to the lost or stolen keys connected to his identity.

6.3.3 Nefarious smart contracts

Executing smart contracts may expose risks [52], like intellectual property theft. The validating nodes carry out smart contracts, while the ledger logs the code, inputs, and outputs. The user's privacy would be jeopardised by the node that has access to the data which is being processed in the transaction. Additionally, for the virtual computer of the blockchain, for instance, the EMV, smart contracts are typically compiled to bytecode. The user should make sure that the code actually translates into bytecode in the transaction before the execution of the smart contract. The smart contract's vulnerability analysis can be performed using an open-source Oyente program and other smart contract analysis tools [53]. The odds and evens gambling sport as a smart contract is one example of a privacy attack [54]. Intel SGX [55] is an example where smart contracts have been employed in the trustworthy execution context, albeit there are security risks associated with this choice [56]. To improve privacy in smart contracts, [57] adopts an interdisciplinary strategy that is based on formal verification employing SMPC and proof-carrying code.

6.3.4 Privacy of on-chain data and non-erasable data

The integrated view of privacy includes privacy as confidentiality and control. Data contained in the blockchain is required to be encrypted for preserving secrecy. Additionally, the right to be erasure is included in control's definition of privacy; yet, the immutability of blockchain introduces a significant difficulty. This way, anonymity is administered using the hashed personal data rather than pseudonymity but not anonymity is provided by hashed personal data. Digital identifiers should either not be entered into the ledger or, at the very least, be utilized separately for each contact. The digital identifier can also be regarded as personal information and should not be entered into the ledger. However, modern blockchain solutions frequently store the public keys for DID on the blockchain. Personal data of any kind should not be kept on-chain to ensure the right to erasure under GDPR [6]. Since the GDPR does not apply to completely anonymous data, it is advisable to either keep personal data off-chain or completely anonymize the information. Utilizing the InterPlanetary File System (IPFS) protocol, for instance, just necessitates the provision of a link to the data, a date, and a hash of the external data for verification (ideally randomly generated). After off-chain deletion, it makes the on-chain reference useless and allows data erasure.

A block matrix data structure for the preservation of integrity along with erasing proficiency and offers methods for enabling erasure in the blockchain has been presented in [58]. It enables the continuous addition of hash-linked records with simultaneous deletion. Similar to this, the authors of [59] introduced Lition which is a public blockchain that permits the storing and erasing of personal information data. To govern the blockchain, a trustworthy knowledge peer of nodes must be established, and they must agree (e.g., by signing a legal contract) to not hold genuine data hashes and to remove data at the user's request (without keeping backup copies).

6.3.5　*Cryptographic-privacy performance*

To guarantee complete anonymity in blockchain, cryptographic mechanisms, for instance, ZKP [60] and ZK-SNARKS [61] are required. Additionally, because the majority of ZKP solutions require computing time to develop and validate proofs, they are inefficient for large-scale applications. The computational issues identified by classic ZKPs are addressed by novel ideas which are based on non-interactive zero-knowledge proofs of knowledge (NIZKPoKs), such as [62], that utilize less evidence than conventional ZKP to boost efficiency, or [63], employing symmetric-key primitives.

6.3.6　*Malicious-curious TTPs*

Users will receive attribute-based credentials and DID Documents once the user ID proving operations are managed by the SSI IdM deployed on the permissioned blockchain. The submitted legitimate credentials and crypto-claims must also be approved by the SSI IdM. It denotes that the blockchain platform, which serves as both the credential's issuer and validator, must have transparent operating procedures and trustworthy code. If not, there may be an issue with the blockchain platform and user privacy would be violated. In fact, the inspection capabilities planned for some SSI IdMs, which would enable de-anonymization and reveal the user's real identity hidden behind a pseudonym, may become a focus of attacks and shortcoming.

6.4　Review of blockchain privacy provisioning solutions

This section outlines the key privacy provisioning methods that can be utilized in blockchain to enable anonymity and transaction privacy (6.4.1), improve data anonymization (6.4.2), and maintain data confidentiality (6.4.3).

6.4.1　*Key privacy provisioning approaches in blockchain*

This section presents the cryptographic approaches that can serve as a framework to ensure privacy preservation in the blockchain. These include Ring Signatures, zkSNARK, Commitment schemes, ZKP, secure multi-party computation approach (SMPC), and Homomorphic Hiding scheme.

6.4.1.1   Secure multi-party computation

Utilizing secret sharing, secure multi-party computation (SMPC) [64] divides the state of the program and data (such as the states of a smart contract on a blockchain) among N participants. To produce the outcome and disclose program states or data, M parties of N must cooperate and work together to accomplish distributed computation of certain inputs. Only a portion of the input is sent to each party, and they each hold a point on a distinct polynomial to designate a variable that creates a portion of the data. The bulk of participants in this strategy must be sincere. In addition, it may be challenging for the participants for presenting their work as part of the MPC, making it challenging to manage participant incentives. MPC is now more suited for private/permissioned blockchains as a result. Additionally, because nodes must exchange data in order to calculate the MPC, SMPC involves network delay. In addition to garbled circuits (GC), homomorphic encryption (HE), oblivious RAM structures, and linear secret sharing (LSS), true SMPC techniques are starting to be employed in production [65]. As stated in [66], a ledger intended to facilitate the interchange of digital assets between numerous blockchain networks, SMPC can also be used with blockchain to split the processing of smart contracts along with accounts and key management without necessitating the involvement of a third party. In this case, storeman nodes manage a smart contract which freezes the assets over the original chain as well as keeps track of a fraction of the source chain account's private keys, prohibiting a node to obtain access to the complete private key for such a real account.

6.4.1.2   Zero-knowledge proofs

With the exception of the fact that the proof itself is right, a party, known as the prover, can demonstrate to another entity, known to be the verifier, that a particular assertion is true using a zero-knowledge proof (ZKP) [67]. A Zero-Knowledge Proof of Knowledge, for instance, can be applied to demonstrate that a claim about knowing a secret value is true while still keeping the prover's knowledge of the secret value hidden. To be a ZKP, a protocol must meet the three requirements, completeness (if the proven statement is true, then the prover is permitted to conduct a successful proof), soundness (except for a little degree of chance, a dishonest prover cannot persuade the verifier that a claim is true if it is false), and zero-knowledge (an algorithm with a polynomial time bound can produce replica of the protocol on its own that are identical to a competent proof among a prover and a verifier).

6.4.1.3   Commitment schemes

Using a commitment scheme [68], a party, Alice, can conceal a secret value while also committing to it so that when she gives Bob the original value, he can determine whether or not Alice is telling the truth. As a consequence, Alice agrees to keep a secret value hidden. In this regard, the authors of [69] demonstrated that any

ZKP may be built using commitment schemes. However, these are also applied in blockchains to connect the owner to the genuine secret attributes or in decentralized calculations such as coin-flipping protocols, as in ZKPs, Zerocoin [70] and Zcash [71]. A commitment scheme can additionally be based either on unconditionally binding (the sender cannot alter the commitment values to a different value than that of the original one) or unconditionally hiding (the sender cannot access the commitment value) (the receiver cannot speculate to what value sender committed) [60]. Therefore, a commitment system is only secure to polynomial bounded computers and is at most computationally concealing or binding. This property is essential for blockchain since the design must consider whether to safeguard the immutable chain's secret value (unconditional hiding) or the ledger from potential attackers in the future (unconditional binding).

6.4.1.4   zkSNARK

Similar to ZKP, zkSNARK (zero-knowledge Succinct Non-Interactive ARgument of Knowledge) [61] offers more possibilities than blockchain technology [39,72]. In this zkSNARK, there is a prover and a verifier. The goal of the prover is to persuade the verifier of the statement by providing evidence. Without re-running the code to check results, the verifier will assume that the prover carried out the instructions correctly. The zkSNARKs may be applied to demonstrate the accurate calculation of any function; in other words, a zkSNARK can be used to demonstrate that a function was run correctly. The node wishing to execute a transaction with blockchain technology, which modifies the state of the ledger, can conceal the procedure to execute a script or smart contract and the input parameters. The zkSNARK can be uploaded by the nodes to demonstrate that the right computations have been made instead of disclosing those parameters, and the other peers will accept it as proof. Due to its conciseness, the proof may be put in a transaction, and due to the speed of verification, any other node can quickly and effectively verify the proof. In the blockchain-based token systems Zerocash [19] and Zcash [71], often known as cryptocurrencies, zkSNARKs are used. Any cryptocurrency must deal with the issue of token duplication. The systems use zkSNARKs during the transaction generating process to protect user privacy and eliminate double-spending. A user must verify the transaction's legitimacy before transferring tokens from an ongoing transaction to another user. Unlike in Bitcoin, where each validator node independently verifies each transaction, in this system, they verify the prover's declaration that the input amount and the output amount are correct and the private keys match the input spending transactions. In addition to ZKP, Zcash includes a commitment method based on hash commitments and nullifiers for keeping track of transactions that have already been spent.

6.4.1.5   Homomorphic hiding

Homomorphic encryption [73], which is derived from privacy homomorphism proposed by [74], is another way to share and manipulate data without disclosing private values. It works by having the encryption function possessing certain characteristics that enable users to obtain the similar encrypted outcome as they would have if they would have done the same thing to the cleartext and then encrypted to ciphertext with the same encryption function. An example of homomorphic hiding is the RSA encryption algorithm. In order to generate zkSNARKs and privately distributed computations, homomorphic hiding is utilized. The additive and multiplicative homomorphic features of Bitcoin's ECDSA key pairs make them a direct application of homomorphic encryption in blockchain technology.

6.4.1.6 Ring Signatures

Ring signatures [75–77] are a kind of digital signature used by one of a group of people who all have public and private keys, but somehow the signature alone does not identify the signer. Not the algebraic structure, but the shape that represents the signature is where the name originates. Group Signatures, which predated Ring Signatures, were introduced in 1991 [78]. Group Signatures define a Group Manager concept, which may de-anonymize any signature and defines the list of individuals in a group. However, a Ring Signature system allows any user to construct their own group of users and endorse a message without letting anyone else know who the genuine signer is. The mathematical foundation for ring signatures is that there is a procedure that is calculated using only public keys, i.e., verification, but having access to a private key allows one to select a value that causes the function to output a desired, predetermined value, i.e., signature. Beginning with an arbitrary glue value v, the signature process applies the function iteratively to the previously calculated value and as well as a random seed. Utilizing the private key, a few of these kinds of random seeds are then modified with a particular value, with the goal of having the finally calculated value of a function equal to v and thus closure of the "ring." Without the requirement for a specific node to actively engage in a particular transaction to enhance privacy, ring signatures are used in Blockchain to hide the sender's identity by applying various public keys from earlier transactions in the chain at random.

The linkability attribute of some linkable ring signatures [79] allows for the detection of double spending while maintaining complete anonymity for the signer, such as when identifying double votes in electronic voting. CryptoNote [80], a blockchain application utilized in digital currencies like Bytecoin or Monero [41], is one example. With Ring Confidential Transactions [81] for value obfuscation, Stealth Addresses [82] for recipient privacy, and Ring Signatures for sender privacy, Monero, a cryptocurrency based on CryptoNote, aims to achieve strong privacy and anonymity. Sun *et al.* recently proposed RingCT [83], a traceable ring signature system for Monero, which has the length of signature and transactions autonomous from the numerous groups.

6.4.2 Anonymization methods for data

6.4.2.1 Mixing

In 1981, the authors of [84] developed the method for mixing the address such that the e-mail usage is anonymized. After that, these methods have been applied to anonymize several services. The basic step in applying such services is to organize a sizable group of users who bundle their messages together, deferring them, and then sending them again all at once or in some random order. The user activity of creating the message and the message traveling the network due to the aggregation and delay of communications has no connection. This technique focuses solely on the network's time correlation and ignores whatever personally identifiable information (PII) that the communication could contain. The mixing scheme in the blockchain is used to hide a token's past. Prior addresses can be connected to new ones through a transaction's history, and when various input addresses are utilized, all of them are assumed to belong to the same owner. Users of Bitcoin can make separate accounts for each transaction in the form of a public-key pair rather than recycling previously completed transactions. The transaction history's addresses are no longer linked because a mixing strategy was used. A mixing service (like [16] or [85]) is a type of anonymous service provider that divides a user's money into smaller amounts before mixing these amounts at random to break the connection between the user and the transaction. Coins can be mixed by the users for creating a single mixing transaction based on their addresses while retaining the ability to check that the right number of coins were delivered to the specified output addresses. The history of the token is hampered by the use of mixed protocols like CoinJoin [85], Ring Signature block-chains like Monero [40], and ZKP blockchains like Zero coin [70], which hide the owner's addresses in a list of potential owners. For mixing protocols to work, users must coordinate, and the mixing is frequently handled by a TTP server.

6.4.2.2   Differential privacy

To deal with privacy preservation, differential privacy [86] investigates whether a data analysis technique exposes information about a person or not. It involves introducing some random noise to data queries therefore any statistical analysis carried out on the complete set will be considered similar to the true findings, but that extrapolation over any specific person will be difficult. Differential privacy can be employed in the blockchain context for accessing private databases through the queries that collect the data as well as obtaining individual data from sources with statistical fluctuations while minimising the PII gathered from people. For private blockchains that permit third parties to use their anonymized data, the first database scenario is appropriate. Blockchains that collect log or sensor data are relevant in the second scenario, where the utilization of an undivided chain could be made for statistical analysis. For instance, authors in [86] utilize differential privacy when carrying out federated learning and then applying the potential of blockchain for recording crowdsourcing processes to prevent an adversary from inferring sensitive personal information.

6.4.3   Methods for data protection

A block's structure uses an interlinked list of hash pointers, so if a transaction or block is removed or changed, the block's hash pointer will change, violating the integrity of all ensuing transactions. This contravenes the GDPR's principles and laws protecting privacy. Through various encryption techniques, the records saved on the blockchain can be secured, achieving secrecy and, as a result, a comprehensive understanding of secrecy and privacy. Different encryption and storage techniques might be used, depending on who will be using the enciphered data. In the case of conventional symmetric and asymmetric encryption, the data originator could submit the encrypted transaction. They would either employ an implementation of a decentralized PKI on the blockchain, like in Sovrin [51], to manage public keys later on or they would distribute their decryption key off-ledger.

Further strategies for distributing encrypted data among numerous peers in a chain centre on granting a group of nodes the right to decrypt the information on the basis of a set of predetermined criteria. In this sense, encryption methods like Key-Policy Attribute-Based Encryption (KP-ABE) or Ciphertext-Policy Attribute-Based Encryption (CP-ABE) [87], which enable the definition of access control mechanism within the encryption itself, enable the restriction of data decryption to only users with the necessary attributes.

Secret sharing is a different strategy that the authors of [88] and [89] independently developed. When t out of N nodes cooperate or when one node acquires t out of N shares of the fragmented document, the original document can only be recovered. The original document can only be restored when t out of N nodes cooperate or when one node acquires t out of N shares of the fragmented document. It permits splitting a document into N separate parts and giving each piece to N different nodes. Another name for this is a (t, N)-threshold system. The theory is that two points create a distinct line and can be used to split and rebuild a document. Draw a line and assign a random position along it to each of the N nodes once you have divided the document into two points in the plane. Reassembling the line and obtaining the original file is possible for each collaborative pair of nodes. The $(2, N)$-threshold is utilized in this method. It is sufficient to use a polynomial with degree $t - 1$ rather than a line to accommodate a higher threshold. Interpolation yields the original polynomial corresponding to the broken document with t distinct points. The situation in which replicating the data across all N storage nodes at time $t = 1$ is similar.

The blockchain instance could become unnecessarily big due to the volume of the ciphered data, as well as the chain's immutability could lead to future privacy issues if the decrypting keys are misplaced or stolen. As an alternative, large amounts of ciphered data might be stored in decentralized off-ledger databases like IPFS [90], with each transaction containing the unique resource identification as well as its hash to guarantee data integrity and existence. By rewarding trustworthy storage nodes with blockchain tokens, enforcing privacy controls to safeguard the data, and using hashes in the transactions to ensure transactional integrity, incentive-based decentralized storage [91–95] can be combined with blockchain technology. Depending on the blockchain's intended usage, some transactions might just be used to verify the chain's hash integrity, such as old transactions that have already been spent, or they might contain private information that the user wants to remove from the chain. Removal of a transaction without disturbing the chain's hash integrity validation is possible by altering the blockchain data structures, according to some theories [58,96]. It changes a blockchain's immutability property because the validation of the hash would still work and the network's consensus rules allow the deletion of a transaction. However, resolution of privacy issues is not assured. The data is replicated throughout every blockchain node, and some nodes can keep storing it long after the chain has been removed.

6.5   Analysis of privacy provisioning strategies

Generally, privacy provisioning strategies on Blockchain can be divided into four major subsets. The taxonomy of privacy provisioning on blockchain strategies is depicted in Table 6.1.

Here is a summary of the four categories and techniques.

6.5.1   SMPC

SMPC splits the state of smart contract execution along with key management without assisting of any third-party involvement.

6.5.2   Identity data anonymization

This approach includes the zero knowledge proofs, mixing for concealing the prover and verifier, and the homomorphic cryptosystem to preserve the identity of user during the transactions in blockchain. To achieve the anonymity of user ring signature and to hide the transaction ring confidential transaction (RingCT) is used.

6.5.3   Transaction data anonymization

It incorporates privacy provisioning methods designed to safeguard the confidentiality of the transactions on the blockchain. It uses methods including mixing, differential privacy, ZKPs, homomorphic hiding, and anonymizing exchanged currencies (to hide the amount in a transaction).

6.5.4   On-chain data protection

This mechanism includes public-key encryption, and secret sharing of cryptographic credentials to achieve data security on a blockchain. Several privacy provisioning approaches are being used to achieve not only anonymization of sender and receiver but also able transaction data, including ZKPs and homomorphic hiding (e.g. operated coins).

Table 6.2 lists the key benefits and drawbacks of the privacy mechanisms and cryptographic principles used in blockchain [100].

Table 6.1   Blockchain privacy preserving mechanism

Categories	Privacy preserving mechanisms
Smart contracts and key management	Secure multi-party computation (SMPC)
Identity data anonymization	ZKP, Ring Signature, mixing, commitment schemes, and homomorphic hiding
Transaction data anonymization	Mixing, differential privacy, ZKPs, homomorphic hiding
On-chain data protection	Secret sharing of cryptographic credentials, public key encryption techniques, and attribute-based encryption approaches

Table 6.2 Summary of privacy techniques

Privacy techniques	Short description	Advantages	Disadvantages
Commitment Scheme [68]	Bind the user to a value while hiding it	Computationally effective binding and concealing	Either unconditional binding or Unconditional hiding but not both
ZKP [67]	Evidence of a claim without revealing any personal data known as zero-knowledge	Demonstrate any ignorant claim to be false	Size; efficiency
Homographic hiding	Calculations using numbers in ciphertext convert to numbers in cleartext	Calculations using numbers in ciphertext convert to numbers in cleartext	Often only a few homomorphic computations
zkSNARK [72,73]	Proof of the accurate calculation of a given code in zero-knowledge	Concise; Zero-Knowledge	Trusted setup phase Attacks from provers with high computational power Poor computational efficiency of the prover Utilization of smart contracts that are inefficient
STARK [97,98]	zSNARK without a trusted setup phase	Transparency: setting up without trust	Low level of maturity
Ring Signatures [78]	To conceal the true signer of a message, sign it using a private key and N public keys	Not reliant on a reliable third party Custom sets are automatically defined by users Deviations like threshold signatures	Challenging coordination and management
Mixing [84]	Organize a group of users to carry out tasks while concealing the creator	Works in addition to existing solutions Efficiency	Coordination of several users Utilization of mixing servers

(*Continues*)

Table 6.2 (Continued)

Privacy techniques	Short description	Advantages	Disadvantages
Differential Privacy [86,99]	Change the statistical treatment of the data so that statistical studies as a whole have relevance but that the personal data is impossible to recover	Data privacy for each person Statistical utility	Directly relevant to blockchain
Attribute-based encryption [87]	Data that has been encrypted can be decoded if the user possesses the required characteristics	Authorities are determined by policies	Authentication system for attribute certificates
Secret sharing [88,89]	A document is divided up and distributed among N parties. Only with t-out-of-N cooperation can the document be rebuilt	Not every node is required to recover the document	Collusion attacks
Transaction removals [58,96]	In order to ensure that the integrity computation is accurate, a transaction is substituted in the chain	Right to eliminate personal information	Eradication is not assured Consensus approval is required for the deletion action

These solutions largely focus on the correlation and mixing of transaction privacy in regard to the privacy issues in blockchain that were discussed in the previous section. The usage of ZKP over accumulators, Ring Signatures, or mixing protocols allows for the concealment of multi-entry transactions as well as transactions with modifications that link numerous addresses to the same user. By using commitments to hide the transaction's specifics and avoiding grouping potential owners' pool of owners, zkSNARKs offers an alternative solution to this correlation. The transaction author validated the transaction's legality, which the validator nodes rely on with zero knowledge.

In ZKP, the prover proves the statement to the verifier without disclosing any sensitive details to the verifier. Other approaches such as the non-interactive zero knowledge protocol also preserve the privacy of e-administration.

While blockchain is not suited for handling massive volumes of data, it does offer integrity and evidence for the presence of other controlled or distributed cloud storage services, such as IPFS. For assaults by the most $t-1$ colluders, privacy is provided by splitting a document into many pieces that require t out of n to reconstruct it, and availability is provided by the utmost $n - t$ unavailable nodes.

The issues of data protection legislation, like GDPR, are addressed through solutions like differential privacy and transaction erasure, which preserve citizens' rights to privacy. Differential privacy is helpful in IoT scenarios for smart cities since it allows for the collection and statistical manipulation of sensor data without impairing the city's utility. The deletion of transactions is not assured, though, because of the distributed nature of the blockchain. Non-deleted transaction privacy is improved through encryption, and attribute-based encryption (ABE) systems enable key distribution based on credentials rather than policies. If the blockchain does not authorize transaction removal, any encrypted data remains susceptible to various attacks.

6.6 Conclusions

This chapter reviews the state-of-the-art for blockchain privacy preserving protocols on blockchain technologies. On-chain data privacy, linkability of transactions in blocks, cryptographic keys management, and usability are only a few of the open research challenges and problems that are associated with privacy provisioning on blockchain that has been highlighted. Based on this, the study examined blockchain platforms, and existing privacy provisioning technologies, namely, secure multi-party computation, zero-knowledge proofs, mixings, post-quantum computing cryptography, etc. Despite significant research efforts to develop and incorporate existing anonymity or cryptographic privacy strategies, current blockchain strategies are still unable to fully address these privacy issues. The development of a fully privacy provisioned and self-sovereign digital identity model on the blockchain is hampered by this condition, which undercuts user rights such as the right to withdraw consent, the right to the erasure of data, and the ability to become anonymous in certain circumstances. The existing privacy provisioning techniques can be applied to the blockchain transaction of decentralized social media. Also, for blockchain privacy provisioning to be enhanced and improved, effective crypto-privacy algorithms are required.

References

[1]   Z. Zheng, S. Xie, H.-N. Dai, and H. Wang, "Blockchain challenges and opportunities: a survey," *Int. J. Web Grid Services*, vol. 14, no. 4, pp. 352–375, 2018.

[2]   R. Panetta and L. Cristofaro, "A closer look at the EU-funded my health my data project," in *Proceedings of the Digital Health Legal*, Nov. 2017, pp. 10–11, doi: 10.5281/zenodo.1048999.

[3]   M. Conoscenti, A. Vetrò, and J. C. D. Martin, "Blockchain for the Internet of Things: a systematic literature review," in *Proceedings of the IEEE/ACS 13th International Conference on Computer Systems Applications (AICCSA)*, Nov. 2016, pp. 1–6.

[4]   F. R. Batubara, J. Ubacht, and M. Janssen, "Challenges of blockchain technology adoption for e-government: a systematic literature review," in *Proceedings of the 19th Annual International Conference on Digital Government Research: Governance in the Data Age*, New York, NY, 2018, pp. 76:1–76:9.

[5]   L. Li, J. Liu, L. Cheng, *et al.*, "Creditcoin: a privacy-preserving blockchain-based incentive announcement network for communications of smart vehicles," *IEEE Trans. Intell. Transp. Syst.*, vol. 19, no. 7, pp. 2204–2220, 2018.

[6]   Regulation (EU) 2016/679 of the European Parliament and of the Council of 27 April 2016 on the Protection of Natural Persons With Regard to the Processing of Personal Data and on the Free Movement of Such Data, and Repealing Directive 95/46/EC (General Data Protection Regulation), document 32016R0679, May 2016, vol. L119, pp. 1–88. http://eur-lex.europa.eu/legalcontent/EN/TXT/?uri=OJ:L:2016:119:TOC

[7]   M. Vukolić, "The quest for scalable blockchain fabric: Proof of work vs. BFT replication," in J. Camenisch and D. Kesdoğan (eds.), *Open Problems in Network Security*, Cham, Switzerland: Springer, 2016, pp. 112–125.

[8]   X. Li, P. Jiang, T. Chen, X. Luo, and Q. Wen, A survey on the security of blockchain systems, *Fut. Gener. Comput. Syst.*, vol. 107, pp. 841–853, 2020, ISSN 0167-739X.

[9]   E. Androulaki, G. O. Karame, M. Roeschlin, T. Scherer, and S. Capkun, "Evaluating user privacy in bitcoin," in A.-R. Sadeghi (ed.), *Financial Cryptography Data Security*, Berlin, Germany: Springer, 2013, pp. 34–51.

[10] P. Koshy, D. Koshy, and P. McDaniel, "An analysis of anonymity in bit-coin using P2P network traffic," in N. Christin and R. Safavi-Naini (eds.), *Financial Cryptography and Data Security*, Berlin, Germany: Springer, 2014, pp. 469–485.

[11] F. Reid and M. Harrigan, "An analysis of anonymity in the bitcoin system," in *Proceedings of the IEEE 3rd International Conference on Social Computing (SocialCom) Privacy, Security, Risk and Trust PASSAT (PASSAT)*, Boston, MA, Oct. 2011, pp. 1318–1326.

[12] J. Herrera-Joancomartí, "Research and challenges on bitcoin anonymity," in J. Garcia-Alfaro, J. Herrera-Joancomartí, E. Lupu, J. Posegga, A. Aldini, F. Martinelli, and N. Suri (eds.), *Data Privacy Management, Autonomous Spontaneous Security, and Security Assurance,* Cham, Switzerland: Springer, 2015, pp. 3–16.

[13] M. Crosby, P. Pattanayak, S. Verma, and V. Kalyanaraman, "Blockchain technology: beyond bitcoin," *Appl. Innov.*, vol. 2, pp. 6–10, 2016.

[14] C. Lundkvist, R. Heck, J. Torstensson, Z. Mitton, and M. Sena, Uport: A Platform for Self-Sovereign Identity, 2017. https://whitepaper.uport.me/ uPort_whitepaper_DRAFT20170221.pdf

[15] A. Tobin and D. Reed, The Inevitable Rise of Self-Sovereign Identity. The Sovrin Foundation, 2016. https://sovrin.org/wp-content/uploads/2017/06/ The-Inevitable-Rise-of-Self-SovereignIdentity.pdf

[16] J. Bonneau, A. Narayanan, A. Miller, J. Clark, J. A. Kroll, and E. W. Felten, "Mixcoin: anonymity for bitcoin with accountable mixes," in *Proceedings of the International Conference on Financial Cryptography and Data Security*, Berlin, Germany: Springer, 2014, pp. 486–504.

[17] E. Heilman, L. Alshenibr, F. Baldimtsi, A. Scafuro, and S. Goldberg, "TumbleBit: an untrusted bitcoin-compatible anonymous payment hub," in *Proceedings of the Network and Distributed System Security Symposium*, San Diego, CA, 2017. https://open.bu.edu/handle/2144/ 29224

[18] T. Ruffing and P. Moreno-Sanchez, "ValueShuffle: mixing confidential transactions for comprehensive transaction privacy in bitcoin," in *Financial Cryptography and Data Security*, Cham, Switzerland: Springer, 2017, pp. 133–154.

[19] E. B. Sasson, A. Chiesa, C. Garman, *et al.*, "Zerocash: decentralized anonymous payments from bitcoin," in *Proceedings of the IEEE Symposium on Security and Privacy (SP)*, May 2014, pp. 459–474.

[20] X. Yi, E. Bertino, F. Y. Rao, K. Y. Lam, S. Nepal, and A. Bouguettaya, Privacy-preserving user profile matching in social networks. *IEEE Trans. Knowl. Data Eng.*, vol. 32, no. 8, pp. 1572–1585, 2019.

[21] M. Li, N. Cao, S. Yu, and W. Lou, "Findu: privacy-preserving personal profile matching in mobile social networks," in *2011 Proceedings of the IEEE INFOCOM*, Apr. 2011, IEEE, pp. 2435–2443.

[22] Z. Yang, B. Zhang, J. Dai, A. C. Champion, D. Xuan, and D. Li, "E-smalltalker: a distributed mobile system for social networking in physical proximity," in *2010 IEEE 30th International Conference on Distributed Computing Systems,* Jun. 2010, IEEE, pp. 468–477.

[23] M. Von Arb, M. Bader, M. Kuhn, and R. Wattenhofer, "Veneta: serverless friend-of-friend detection in mobile social networking," in *2008 IEEE*

International Conference on Wireless and Mobile Computing, Networking and Communications*, Oct. 2008, IEEE, pp. 184–189.

[24]   S. Nakamoto, Bitcoin: A Peer-to-Peer Electronic Cash System, 2008. https://bitcoin.org/bitcoin.pdf

[25]   V. Gatteschi, F. Lamberti, C. Demartini, C. Pranteda, and V. Santamaría, "To blockchain or not to blockchain: that is the question," *IT Prof.*, vol. 20, no. 2, pp. 62–74, 2018.

[26]   M. Bartoletti and L. Pompianu, "An empirical analysis of smart contracts: platforms, applications, and design patterns," in *Proceedings of the International Conference on Financial Cryptography and Data Security*, Cham, Switzerland: Springer, 2017, pp. 494–509.

[27]   P. Jayachandran, The Difference Between Public and Private Blockchain— Blockchain Unleashed: IBM Blockchain Blog, 2017. https://www.ibm.com/blogs/blockchain/2017/05/thedifference-between-public-and-private-blockchain/

[28]   D. Ron and A. Shamir, "Quantitative analysis of the full bitcoin transaction graph," in A.-R. Sadeghi (ed.), *Financial Cryptography and Data Security*, Berlin, Germany: Springer, 2013, pp. 6–24.

[29]   M. Ober, S. Katzenbeisser, and K. Hamacher, "Structure and anonymity of the bitcoin transaction graph," *Fut. Internet*, vol. 5, no. 2, pp. 237–250, 2013.

[30]   M. Fleder, M. S. Kester, and S. Pillai, "Bitcoin transaction graph analysis," 2015, arXiv:1502.01657. https://arxiv.org/abs/1502.01657

[31]   M. Spagnuolo, F. Maggi, and S. Zanero, "BitIodine: extracting intelligence from the bitcoin network," in *Proceedings of the International Conference on Financial Cryptography and Data Security*, Berlin, Germany: Springer, 2014, pp. 457–468.

[32]   S. Meiklejohn and C. Orlandi, "Privacy-enhancing overlays in bitcoin," in *Proc. Int. Conf. Financial Cryptogr. Data Secur*, Berlin, Germany: Springer, 2015, pp. 127–141.

[33]   A. Kosba, A. Miller, E. Shi, Z. Wen, and C. Papamanthou, "Hawk: the blockchain model of cryptography and privacy-preserving smart contracts," in *Proceedings of the IEEE Symposium on Security and Privacy (SP)*, May 2016, pp. 839–858.

[34]   J. Herrera-Joancomartí and C. PØrez-Solà, "Privacy in bitcoin transactions: new challenges from blockchain scalability solutions," in *Modeling Decisions for Artificial Intelligence*, Cham, Switzerland: Springer, 2016, pp. 26–44.

[35]   T. Ruffing, P. Moreno-Sanchez, and A. Kate, "CoinShuffle: practical decentralized coin mixing for bitcoin," in M. Kutyłowski and J. Vaidya (eds.), *Computer Security—ESORICS,* Cham, Switzerland: Springer, 2014, pp. 345–364.

[36]   L. Valenta and B. Rowan, "Blindcoin: blinded, accountable mixes for bitcoin," in M. Brenner, N. Christin, B. Johnson, and K. Rohloff (eds.), *Financial Cryptography and Data Security*, Berlin, Germany: Springer, 2015, pp. 112–126.

[37] E. Heilman, F. Baldimtsi, and S. Goldberg, "Blindly signed contracts: anonymous on-blockchain and off-blockchain bitcoin transactions," in *Proceedings of the International Conference on Financial Cryptography and Data Security*, Berlin, Germany: Springer, 2016, pp. 43–60.

[38] S. Goldfeder, H. Kalodner, D. Reisman, and A. Narayanan, "When the cookie meets the blockchain: privacy risks of Web payments via cryptocurrencies," *Proc. Privacy Enhancing Technol.*, vol. 2018, no. 4, pp. 179–199, 2018.

[39] N. Bitansky, R. Canetti, A. Chiesa, and E. Tromer, "Recursive composition and bootstrapping for SNARKS and proof-carrying data," in *Proceedings of the 41st Annual ACM Symposium on Theory of Computing*, 2013, pp. 111–120.

[40] A. Biryukov, D. Khovratovich, and I. Pustogarov, "Deanonymisation of clients in bitcoin P2P network," in *Proceedings of the 2014 ACM SIGSAC Conference on Computer and Communications Security*, 2014, pp. 15–29.

[41] S. Noether, "Ring signature confidential transactions for Monero," IACR Cryptol. ePrint Arch., Tech. Rep. 2015/1098, 2015.

[42] R. Dingledine, N. Mathewson, and P. Syverson, "Tor: The second-generation onion router," in *Proceedings of the USENIX Security*, 2004, pp. 1–18.

[43] B. Zantout and R. Haraty, "I2P data communication system," in *Proceedings of the ICN*, 2011, pp. 401–409.

[44] A. Biryukov and I. Pustogarov, "Bitcoin over Tor isn't a good idea," in *Proceedings of the IEEE Symposium on Security and Privacy (SP)*, May 2015, pp. 122–134.

[45] N. T. Courtois and R. Mercer, "Stealth address and key management techniques in blockchain systems," in *Proceedings of the ICISSP*, 2017, pp. 559–566.

[46] L. Er-Rajy, A. El Kiram My, M. El Ghazouani, and O. Achbarou, "Blockchain: bitcoin wallet cryptography security, challenges and countermeasures," *J. Internet Banking Commerce*, vol. 22, no. 3, pp. 1–29, 2017.

[47] S. Eskandari, J. Clark, D. Barrera, and E. Stobert, "A first look at the usability of bitcoin key management," 2018, arXiv:1802.04351. https://arxiv.org/abs/1802.04351

[48] R. Gennaro, S. Jarecki, H. Krawczyk, and T. Rabin, "Secure distributed key generation for discrete-log based cryptosystems," *J. Cryptol.*, vol. 20, no. 1, pp. 51–83, 2007.

[49] S. Barber, X. Boyen, E. Shi, and E. Uzun, "Bitter to better—How to make bitcoin a better currency," in *Proceedings of the International Conference on Financial Cryptography and Data Security*, Berlin, Germany: Springer, 2012, pp. 399–414.

[50] M. Egorov, M. Wilkison, and D. Nuæez, "NuCypher KMS: Decentralized key management system," 2017, arXiv:1707.06140. https://arxiv.org/abs/1707.06140

[51] S. Foundation, "Sovrin: a protocol and token for self-sovereign identity and decentralized trust," Sovrin Found., Northampton, MA, USA, Tech. Rep., 2018. https://sovrin.org/wp-content/uploads/Sovrin-Protocol-and-Token-White-Paper.pdf

[52] N. Atzei, M. Bartoletti, and T. Cimoli, "A survey of attacks on Ethereum smart contracts (SoK)," in *Proceedings of the 6th International Conference on Principles of Security and Trust*, vol. 10204. New York, NY: Springer-Verlag, 2017, pp. 164–186.

[53] H. Hasan and K. Salah, "Proof of delivery of digital assets using blockchain and smart contracts," *IEEE Access*, vol. 6, pp. 65439–65448, 2018.

[54] N. Atzei, M. Bartoletti, and T. Cimoli, "A survey of attacks on Ethereum smart contracts (SoK)," in M. Maffei and M. Ryan (eds.), *Principles of Security and Trust*, Berlin, Germany: Springer, 2017, pp. 164–186.

[55] V. Costan and S. Devadas, "Intel SGX explained," *IACR Cryptol. ePrint Arch.*, vol. 2016, no. 86, pp. 1–118, 2016.

[56] A. Moghimi, G. Irazoqui, and T. Eisenbarth, "CacheZoom: how SGX amplifies the power of cache attacks," in *Proceedings of the International Conference on Cryptographic Hardware and Embedded Systems*, Cham, Switzerland: Springer, 2017, pp. 69–90.

[57] D. C. SÆnchez, "Raziel: private and verifiable smart contracts on blockchains," *IACR Cryptol. ePrint Arch.*, vol. 2017, pp. 878, 2017.

[58] D. R. Kuhn, "A data structure for integrity protection with erasure capability," NIST, Gaithersburg, MD, Tech. Rep., May 2018. https://csrc.nist.gov/publications/detail/white-paper/2018/05/31/data-structure-for-integrity-protection-with-erasure-capability/draft

[59] B. Stein, K. Kuznecov, S. Lee, and J. Müller, "A public blockchain solution permitting secure storage and deletion of private data—Draft," *Lition Foundation*, Berlin, Germany, Tech. Rep., 2018. https://www.lition.io/docs/Lition_TechnicalWhitePaper_V0.7.1.pdf

[60] J. Pieprzyk, T. Hardjono, and J. Seberry, *Computer Security Fundamentals*, Berlin, Germany: Springer, 2013.

[61] B. Parno, J. Howell, C. Gentry, and M. Raykova, "Pinocchio: nearly practical verifiable computation," in *Proceedings of the Symposium on Security and Privacy (SP)*, May 2013, pp. 238–252.

[62] B. Bünz, J. Bootle, D. Boneh, A. Poelstra, P. Wuille, and G. Maxwell, *Bullet Proofs: Efficient Range Proofs for Confidential Transactions*, Stanford University, Stanford, CA, Tech. Rep. 2017/1066, 2017.

[63] S. Ames, C. Hazay, Y. Ishai, and M. Venkitasubramaniam, "Ligero: lightweight sublinear arguments without a trusted setup," in *Proceedings of the ACM SIGSAC Conference on Computer and Communications Security (CCS)*, New York, NY, 2017, pp. 2087–2104.

[64] R. Cramer and I. B. Damgård, *Secure Multiparty Computation*. Cambridge, UK: Cambridge University Press, 2015.

[65]   D. W. Archer, D. Bogdanov, B. Pinkas, and P. Pullonen, "Maturity and performance of programmable secure computation," *IEEE Security Privacy*, vol. 14, no. 5, pp. 48–56, 2016.

[66]   Wanchain Foundation, Building Super Financial Markets for the New Digital Economy, 2018. https://www.wanchain.org/files/Wanchain-Whitepaper-EN-version.pdf

[67]   S. Goldwasser, S. Micali, and C. Rackoff, "The knowledge complexity of interactive proof systems," *SIAM J. Comput.*, vol. 18, no. 1, pp. 186–208, 1989.

[68]   G. Brassard, D. Chaum, and C. CrØpeau, "Minimum disclosure proofs of knowledge," *J. Comput. Syst. Sci.*, vol. 37, no. 2, pp. 156–189, 1988.

[69]   M. Blum, "How to prove a theorem so no one else can claim it," in *Proceedings of the International Congress on Mathematicians*, 1986, pp. 1444–1451.

[70]   I. Miers, C. Garman, M. Green, and A. D. Rubin, "Zerocoin: anonymous distributed E-cash from bitcoin," in *Proceedings of the IEEE Symposium on Security and Privacy (SP)*, May 2013, pp. 397–411.

[71]   Zcash. (2018). Zcash—How ZK-Snarks Work in Zcash. https://z.cash/technology/zksnarks.html

[72]   E. Ben-Sasson, A. Chiesa, D. Genkin, E. Tromer, and M. Virza, "SNARKs for C: verifying program executions succinctly and in zero knowledge," in *Advances in Cryptology—CRYPTO*, Berlin, Germany: Springer, 2013, pp. 90–108.

[73]   C. Gentry, "Fully homomorphic encryption using ideal lattices," in *Proceedings of the 41st Annual ACM Symposium on Theory of Computing (STOC)*, New York, NY, 2009, pp. 169–178.

[74]   R. L. Rivest, L. Adleman, and M. L. Dertouzos, "On data banks and privacy homomorphisms," *Found. Secure Comput.*, vol. 4, no. 11, pp. 169–180, 1978.

[75]   N. Van Saberhagen, Cryptonote v2.0, 2013. https://cryptonote.org/whitepaper.pdf

[76]   B. K. Chaurasia and S. Verma, "Conditional privacy through ring signature in vehicular Ad-hoc networks," In M.L. Gavrilova and C.J.K. Tan (eds.), *Transactions on Computer Science, XIII, LNCS 6750*, Berlin Heidelberg: Springer-Verlag, 2011, pp. 147–156.

[77]   R. L. Rivest, A. Shamir, and Y. Tauman, "How to leak a secret," in *Proceedings of the International Conference on the Theory and Application of Cryptology and Information Security*, Springer, 2001, pp. 552–565.

[78]   D. Chaum and E. van Heyst, "Group signatures," in *Proc. Workshop Theory Appl. Cryptograph. Techn.*, Springer, 1991, pp. 257–265.

[79]   J. K. Liu, V. K. Wei, and D. S. Wong, "Linkable spontaneous anonymous group signature for ad hoc groups," in H. Wang, J. Pieprzyk, and V. Varadharajan (eds.), *Information Security and Privacy*, Berlin, Germany: Springer, 2004, pp. 325–335.

[80] J. Camenisch and E. Van Herreweghen, "Design and implementation of the idemix anonymous credential system," in *Proceedings of the 9th ACM Conference on Computer and Communications Security (CCS)*, New York, NY, 2002, pp. 21–30.

[81] S. Noether and A. Mackenzie, "Ring confidential transactions," *Ledger*, vol. 1, pp. 1–18, 2016.

[82] P. Todd, Stealth Addresses, Post on Bitcoin Development Mailing List. Accessed: Nov. 11, 2019. https://lists.linuxfoundation.org/pipermail/bitcoin-dev/2014-January/004020.html

[83] S.-F. Sun, M. H. Au, J. K. Liu, and T. H. Yuen, "RingCT 2.0: a compact accumulator-based (linkable ring signature) protocol for blockchain cryptocurrency Monero," in S. N. Foley, D. Gollmann, and E. Snekkenes (eds.), *Computer Security—ESORICS*, Cham, Switzerland: Springer, 2017, pp. 456–474.

[84] D. L. Chaum, "Untraceable electronic mail, return addresses, and digital pseudonyms," *Commun. ACM*, vol. 24, no. 2, pp. 84–90, 1981.

[85] G. Maxwell, "CoinJoin: Bitcoin privacy for the real world," in *Proceedings of the Post Bitcoin Forum*, 2013. https://bitcointalk.org/index.php?topic=279249.0

[86] Y. Zhao, J. Zhao, L. Jiang, R. Tan, and D. Niyato, "Mobile edge computing, blockchain and reputation-based crowdsourcing IoT federated learning: a secure, decentralized and privacy-preserving system," 2019, arXiv:1906.10893. https://arxiv.org/abs/1906.10893

[87] J. Bethencourt, A. Sahai, and B. Waters, "Ciphertext-policy attribute based encryption," in *Proceedings of the IEEE Symposium on Security and Privacy (SP)*, May 2007, pp. 321–334.

[88] A. Shamir, "How to share a secret," *Commun. ACM*, vol. 22, no. 11, pp. 612–613, 1979.

[89] G. R. Blakley, "Safeguarding cryptographic keys," in *Proceedings of the AFIPS Conference*, vol. 48, pp. 313–317, 1979.

[90] J. Benet, "IPFS—Content addressed, versioned, P2P file system," 2014, arXiv:1407.3561. https://arxiv.org/abs/1407.3561

[91] A. Miller, A. Juels, E. Shi, B. Parno, and J. Katz, "Permacoin: repurposing bitcoin work for data preservation," in *Proceedings of the IEEE Symposium on Security and Privacy (SP)*, May 2014, pp. 475–490.

[92] J. Benet and N. Greco, *Filecoin: A Decentralized Storage Network*, Protocol Labs, San Francisco, CA, USA, Tech. Rep., 2018. https://filecoin.io/filecoin.pdf

[93] D. Irvine, "Maidsafe.net," U.S. Patent Appl. 12/476,229, Mar. 11, 2010.

[94] S. Wilkinson, T. Boshevski, J. Brandoff, *et al.*, STORJ: A Peer-to-Peer Cloud Storage Network, 2018. https://storj.io/storj.pdf

[95] D. Vorick and L. Champine, "Sia: simple decentralized storage," *Nebulous*, Boston, MA, Tech. Rep., 2014, vol. 8, 2018. https://assets.coss.io/documents/white-papers/siacoin.pdf

[96] V. Demianets and A. Kanakakis, Distributed Ledger With Secure Data Deletion—Revision 1.4. Stockholm, Sweden, 2016.

[97] R. S. Wahby, I. Tzialla, J. Thaler, and M. Walfish, "Doubly-efficient zkSNARKs without trusted setup," in *Proceeding of the IEEE Symposium on Security and Privacy*, May 2018, pp. 926–943.

[98] C. Dwork and A. Roth, "The algorithmic foundations of differential privacy," *Found. Trends Theor. Comput. Sci.*, vol. 9, no. 3–4, pp. 211–407, 2014.

[99] J. B. Bernabe, J. L. Canovas, J. L. Hernandez-Ramos, R. T. Moreno, and A. Skarmeta, Privacy-preserving solutions for blockchain: review and challenges. *IEEE Access*, vol. 7, pp. 164908–164940, 2019.

[100] B. K. Chaurasia, S. Verma, and S. M. Bhasker, "Message broadcast in VANETs using Group Signature," in *Fourth International Conference on Wireless Communication and Sensor Networks*, 2008, pp. 131–136.

Chapter 7

Blockchain-based knowledge graph for high-impact scientific collaboration networks

Yao Yao[1], Meghana Kshirsagar[1], Gauri Vaidya[1], Junying Liu[2], Yongliang Zhang[3] and Conor Ryan[1]

Abstract

In this book chapter, we introduce a framework leveraging the *intelligence of the crowd* to improve the quality, credibility, inclusiveness, long-term impact and adoption of research, particularly in the academic space. This integrated platform revolves around a central knowledge graph (KG) which interacts through artificial intelligence (AI) algorithms with the community. In combination with Internet of Things (IoT) technology and blockchain, a highly productive environment including liquid governance and arbitration is created to fairly acknowledge and attractively incentivize contributions of valuable intellectual property (IP) to this knowledge base. In the proposed platform, various stakeholders customize their terms of agreement to be followed while validating the transactions on blockchain, known as *smart contracts*. Through the interaction of smart contracts and stakeholders, the agreement based on objective (scientific) criteria will gradually emerge from the simulated interaction and, if applicable, its experimental/empirical verification.

Keywords: Social media; Knowledge graph; Consortium blockchain; MultiChain; Smart contracts; Scientific collaborations

7.1 Introduction

Projects in fundamental science aim to produce outcomes that are eventually beneficial for public commons, i.e., they serve the good of people and societies through advancing knowledge, culture and lives. This fact brings about the proclivity that

[1]Biocomputing and Developmental Systems (BDS) Lero, The Science Foundation Ireland Research Centre for Software Department of Computer Science and Information Systems, University of Limerick, Ireland
[2]The School of Pharmacy and Pharmaceutical Sciences, Trinity College Dublin, Ireland
[3]School of Engineering, University of Limerick, Ireland

all research activities are inherently required for collaboration with others. Following the increase of the complexity of modern society, this proclivity has also become imperative. However, establishing a successful interdisciplinary collaboration between multiple stakeholders usually is a challenge today.

The main challenge comes from two aspects: one is about value validation and another one is about knowledge understanding [1]. In general, for any research, the genuine value of research is based on credible results that withstand independent validation in compliance with widely accepted standards and methods and are slated to make a positive impact in society. The traditional evaluation based on peer-review of publications worked well in assessing specific research topics in domains familiar to the reviewers, but it becomes less efficient and accurate when there is a need to assess several types of research from different domains. Furthermore, this evaluation is not available to be applied to unpublished results or confidential data. Aside from the value validation problem, different expertise within a single project also elicits conflicts that limit the efficiency and scalability of research collaboration from different domains.

The consensus on terminology and knowledge is an essential factor to determine the success of the research collaboration. However, the corresponding integration usually is insufficient for implementing complicated interdisciplinary collaboration. Following the development of any new scientific research, the collaboration process usually requires complex and hierarchical sharable knowledge which is often only partially understood in its full depth by the entire community, and often severely lacks a comprehensive translation platform through different domains. For enabling efficient collaboration and interaction in the community, each stakeholder has to be able to gain a quite comprehensive view of the global knowledge [2]. To achieve such a holistic view on knowledge, we need to dynamically integrate knowledge with complex context and assuredly protect the privacy, congruence, and security of data. For example, avoiding pernicious tampering will be the essential premise for implementing knowledge integration in collaboration. In our research, we utilize several disruptive approaches such as knowledge integration, holistic knowledge management, and blockchain-based networks enabled by the latest data technologies to address the discussed challenges above. The original intent and objective of this study was to introduce the blockchain-based knowledge base into the online scientific collaboration network. The broader objective was also to explore other related possibilities of applying blockchain technology to facilitate the consensus establishment in general collaboration.

The structure of the chapter is as follows. Section 7.2 discusses the two key technologies adapted in this chapter for scientific collaboration, namely Blockchain and Knowledge Graphs. Section 7.3 presents the methodology of the proposed architecture for scientific collaborations, with their possible use cases in diverse domains in Section 7.4. Section 7.5 concludes the chapter with a summary of the chapter with a view to future works.

The major contributions of the chapter can be summarized as below:

• The study presents a blockchain-based knowledge graph platform that can be used to coordinate scientific collaboration.

- We discuss the related concepts of using blockchain technology to reach the consensus in an online community.
- The proposed system has the potential to facilitate interdisciplinary research collaboration on a highly extendable scale by providing reliable value validation and comprehensive knowledge integration. The key contributions of the chapter can be summarized as follows:
  - ○ Establishing a federated blockchain network, analogous to social media platforms, for scientific collaboration.
  - ○ Presentation of use cases from healthcare industry, pharmaceutical domains, and material science demonstrating the dual advantages of blockchains and knowledge graphs.
  - ○ Applying the network to solve complex tasks, writing grant applications through consortia formation, utilizing shared resources, methodologies, technologies for mutual benefits.

7.2 Background

This section discusses the current works related to use of blockchain in collaborative networks. We also briefly introduce some key concepts used throughout the chapter.

7.2.1 Related works

Recently, the use of blockchain has been widened into diversified domains for multiple operations because of its key properties of immutability, fairness, decentralized smart contracts, and data security. This has also inspired researchers to employ blockchains in collaborations with an aim to reduce transaction costs and work cycles. There has been some recent work related where researchers have used blockchains in collaborative networks. Table 7.1 summarizes the literature with their application domains, blockchain platform, and key features.

7.2.2 Blockchain

A blockchain [9] is a decentralized platform storing the records of valid transactions with a mechanism for validating those transactions using the peers in the blockchain network without the intervention of any third party. The key features of blockchain, such as digital data storage and integrity with dispute resolution mechanisms, have attracted industries for implementing them in applications [10–12].

The key features of a blockchain can be summarized as:

- *Immutable records*: Once transactions are appended to a blockchain, they cannot subsequently be changed. This makes them secure and easy to verify for future reference, e.g., insurance claims and medicine prescriptions.
- *Data ownership*: Data ownership cannot be changed once a transaction is added to a blockchain. This ensures that the data is always being used for legitimate purposes.

Table 7.1   Literature review on using blockchains for collaboration

Field of colla-boration	Applications	Blockchain technology	Stakeholders
ChainGov [3]	Mobile decentralized system that facilitates collaborations between immigrants and governments	–	Governments, social companies, immigrants
Collaborative Medical Decision-Making [4]	Local reference-based consortium blockchain scheme	Multichain 2.0	Patient, cured patient, doctor, insurance company
EPCglobal Network [5]	Computer network used to share product data between trading partners	Hyperledger	Trading partners
E-Voting Scheme [6]	Blockchain based e-voting application	Hyperledger	Voting participants, government, organizers
Public Philanthropy Logistics Platform [7]	Model for evaluating philanthropy material donations for social welfare	Ethereum	Fundraisers, recipients, public welfare organization department, supervisory department
Cardossier [8]	System for managing car data and seeking to improve collaboration	Enterprise blockchain	Businesses, government agencies, public agencies

- *Decentralized data*: Blockchain enables the collaboration of independent stakeholders such as hospitals, insurance services, health care services for better management of services, as the data is shared with each peer in the network. This also makes data available anytime and anywhere, as there is no point of failure.
- *Data security*: The data uploaded on blockchain is secure as it uses the cryptographic hash functions for hashing purposes, e.g., SHA-256 is used to ensure anonymity and generate user addresses in proof-of-work algorithms.

The entities taking part in the blockchain network are termed as the nodes. The transactions in the network are confirmed by following certain fault-tolerant protocols, which are agreed upon by all the participating nodes in the network, known as consensus algorithm. The process for transaction verification is illustrated in Figure 7.1. A consensus algorithm drives the verification of transactions on any blockchain network with added security of computational complexity of mining. Mining is the process of validating the transactions in terms of finding a solution to complex cryptographic equations and rewarding the entities finding the optimal solution to the equations, called as miners, with a currency called as cryptocurrency. The general concept of mining is shown in Figure 7.2. There are different variants of consensus algorithms according to the nature of participating nodes in the network and the kind of data dealt with. As an instance, in a proof-of-work consensus algorithm, all the participating nodes compete for finding a

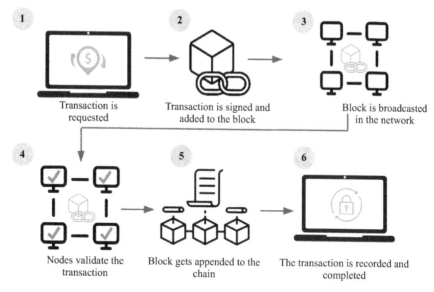

Figure 7.1 Illustration of transaction update and data storage on the blockchain network

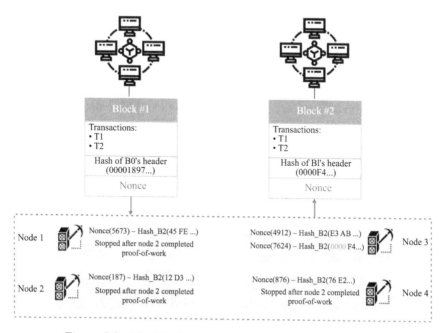

Figure 7.2 The blocks maintained by nodes on the network

solution to a cryptographic equation while in proof of stake, the nodes compete to stake their maximum assets to receive maximal rewards. Another form of consensus algorithm exists where all the participant nodes in the network vote for validating a transaction, called voting-based-consensus. Such consensus algorithms make the blockchain more secure. This security and ease of retrieval of data from the blockchain for data analysis enables a blockchain to be used as a global decentralized database [13].

While a traditional database may be accessible to any number of people, it is often owned and managed by a small number of servers that have complete control over how it works and the data within it. Such architecture may bring security issues in a complex network with massive transactions because the verification and identification of transactions could become too expensive due to the increase of complexity. Blockchain, as a trust-less and fully decentralized peer-to-peer immutable data storage solution, provides a powerful method to address the above issues. Blockchain is a chronological sequence of blocks including a list of complete and valid transaction records. Blocks are linked to the previous block by a reference (hash value), and thus forming a chain. The block preceding a given block is called its parent block, and the first block is known as the genesis block [9].

There are a wide variety of blockchains, although the fundamental ideas are the same, just with minor changes to the parameters and consensus algorithms. There are two major types of blockchain, permissioned (private) and permissionless (publicly accessible). In a permissionless blockchain, all transactions are open to all nodes in the blockchain and the validation of transactions is founded on pre-existing rules. All participants can view the transactions while remaining anonymous. Permissioned blockchains can be seen as an additional blockchain security system, as they maintain an access control layer to allow certain actions to be performed only by certain identifiable participants [14]. For this reason, these blockchains differ from public and private blockchains. A permissioned blockchain uses the advantages of blockchain while maintaining the authority of control in the network because only certain nodes can add and validate the transactions. The transactions can also be viewed by certain nodes that are relevant to them. Permissioned blockchain examples include Corda [15], Hyperledger Fabric [16], Ethereum [17], Multichain [18], and Quorum [19]. Another platform for blockchain where multiple organizations govern the platform as a permissioned blockchain is the Consortium or Federated Blockchain [20]. The blockchain will be governed as a consortium, as we need to have only a decentralized version and one that supports transactions without any fees. Technologies that can be used to build consortium networks are Ethereum, MultiChain, and Hyperledger.

The key concepts of blockchain, such as immutable records, data ownership and decentralized data, enable the decentralization of the collaboration process in order to make it fairer. It also creates a digital community which, through leveraging blockchain technology can realize an "incentive-based" ecosystem to reward participants for the production and sharing of fruitful scientific work and knowledge.

7.2.3   Semantic technology and knowledge graph

Semantic technology is used to help machines understand data. This technology focuses on converting human expert knowledge and semantic statements into a machine-accessible format. The most well-known technologies to enable the encoding of semantics with a computational model are resource description framework (RDF) and web ontology language (OWL). In our current research, we use RDF as the format to represent knowledge graphs. There is much previous research that suggests that a combination of semantic technology such as KG has the potential to combine with blockchain and AI technology for facilitating online collaboration [21–23].

7.2.4   Resource description framework

The resource description framework (RDF) is a family of World Wide Web Consortium (W3C) [24] specifications originally designed as a data model for metadata. It has come to be used as a general method for conceptual description or modelling of information that is implemented in web resources, using a variety of syntax notations and data serialization formats. In RDF format, the body of knowledge modeled by a collection of statements may be subjected to reification, where each statement (i.e., each triple subject-predicate-object altogether) is assigned a Uniform Resource Identifier (URI) [24] and treated as a resource about which additional statements can be made. Each of the statements following the above syntax can be regarded as an RDF triple and many RDF triples can consist of a knowledge graph that represents the particular knowledge model. An RDF triple is the basic component for constituting knowledge.

7.2.5   Knowledge graph on the blockchain network

A knowledge graph (KG) is a tool for representing knowledge. It uses a graph-structured model or topology to represent a collection of knowledge. In this research, we use RDF to support a hierarchical KG. The KG can be regarded as a knowledge base used by diverse AI programs to enhance their understanding and learning efficiency with information gathered from a variety of sources [25]. It can present interlinked descriptions of its entities, i.e., objects, events, and situations, as well as abstract concepts with free-form semantics.

In a KG, the basic components that are used to represent knowledge are called semantic triples. As the name indicates, a triple is a set of three entities that codify a statement about semantic data in the form of subject-predicate-object expressions. The computational program can extract knowledge from data and convert that knowledge into semantic triples which it then stores in a hierarchical KG. In our proposed platform, the customized computational agents will collect the relevant record of stakeholders' behavior during the collaboration and extract the consensus and knowledge from the record data. After the verification of all stakeholders on the blockchain network, such consensus and knowledge will be updated by the KG on the blockchain.

7.3   Methodology

By combining the agent-based knowledge integration framework with blockchain technologies, we propose a novel platform that addresses these discussed challenges in the knowledge integration of scientific collaboration. In the proposed system, computational agents constitute an online platform for coordinating the collaboration process and communicate with other agents or stakeholders for establishing the possible online network. Various stakeholders of the private consortium can be researchers belonging to a specific university, focused research groups, governmental research bodies, funding agencies, etc. [26]. These stakeholders can customize their agents, and then submit them on a permissioned blockchain, in this case, MultiChain. Through the interaction of agents and stakeholder's agreement based on objective (scientific) criteria will gradually emerge from the simulation and, if applicable, its experimental/empirical verification. Such consensus will be recorded as validated KGs of the collaboration community on a designated blockchain where it is protected by encryption and managed by customized smart contracts.

7.3.1   *Knowledge graphs for managing efficient crowdsourcing in collaboration*

A key aspect of our platform is the integration of relevant data and knowledge which could empower network participants or stakeholders to propose "bounties" or "tasks" on the platform by enlisting the services of another stakeholder who has expertise in the required area and can meet the demands of the proposed project for some predefined reward that is paid out on completing the task, either by the person who lists the bounty themselves or through an on-chain treasury or else through outside funding.

The integration implemented on our platform can be regarded as a type of crowdsourcing. Crowdsourcing is a model where individuals or organizations obtain goods or services, including ideas, voting, micro-tasks, and finances from a large, relatively open, and often rapidly evolving group of participants. Crowdsourcing has a great potential to flexibly engage massive resources at favorable value-for-money. However, crowdsourcing, as legacy academic research, also tends to suffer from the challenges of implementing solid verification, sophisticated administration, governance and complicated identity management today, especially when involving a large group of widely autonomous participants. Solving these conundrums in crowdsourcing, by what will here be referred to as "competitive parallelization," is critical for delivering an appropriate and efficient application. In this study, we utilize the latest semantic technologies and hierarchical KGs to support automated coordination of the crowdsourcing application in academic collaboration via blockchain technology. This way, a knowledge integration framework overcomes the complexity of crowdsourcing on a large scale.

In our framework, we take the record of user transactions on the blockchain and deploy particular knowledge graphs to capture the corresponding concepts and patterns that are included in the transaction logs. The knowledge also includes user

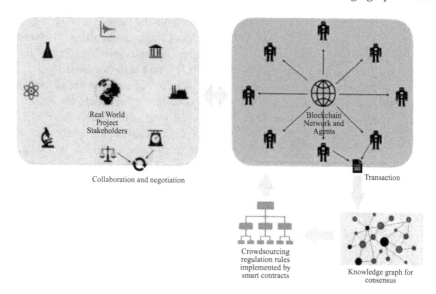

Figure 7.3   The illustration of the crowdsourcing framework

profiles that represent all-critical credibility, impact, and adoption. After knowledge extraction from transactions, the system will convert and gradually update those concepts and their respective contexts. The resulting KGs will thus gradually accumulate, validate, and refine the knowledge underpinning community consensus. Later on, the knowledge in the KG (i.e., the credentials of a particular user, the profile of stakeholders, and so on) will conduct agents to regulate future transactions on the blockchain. Figure 7.3 illustrates the general structure of our framework and crowdsourcing in the real world will relate to it.

There are vast amounts of data coming from two primary sources – the first is researchers' communication through sources such as mobile applications, web mails, blogs, and the second is the literature data associated with the publications of relevant research. These data reside as RDF stores in various databases and, to protect the privacy and security against malicious tampering, the knowledge from the RDF stores is integrated and conceptually represented in the form of KGs. Each KG can further be used to provide insights into crucial information, such as researcher profile, credentials, expertise, and capabilities, which can be accessed by all stakeholders, such as funders, employers, other researchers, collaborators, laboratory technicians, industrial partners, or students who are authenticated users on the blockchain. Through modeling and representation of semantic concepts, KGs can help to prevent points of failure leading to misinformation.

7.3.2   Construction of the blockchain networks

Consortium networks for building scientific collaboration networks are useful as the infrastructure rules are easy to manage and regulate, and external interference can be avoided. Also, in a consortium, members have the facility to alter previous information, which is not possible with other blockchain mechanisms. As there is focused group participation in such networks, the transaction throughput is fairly high. The scalability of nodes is limited from a few dozen to hundreds.

The architecture for the proposed system of scientific collaborations using the Consortium blockchain network is as illustrated in Figure 7.4. There are groups of people socially connected with a mutual interest who will collaboratively work together and explore or share ideas about complex challenging problems. The infrastructure for the scientific collaboration between research bodies will be analogous to social media platforms and powered through a consortium blockchain as noted above. These are permissioned blockchains, which are essentially a hybrid of the public and private blockchain, and can be scaled depending on the mutual interests of all participating groups.

With such a consortium, interested participants can join and get access to the shared data thus avoiding the procedure of building it from scratch. Such a network allows all participants at each node to work as teams and thereby enhance efficiency when solving complex problems together, thereby reducing developmental costs and time. Due to coordination of actions and expertise exchange, duplication regarding the same work can be avoided and instead stakeholders would share responsibilities. As the blockchain is permissioned, the access is allowed for only members of predetermined groups participating in the consortium. Because in Consortium or Federated blockchain multiple organizations govern the platform, all members who have access to the network supervise the group and it is semi-decentralized. All the operations in the form of transactions are approved by predefined experts representing each focused group and together they define a governance model which prescribes the rules of engagement among different organizations participating in the network.

All participating nodes agree to a protocol which is followed by all the members to append the blocks to the chain. The consensus algorithms implemented will be proof of work and proof of stake. Due to the approval by only a fixed number of experts resulting in a system implementing a voting-based approach, the speed of such networks is remarkable and latency is very low. Also, it is protected from

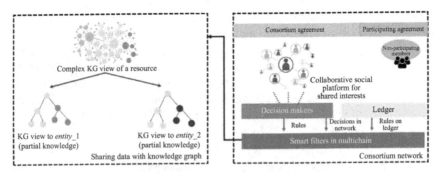

Figure 7.4   Proposed system architecture

monopoly and the so-called 51% attack, as each focused group has a member representation for validating the creation of blocks, establish rules, delete erroneous transactions, etc., the biggest advantage of bringing focused group in the form of a blockchain analogous social network is the absence of transaction fees in the consortium blockchain.

Due to voting-based validation, the difficulty level is relatively less complex and hence such networks do not suffer from massive energy usage. The network enables greater privacy as the verified information is not made public, rather is available within the consortium members thus creating a high level of trust and confidence. We propose the use of multichain for creating our blockchain-powered scientific collaborative social network. MultiChain provides a simple API and a command line interface to preserve and set up a chain. The chain holds its own native currencies or issues assets. Users cannot exchange existing cryptocurrencies on MultiChain unless someone trusted acts as a bridge in the middle, holding some cryptocurrency and issuing tokens on MultiChain to represent it. MultiChain is an off-the-shelf platform for the creation and deployment of private blockchains, either within or between organizations. It aims to overcome a key obstacle to the deployment of blockchain technology in the institutional financial sector, by providing the privacy and control required in an easy-to-use package [18].

The proposed system, unlike a social network, connects the organizations with mutual interest sharing a public ledger, called as nodes. The nodes will be different focus groups, universities, research bodies, governmental departments, industries all of whom are working in the same domain to address a societal need. Each group is represented by a designated expert, representing miners. Incentives can be access to shared resources resulting from collaboration such as high computing machines, software, and sensitive data-sets. A consensus algorithm will be proof of authority and it will be concerned with setting research goals and collecting and agreeing to answers on research objectives. The system will associate a score with each user account and the specific account will be rewarded when it exceeds a predefined threshold. We will follow the combination of proof of capacity and proof of authority as the choice of consensus mechanism algorithms for entering information on the block. Proof of authority will authorize all the users by an authentication mechanism who are allowed to enter information, whereas proof of capacity can allocate equal-sized hard disk space to all authorized users [25]. The system can be further extended to enable data sharing among multiple diverse domains.

The proposed system is an integration of blockchain and KGs. Blockchain will be used as a decentralized database for storing research information, while the KGs will use distributed ledgers to secure keys, and distributed ledgers use knowledge graphs to provide the necessary context and provenance for those keys.

7.3.3 *Agent-based modelling and collective intelligence for knowledge extraction and knowledge integration*

To efficiently implement the verification and identification required for crowd-sourcing, we need a comprehensive knowledge base to properly conduct daily management. The knowledge in such a knowledge base needs to deliver exact responses to the program based on the particular context of the encountered scenarios. The transaction logs, user feedback, and relevant literature include massive amounts of knowledge that can be used to support this function; however, such knowledge is latent in data and cannot be captured directly by programs.

To extract the knowledge from data and integrate knowledge into the knowledge base, we will adopt a hierarchical, agent-based model to analyze the relevant data of crowdsourcing. This proposed approach has been introduced by our recent paper [27,28]. Each stakeholder can define and customize their agents to implement the particular smart contracts on the blockchain and follow the corresponding data policies during the collaboration process like in [29].

7.3.4   Data integration and protection on blockchain

The relevant data of crowdsourcing in our system has been stored in a distributed manner and multiple data stakeholders keep their data partition at the local dataset. The granularity of holistic crowdsourcing data allows the application of flexible and secure data-sharing policies here. We use blockchain as a bridge to connect all distributed data stakeholders in the system and set up diverse smart contracts to regulate the transactions through blockchain.

As discussed above in Section 7.2, when a smart contract has verified the users based on the knowledge from KGs, it will send the secure communication code to related stakeholders and initialize a data communication channel. The participating nodes in the network then verify the transactions, and later added after hashing to the existing blockchain network. A similar approach has been discussed in a previous paper of the data sharing in healthcare for electronic health records [30].

During the communication process, if the credential of users has been suspected, or the data owner has a problem responding to the request, an alerting transaction will be submitted through blockchain. All transactions on the blockchain remain with all stakeholders, and such transparency makes any tampering very difficult. During this data sharing process, all data will always be stored locally, and only the authorized sharing data will be accessible to users through the assigned agents. The smart contracts on blockchain ensure each stakeholder can only access the related part of the data. The congruency and granularity of shared data will be guaranteed with knowledge from knowledge graphs. By this, data privacy and security can be well protected while still enabling the necessary data sharing between genuine stakeholders.

The blocks are secured by any one of the cryptographic secured hash algorithms such as SHA-256 [18]. Only updates will be possible and altering and deletion of data is impossible leading to immutability and security. These blocks are then chained together using a cryptographic hash function in an append-only structure. That means new data is only appended in the form of additional blocks chained with previous blocks since altering and deleting previously confirmed data is impossible. As previously discussed, any modification of one of the blocks will generate a different hash value and different link relation. Hence, achieving immutability and security. The example of an application can be seen in our previous research [31].

7.4   Scenarios and use cases

This section covers some possible use cases that have been discussed with a few experts who are interested in using our proposed platform to facilitate their collaboration. In these use cases, we identified the requirements of expert users under different contexts and discussed the possible solutions which are based on our proposed platform. Through these examples, we present a more concreted prospect about applying blockchain-based knowledge graph in general scientific collaboration and examine the potential advantage of this platform.

7.4.1   *Using blockchain and knowledge-driven application in international collaboration of grant application in pharmaceutical research*

The collaboration of funding application poses significant challenges on the process which comply with the EU General Data Protection Regulation (GDPR) [32] where blockchain might provide a reasonable and flexible means of fostering collaboration, especially in international partnerships of different institutions or organization from the countries outside Europe, such as the USA, China, and the UK. In this sense, the combination of blockchain, semantic technology, and AI offers a promising alternative to centralized workflow management systems. For example, if required, smart contracts can allow the automated activation of specific steps of the workflow and its monitoring. Therefore, blockchain is a system of record based on a distributed immutable ledger that is shared, replicated, and continuously synchronized among peers hosted by participants of a decentralized network. In a blockchain, every record is timestamped and has a cryptographic signature, thus making the ledger an auditable and immutable history of all transactions in the network.

The EU grants often involve more than 10 participants from different fields and countries. The EU encourages the leading institute to choose collaborators from within the EU participant pool and from three other associated countries to form a strong consortium. Therefore, the process of grant application faces genuine challenges related to the requirements of GDPR. With the proposed system powered with consortium blockchain, the collaboration will be more efficient and coherent. For example, consider an application in pharmaceuticals, the consortium formed would have to have all required skills, experience, and resources available coherently and in a complementary manner. The partners would each bring a high level of expertise to develop a multi-disciplinary team covering a representative selection of academic partners in the project's key technology areas, including AI, virology, multi-omics, biomedical, immunoassay, bioinformatics, and pharmaceuticals.

The appropriateness of collaboration is as follows:

- The collaboration is built up from representatives across drug development paths and at least one partner covering each aspect of the pathway.
- All partners (such as producers, manufacturers, retailers, suppliers, and others working together in the relevant supply chain processes with the aim of

increasing safety and transparency) have experienced organization with significant research and development capacities and know-how corresponding to the technical development and demonstration work. The partners provide state-of-the-art research infrastructure, management resources, and capacities as depicted in the partner descriptions of the following section.

- The collaboration members possess broad experience in carrying out publicly funded research projects concerning the particular needs on management, cross-border cooperation, and scheduling.
- Close interrelations among several partners existing from previous collaboration or research projects ensure a trustful and effective communication and teamwork within and across the tasks. All partners would provide a proven track record of outstanding expertise and skills in their respective areas.

With the proposed approach in grant applications, there would be multiple participants that could access information stored in the hub (e.g., TeamCloud) [33]. TeamCloud will act as the project's internal document repository where all the files will be exchanged within the consortium, including intermediate versions of the deliverables, meeting's material (agenda, notes, presentations, omics data, minutes, etc.), and any other document used.

Importantly, participants will also be able to access the smart contracts executed on the blockchain. The smart contracts in grant applications collaborations will specify how proposals progress along their lifecycle (e.g., when the work package has been submitted then forwarded to its collaborator of the same work package) and also constraints within or between work packages. The necessary specifications and settings will be stored as knowledge on the knowledge graph which is accessible to all verified stakeholders and relevant smart contracts. By this, a consensus of collaboration would be established on the knowledge graph. The fact that consensus of collaboration can be viewed and agreed upon by the participants is central to enabling transparency and auditability of all processing on the blockchain. Collectively, the proposed consortium-blockchain powered knowledge sharing will provide a trusted data repository of consortium information, communicating knowledge between participants, storing experimental logs and datasets, and managing intellectual property rights.

7.4.2   *EHR data integration and collective diagnosis modeling through blockchain protected network for scientific collaboration*

An electronic health record (EHR) is a digital version of a patient's paper chart and such data usually is stored respectively when the same patient moves between different organizations. The collection of data from different sources and compilation of such discrete data is known as Data Integration on EHR [34]. The compilation involves the extraction, mapping, cleansing, and transformation of data. Data integration is imperative in healthcare research today. The benefit of data integration, especially for EHR data integration, to health care research is not only to allow analytics tools to produce useful insights and information, but also to increase the reusability and verifiability of the relevant expertise. To achieve a successful data integration between multiple stakeholders in healthcare, research needs to efficiently coordinate the distributed data sources and integrate various access principles of these data sources.

Due to the sensitivity and professionalism of healthcare data and knowledge, implementing data integration in healthcare research usually faces a challenge. In this scenario, health data is retrieved from various discrete health-related systems and e-sources such as electronic devices, EHRs, web services, E-health reports, and many more. All the stakeholders in the healthcare industry will be able to access relevant information from the EHR data that is relevant to their context [30].

There is a similar application of using KG to guide web information retrieval in our previous research [31]. Following up the same approach, we propose to use the consortium-based blockchain powered with KG for efficient information retrieval. This proposed platform has the potential to combine with technology like wearable devices, the Internet, and IoT to dynamically access information, connect people, and then manage received information and respond to the health sector efficiently and intelligently. In the era of IoT, blockchain-based data integration is proposed as a smart infrastructure based on sensors, IoT devices, etc. that generate information and process this information using technologies like cloud computing on the servers. In addition, various health tests and medical devices are gathering lots of crucial data which can affect life and death scenarios. Integrating the data from these sources will provide a collective diagnosis model and such models will be able to more comprehensively understand the health problems of patients. In any case of emergency, the data can be retrieved in a format of a knowledge graph for prompt diagnosis. With the help of the proposed approach, all stakeholders can share their knowledge and data on a safe and protected platform and this greatly extends the benefit of data integration while preventing the abuse of private data. This is illustrated in Figure 7.5.

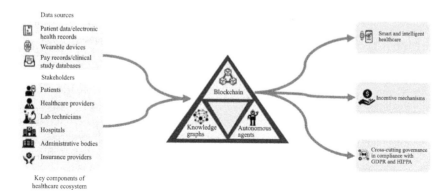

Figure 7.5　EHR data integration platform for scientific collaboration

7.4.3   Computational knowledge sharing in the research of material science

The traditional research and development process of materials experienced discovery, development, property optimization, systems design and integration, certification, manufacturing and deployment, usually taking 10–20 years from the discovery of materials [35]. In most cases, the developments of materials are carried out through a large number of trial-and-error experiments, which are time-consuming and uncertain. For example, quantum dots (QDs) [36] are small-sized semiconductor nanocrystals with a diameter from several nanometers to tens nanometres. By tailoring the size, shape, phase, composition and structure, the properties of QDs can be well-tuned, resulting in advanced functional materials with excellent optical properties such as high color purity, tunable emission peak, and high photoluminescence efficiency. However, one major obstacle hindering their development is Edisonian (trial and error)-based QD synthesis, discovery, and optimization methods.

During the synthesis, the moisture, vacuum level, temperature, duration of reaction, amount of the chemical, the purity of the chemical and so on, can lead to the growth and structure of QDs. Thus, every factor needs to be considered to make a successful synthesis, and it is even more difficult to get the QDs with specific properties and structures, as each synthesis requires a significant investment of time and resources.

With one common example, cadmium selenide QD synthesis, it takes at least two hours to prepare the precursor and two hours to complete the whole reaction process if there is no other abnormal condition. At the end of the purification, basic testing takes at least two hours. Generally, the implementation of each relevant experiment in this domain is often expensive (a successful synthesis requires at least tens to hundreds of Euros) and the results of the experiments are easily perdurable with various factors affecting the synthesis reaction.

In this scenario, the knowledge about the correlation between factors and the reaction process is critical for efficiently achieving the research targets. Such knowledge has to be gained from massive expensive experiments and the entire knowledge is diversely distributed over many different labs and institutions of the world. With the proposed approach, KGs will be used to integrate the relevant and distributed knowledge and make the integrated knowledge beneficial with all verified stakeholders in this research. By adopting the consortium network with blockchain, all stakeholders can safely share their particular knowledge on the related experiments while accessing other needed knowledge from other participants [37]. The customized smart contracts on the blockchain will ensure the knowledge contributor's incentives and data security. This platform will provide enough references to all participants to avoid some failures and speed up research progress while expediting the learning process on the relevant knowledge discovery. ML techniques, such as multi-output neural networks (NNs), ensemble methods, and Bayesian optimization, provide an exciting opportunity for reshaping the synthesis and optimization of QDs through the ML-based direction of a high-throughput QD synthesizer

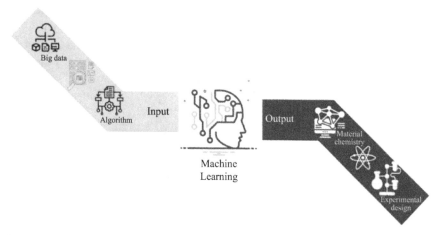

Figure 7.6 Using machine learning (ML) to facilitate experimental design in material science

[38]. One of the biggest problems of deploying such a program to extract the knowledge is that the sample size could be not enough in single research.

The concept of using ML for designing the experiments for material science is shown in Figure 7.6. ML needs a large sample size and includes as many features as possible to create an accurate and reliable model for covering similar experiments. The blockchain-based data and knowledge sharing platform can effectively address the problem of deficient sample data in single research. The integrated experimental data will no doubt greatly improve the understanding of the experimental knowledge.

7.5 Conclusion

Blockchain technology has shown a great potential and has already had a significant impact on many domains. The combination of blockchain and knowledge-driven data analysis techniques provides people with a powerful tool for coordinating complicated interactive transactions in an untrusted network. This tool can be used to solve many essential problems that people may suffer in Social Media Computing and can improve the efficiency and security of Social Media platforms from many aspects. This chapter presents a practical solution of using blockchain and a knowledge-driven system to solve the coordination problems in academic collaborations. It also can be a heuristic example to other social media computing applications based on different domains.

Generally speaking, the interactive activities of a well-formed society always need to follow certain rules and such rules can be understood as the consensus for coordinating the social behaviors of each participant. In our research, we adopted a blockchain network as the platform to provide users with safe and decentralized social media. Through the interaction between users in this social media, the consensus of collective behavior in the society would be self-organized gradually and it would be stored into the knowledge graph that is maintained in the blockchain network. Throughout the establishment of the consensus, blockchain technology ensures the necessary transparency, fairness, integrity, and authority in each interactive transaction and semantic technology helps to convert the emerging knowledge of consensus into an accessible format.

The relevant scenarios discussed above showed a promising perspective of using our platform to assist the interdisciplinary academic collaboration in different domains. Based on the experience and requests of multiple experts from various backgrounds, we identified the critical problems of the current collaboration in the traditional manner and demonstrated the advantage of our proposed platform on the corresponding applications. In the future, we would extend this approach with the more general meaning of social media and collaborations and improve the structure of the platform to adapt to different contexts.

References

[1] Sonnenwald DH. Scientific collaboration. *Annu Rev Inf Sci Technol.* 2007;41(1):643–681.

[2] Auer S, Kovtun V, Prinz M, Kasprzik A, Stocker M, and Vida ME. Towards a knowledge graph for science. In *Proceedings of the 8th International Conference on Web Intelligence, Mining and Semantics*, 2018, pp. 1–6.

[3] Chiang C, Betanzos E, and Savage S. Exploring blockchain for trustful collaborations between immigrants and governments. In *Extended Abstracts of the 2018 CHI Conference on Human Factors in Computing Systems*, 2018.

[4] Yang J, Onik M, Lee N, Ahmed M, and Kim C. Proof-of-familiarity: a privacy-preserved blockchain scheme for collaborative medical decision-making. *Appl Sci.* 2019;9(7):1370.

[5] Chua P, Li Y, and He W. Adopting hyperledger fabric blockchain for EPC global network. In *2019 IEEE International Conference on RFID (RFID)*, 2019.

[6] Kirillov D, Korkhov V, Petrunin V, Makarov M, Khamitov I, and Dostov V. Implementation of an E-voting scheme using hyperledger fabric permissioned blockchain. *Comput Sci Appl – ICCSA.* 2019;2019:509–521.

[7] Li J, Qu F, Tu X, Fu T, Guo J, and Zhu J. Public philanthropy logistics platform based on blockchain technology for social welfare maximization. In *2018 8th International Conference on Logistics, Informatics and Service Sciences (LISS)*, 2018.

[8] Zavolokina L, Ziolkowski R, and Bauer I. Management, governance, and value creation in a blockchain consortium. *MIS Q Executive.* 2020;19(1):1–17.

[9] Nakamoto, S. Bitcoin: a peer-to-peer electronic cash system. *Decentralized Bus Rev.* 2008;21260.

[10]   Morini M. 2016. From "Blockchain hype" to a real business case for Financial Markets. Available at SSRN 2760184.

[11]   Notheisen B, Hawlitschek F, and Weinhardt C. Breaking down the blockchain hype – towards a blockchain market engineering approach. In *European Conference on Information Systems*, 2017.

[12]   Carson B, Romanelli G, Walsh P, and Zhumaev A. *Blockchain Beyond the Hype: What is the Strategic Business Value*. McKinsey & Company, 2018, pp. 1–13.

[13]   Sultan K, Ruhi U, and Lakhani R. Conceptualizing blockchains: characteristics and applications. arXiv preprint arXiv:1806.03693, 2018.

[14]   Yaga D, Mell P, Roby N, and Scarfone K. Blockchain technology overview. In NIST Interagency/Internal Report (NISTIR) – 8202, 2018.

[15]   Brown RG, Carlyle J, Grigg I, and Hearn M. Corda: an Introduction. Unpublished; 2016. http://dx.doi.org/10.13140/RG.2.2.30487.37284.

[16]   Androulaki E, Barger A, Bortnikov V, *et al.* Hyperledger fabric: a distributed operating system for permissioned blockchains. In *Proceedings of the Thirteenth EuroSys Conference*. New York, NY: ACM, 2018.

[17]   Buterin V. A next-generation smart contract and decentralized application platform. *White Paper*. 2014;3:37.

[18]   Multichain Private Blockchain – White Paper, URL, last (Accessed 18 November 2021).

[19]   Baliga A, Subhod I, Kamat P, and Chatterjee S. Performance evaluation of the quorum blockchain platform, arXiv preprint.

[20]   Dib O, Brousmiche KL, Durand A, Thea E, and Hamida EB. Consortium blockchains: overview, applications and challenges. Int Adv Telecommun, IARIA. 2018. ⟨hal-02271063⟩

[21]   Bellomarini L, Galano G, Nissl M, and Sallinger E. Rule-based blockchain knowledge graphs: declarative AI for solving industrial blockchain challenges. In *Proceedings of the 15th International Rule Challenge, 7th Industry Track, and 5th Doctoral Consortium @ RuleML+RR 2021 co-located with 17th Reasoning Web Summer School {(RW} 2021) and 13th DecisionCAMP 2021 as part of Declarative {AI} 2021*, Leuven, Belgium (virtual due to Covid-19 pandemic), 2021.

[22]   Dhaniya JK. AI-blockchain convergence: realigning synergies for connected organizations. https://www.academia.edu/44718511/AI_Blockchain_Convergence_Realigning_synergies_for_connected_organizations.

[23]   Piscopo A, Phethean C, and Simperl E. What makes a good collaborative knowledge graph: group composition and quality in Wikidata. In *International Conference on Social Informatics*. Cham: Springer, 2017, pp. 305–322.

[24]   Raimond Y and Schreiber G. RDF 1.1 Primer: W3C Note; World Wide Web Consortium: Cambridge, MA, USA, 2014.

[25]   Fensel D, Şimşek U, Angele K, *et al.* Introduction: what is a knowledge graph? In *Knowledge Graphs*. Cham: Springer, 2020, pp. 1–10.

[26]   Qazi M, Kulkarni D, and Nagori M. Proof of authenticity-based electronic medical records storage on blockchain. In *Smart Trends in Computing and Communications*. Singapore: Springer, 2020, pp. 297–306.

[27]   Yao Y, Kshirsagar M, Vaidya G, and Ryan C. Using a bio-inspired model to facilitate the ecosystem of data sharing in smart healthcare. In *Evo*, 2021, p. 25.

[28]   Yao Y, Kshirsagar M, Vaidya G, Ducrée J, and Ryan C. Convergence of blockchain, autonomous agents, and knowledge graph to share electronic health records. *Front Blockchain*. 2021;4:13.

[29]   Chidepatil A, Bindra P, Kulkarni D, Qazi M, Kshirsagar M, and Sankaran K. From trash to cash: how blockchain and multi-sensor-driven artificial intelligence can transform circular economy of plastic waste? *Adm Sci*. 2020; 10(2):23.

[30]   Nagori M, Patil A, Deshmukh S, *et al.* Multichain enabled EHR management system and predictive analytics. In *Smart Trends in Computing and Communications*. Singapore: Springer, 2020, pp. 179–187.

[31]   Mirza A, Nagori M, and Kshirsagar V. Constructing knowledge graph by extracting correlations from Wikipedia Corpus for optimizing web information retrieval. In *2018 9th International Conference on Computing, Communication and Networking Technologies (ICCCNT)*, IEEE, 2018, pp. 1–7.

[32]   Staunton C, Slokenberga S, and Mascalzoni D. The GDPR and the research exemption: considerations on the necessary safeguards for research biobanks. *Eur J Hum Genet*. 2019;27(8):1159–1167.

[33]   https://www.teamcloud.my/., URL last (Accessed 18 November 2021).

[34]   Lenzerini M. Data integration: a theoretical perspective. In *Proceedings of the Twenty-First ACM SIGMOD-SIGACT-SIGART Symposium on Principles of Database Systems – PODS '02*. New York, NY: ACM Press, 2002.

[35]   Tinkle S, McDowell DL, Barnard A, Gygi F, and Littlewood PB. Technology: sharing data in materials science. *Nature*. 2013;503(7477):463–464.

[36]   Valizadeh A, Mikaeili H, Samiei M, *et al.* Quantum dots: synthesis, bioapplications, and toxicity. *Nanoscale Res Lett*. 2012;7:480. https://doi.org/10.1186/1556-276X-7-480

[37]   Han C-Y, Kim H-S, and Yang H. Quantum dots and applications. *Materials (Basel)*. 2020;13(4):897.

[38]   Sarker IH. Machine learning: algorithms, real-world applications and research directions. *SN Comput Sci*. 2021;2(3):160.

Chapter 8

5G multimedia communication and blockchain technology: emerging potential and challenges

Dragorad Milovanovic[1], Tulsi Pawan Fowdur[2] and Zoran Bojkovic[1]

Abstract

The integration of Blockchain (BC) technology with 5G networks is newly emerging area. Driven by the dramatically increased capacity of 5G networks and recent breakthroughs in BC technology, 5G services are expected to contribute to rapid development and bring significant benefits to future society. Multimedia communication can potentially reach a wide range of areas and touch people's lives in profound and different ways. In recent years, great progress has been made in defining approaches, architectures, standards, and solutions. 5G applications have evolved significantly, including voice, video, wireless, information access, and social interaction networks. More interestingly, BC helps establish secure multimedia communication among users and potentially reduces communication latency, transaction costs, and provides global accessibility for all users. Today, social media is a platform for establishing connections, sharing content and social interaction of a huge number of users. Digital media has changed the way we connect and share our experiences. Multimedia content is a key ingredient of social media, and BC integration optimizes content management and immersive communication.

Our aim in the chapter is to discuss the opportunities, challenges, and prospective solutions that BC-based 5G technologies are expected towards the 6G era. An overview of the BC technology in communication systems along with key features of multimedia communication is given. Several aspects of BC integration in 5G such as interoperability and standardization requirements, application and services, security and privacy, robustness and data integrity, resource allocation and management as well as energy efficiency, are analyzed. As concluding remarks, we identified some open issues and future research directions that should be considered in more innovative solutions and studies in this promising area.

[1]University of Belgrade, Serbia
[2]Department of Electrical and Electronic Engineering, University of Mauritius, Mauritius

Keywords: 5G mobile networks; Trust model; Blockchain application; Integration challenges; Multimedia platforms; Immersive communication

8.1   Introduction

Fifth-generation (5G) mobile networks enable and support customized, user-centric multimedia applications, enabling user interconnection and significant benefits for society. However, the widespread application and use of these services impose new challenges such as network reliability, decentralization, control, transparency, risks of data interoperability, data immutability, and privacy which need to be taken into account [1]. Furthermore, conventional techniques may not be sufficient to address the new requirements. An innovative solution is the integration of blockchain technology into 5G networks based on the requirements of decentralization, transparency, anonymity, immutability, traceability, and resiliency. Blockchains has potential to improve existing 5G services and applications that support spectrum sharing, data sharing, network virtualization, resource management, network slicing, privacy, and security [2]. However, there are also various challenges that increase the complexity of the blockchain, including high computing costs and delays. It is important to explore the difficulties we face in this integration in order to continue further development and implementation.

Blockchain (BC) technology is able to address a number of issues related to trust and security in communications networks, enables more efficient resource sharing, boosting trusted data interaction, secure access control and privacy protection, and providing tracing, certification and supervision functionalities for 5G and beyond networks [3–5]. Trust is a concept we have considered in the case of communications, including the interaction between people and computers, as well as social networks. Distributed trust plays a significant role in a 5G heterogeneous infrastructure with improved efficiency and security across a variety of resources. However, this goal is obstructed by a number of trust issues that are often overlooked in network design. Innovative BC technology provides a promising solution. Building on its decentralized nature, BC can establish cooperative trust among separate network entities and enable efficient resource sharing, trusted data interaction, secure access control, and privacy protection for wireless networks.

Proper integration of BC technology enhances the security, cost effectiveness and efficiency of 5G multimedia communication [6–9]. The mobile network includes a list of different requirements, standardized specifications and a wide range of implementation options. Essential security challenges, for example, integrity, authentication, trust, and availability are addressed by the distributed BC concept. End-to-end allocation and sharing of resources, network management and organization of 5G services, are enabled by smart contracts. BC enables new business models and reduces problems in cooperation of network operators and continuous process management. Along with numerous advantages, many challenges have to be met, including standardization requirement, scalability and performance, resource constraints and allocation, energy efficiency and security.

BC eliminates the need for central entity processing to allow two nodes to perform transactions, by simplifying a decentralized, reliable, secure, and immutable ledger. There is no sole point of failure or attack since the blocks are decentralized. All data stored on the BC is transparent to all nodes involved in the transaction and are checked by all peer nodes. Nodes use a consensus algorithm to verify all transactions recorded in blocks in the BC network, in a given time interval. BC is formed by connecting verified blocks using a linked list, or chain of blocks. A BC can be categorized as public, private, and consortium. In a public BC, each node joins the BC network and participates in BC operations. Private BC is limited within the secured network of an organization in which only chosen members become part of the BC network. If scalability and conformance with data privacy rules and other regulatory issues are required, private blocks have to be used [10–12].

The key components and characteristics of BC are as follows:

- **Ledger** is an append-only shared database, which registers all transactions and shares with all concerned participants.
- **Smart contract** is the part of the runnable computer program that is stored on the BC and is run when specific criteria are satisfied.
- **Consensus** refers to the agreement between the nodes participating in the BC network to approve each transaction.
- **Trustless** means that there is no reliance on third parties to ensure the authenticity and protection of information. The network BC nodes uses a consensus algorithm to offer protection to the network and create trust.
- **Transparency** indicates that all transactions are available to all nodes in the network so that each individual transaction is verified independently.
- **Provenance** indicates that all transactions in the network can be traced and checked as changes in data ownership over time.
- **Immutability** indicates that all stored BC data are resistant to unauthorized use. To modify data recorded on the BC, most nodes (51%) in the BC network need to be controlled.

The most important integral components of the BC platform are as follows:

- **Consensus protocol** is necessary in agreement of all nodes participating in the BC network in adding a new block to the set of available blocks. The approval procedure is conducted by a consensus protocol mechanism. The protocols directly influence the properties and functions of the BC platform. The most well-known consensus protocols are proof of work (PoW), proof of stake (PoS), proof of activity (PoA), practical *Byzantine* fault tolerance (PBFT), LibraBFT.
- **Smart contracts** are stored on the BC network and executed under specific situations. Contracts allow distributed automation for all nodes participating in the BC by eliminating the requirement for a third party and thus. The most well-known BC platform that allows smart contract creation is Ethereum which uses the *Solidity* scripting language which is part of the runnable computer program.

Next sections describe several aspects such as interoperability, privacy, robustness, data integrity, resource allocation and management as well as energy efficiency, related to BC integration into the 5G architecture.

8.2   Integration BC trust in 5G mobile networks

Blockchain is an emerging technology for increased efficiency, high security, seamless interoperability, privacy, and low cost 5G networks. Various field trials and proof of concept (PoC) face the challenges of the current application of 5G mobile networks. The basic issue of testing is the registration and management of data from various networks and business processes. The objectives of this technology are to enhance the transparency and trustworthiness of data obtained from different networks. Startups are also emerging that offer BC-based solutions to network operators to improve security, data sharing, and automation. Leading network operators are testing BC use based on early trials, but in very limited applications. Realization of full BC potential is expected in the coming period on the basis of extensive research work so far [13,14].

5G mobile networks offer high data rates, coverage, connectivity and bandwidth, while greatly reducing latency and power consumption. 5G supports different requirements of individual use cases. Baseline scenarios include enhanced mobile broadband (eMBB), massive machine-type communication (mMTC), and ultra-reliable low-latency communication (uRLLC). The realization of various requirements imposes the need to consider the integration of new technologies of radio access technologies, software-defined networking (SDN), virtualization of network functions (NFV), machine learning (ML), and cloud computing (CC). However, the application of these technologies foretells new challenges related to complexity, decentralization, transparency, interoperability, privacy, and security. Thanks to its capabilities such as transparency, data encryption, auditability, immutability, and distributed architecture, BC is a prospective solution to these problems. It is thus necessary to consider the integration of BC into the 5G architecture [15,16].

8.2.1   5G network architecture

The 5G mobile network contains a list of different requirements, standardized specifications, and different implementation possibilities. The Association of Standardization Organizations 3GPP (3rd-Generation Partnership Project) provides a stable platform for implementation and at the same time allows the addition of new functions by developing a system of parallel releases of technical specifications. The 5G study was launched in 2016 with Release-14 to study feasibility. Phase-1 Release-15 and Phase-2 Release-16 laid the foundations of the 5G system, while Release-17 provides improvements and optimizations for extended applications. Release-18 lays balanced concepts for the evolution of 5G-Advanced (see Figure 8.1) as well as the basis for more demanding applications such as extended reality (XR) mobile services. The standard also introduces more intelligence into the network, utilizing ML to adapt to its environment [1].

The 5G network provides wireless connectivity to devices UE (user equipment) smartphones and tablets as well as cars, drones, industrial machines, robots, home appliances, medical devices, and so on. 5G system consists of two main

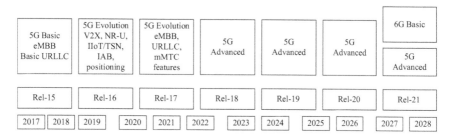

5G Basic eMBB Basic URLLC	5G Evolution V2X, NR-U, IIoT/TSN, IAB, positioning	5G Evolution eMBB, URLLC, mMTC features	5G Advanced	5G Advanced	5G Advanced	6G Basic / 5G Advanced
Rel-15	Rel-16	Rel-17	Rel-18	Rel-19	Rel-20	Rel-21
2017 2018	2019	2020 2021	2022 2023	2024 2025	2026	2027 2028

Figure 8.1   5G standardization time plan in 3GPP

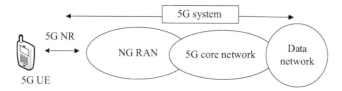

Figure 8.2   5G system consists of 5G NR radio access network and 5GC core network

subsystems: 5G NR radio access network and the 5GC core network (see Figure 8.2). The radio access network (RAN) manages the radio-spectrum, making sure it is both used efficiently and meets the QoS (quality of service) requirements of every user. The core network provides Internet (IP) connectivity for both data and voice services, ensures this connectivity fulfills the promised QoS requirements, tracks user mobility to ensure uninterrupted service, and tracks subscriber usage for billing and charging. 5GC is partitioned into a control plane and user plane by an architectural feature CUPS (*Control and User Plane Separation*). Each 5G gNB base station establishes control plane connectivity between the user equipment and the corresponding 5GC control plane component as well as for each active UE, the base station establishes one or more tunnels between the corresponding 5GC user plane component. Finally, the base station forwards both control and user plane packets between the 5GC and the user equipment.

The 5GC core network is based on service-based architecture (SBA), centered on services that can register themselves and subscribe to other services. The goal is to migrate from telecom-style protocol interfaces to web-based APIs on cloud- and virtualization-based platform. These platforms are programmable, and allow many different functions to be built, configured, connected, and deployed at the scale that is needed at the given time. This enables a more flexible development of new services, as it becomes possible to connect to other components without introducing specific new interfaces. The 3GPP defines SBA architecture, whereby the control plane functionality and common data repositories of a 5G network are delivered by way of a set of interconnected network functions (NFs), each with authorization to access each other's services. Assuming the role of either service

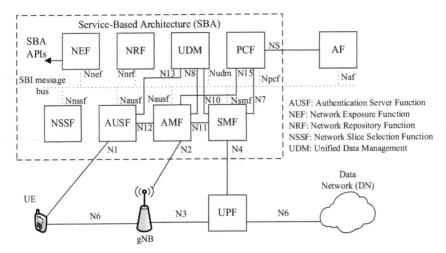

Figure 8.3   5GC service-based architecture (SBA) and set of interconnected NFs

consumer or service producer, network functions are self-contained, independent, and reusable. Each network function service exposes its functionality through a service-based interface (SBI) (see Figure 8.3).

Virtual network functions (VNFs) are implemented in software that is separate from the underlying hardware of an infrastructure that dynamically spans multiple physical locations. Network virtualization and software, as well as Cloud RAN (C-RAN) enable the delivery of various services on demand. Network virtualization provides a means for different services to share physical resources by logically slicing the physical infrastructure. On the other hand, software enables network programmability, flexibility, and adaptability by using programming in the design, implementation, deployment, management, and maintenance of network equipment/components/services. Both network virtualization and software-defined networking (SDN) are important in meeting the requirements of the 5G network, as well as providing end-to-end (E2E) service management and improving end-user QoE. Unification of the service platform was realized using SDN, network function virtualization (NFV), and CC technology (CC).

- **SDN** allows the management of network equipment using software on off-the-shelf hardware, instead of using switches or routers directly. SDN in a 5G network orchestrates and manages applications/functions in a precise manner across the network by separating network control from data planes such that a central control plane manages multiple devices. Unbundling allows flexible and central management with total view of the whole network permitting it to respond quickly to varying network states and end-user requirements.
- **NFV** allows virtualization of all network functions (firewall, VPN, router, switches) implemented on specialized hardware for work on CC infrastructure. NFV separates physical hardware from corresponding network functionalities and enables work to be done in a scalable and flexible way on generic servers in the

cloud. The use of network abstraction and dependency on virtualization are the main common aspects of SDN and NFV. Network control functions are separated from network forwarding functions using SDN and network functions are separated from the hardware on which they operate using NFV. The difference between SDN and NFV differs in the separation of functions and abstraction of resources. SDN shifts decision-making to the level of virtual network control by abstracting physical network resources such as switches and routers. The traffic is directed by the virtual control plane and managed by the hardware. NFV virtualizes all physical network resources under hypervisors, allowing network expansion by deploying virtual machines without the need to add new devices to the network.

- **CC** enables resource sharing by virtualizing the physical infrastructure that is dynamically provided and adapted to the requirements of the application, platform, and heterogeneous computing infrastructure. The physical resources that are shared are servers, networks, warehouses, services, and applications. Cloud-RAN or centralized-RAN (C-RAN) are designed to take advantage of CC and provide flexibility and scalability to RANs to effectively address capacity and coverage issues.

5G mobile networks based on SBA architecture are very dynamic in terms of virtualization and software. The establishment of trust in such an open and varied ecosystem is key to the global adoption of 5G technology. However, a flexible and complex ecosystem poses significant risks to security and privacy. It is proposed to distribute trust to strengthen software and ensure data integrity. Also, trust in communication enables the maintenance of a complete inspection of all events and audit variations associated with data and applications of virtual network functions (VNF) (see Figure 8.4). Standardized and reliable communication is crucial in ensuring the availability of services and preventing data leakage and privacy.

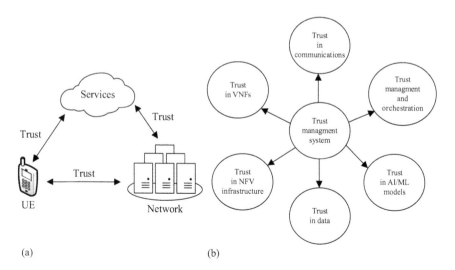

Figure 8.4   (a) 5G trust model and (b) trust management system

The main focus of the NFV Industry Specifications Group (ISG) are security and trust challenges associated with virtualization. Various reports and specifications have been published as guidelines to improve security and confidence unique to NFVs. These reports provide guidelines on VNF packet security, certification management, remote attestation, multilayer host administration, and execution of sensitive NFV components.

The trusted computing group (TCG) formulates specifications and standards for Trusted Platform Modules (TPMs), Trusted Network Communications (TNCs), and Trusted Computing (TC). TPM concentrates on establishing a foundation of hardware-based trust. The TCN architecture specifies compliance, orchestration, and access control, with the goal of improving network visibility, endpoint compliance, network enforcement, and security automation problems. TC specifies trust establishment, platform information exchange, and policies compliance assurance for cloud users. Recently, TCG created a working group to extend trust concepts to virtualized platforms.

The standard development organization ITU-T Study Group 13 (SG13) publishes various recommendations for improved trust in future networks. The conceptual model for reliable networking in trust-oriented network domains includes the characteristics of identifying and assessing the trust of network elements and reliable communication (Table 8.1). ITU-T SG17 group studies security framework based on trust relationship among stakeholders in 5G ecosystem.

The international organization for standardization (ISO) which formulates various standards on software and data quality (ISO/IEC 25000 series) and records/archives management (ISO/TC46/SC11) has also been focusing on the trust in data. A trusted data enabling process model that conforms to the specifications of ISO/TC46/SC11The ITU-T has been developed by the Focus Group on data processing and management (FG-DPM). With regards to blockchain-based data exchange and sharing, the FG-DPM has also specified the requirements, functional models, a platform, and deployment modes.

Table 8.1   ITU-T Study Groups SG13 recommendation related to trust in future networks

Recommendation	Trust in network infrastructure communication
ITU-T Y.3052 (03/17)	• Overview of trust provisioning in ICT infrastructure and services • Explains the concept of trust provisioning and introduces a trust relationship model as well as trust evaluation based on trust indicators and trust index
ITU-T Y.3517 (12/18)	• Overview of inter-cloud trust management
ITU-T Y.3053 Amendment (12/18)	• Framework of trustworthy networking with trust-centric network domains • The model encompasses features of identification and trust evolution of network elements and trustworthy communication between them

8.2.2 Drivers for BC integration

New technologies are being integrated into 5G networks with the aim of solving the problems of previous generations of mobile networks and meeting various new requirements [13]. However, the integration of a number of technologies creates new challenges for security, network resilience, privacy, robustness, and data integrity [4,17,18]. Integration of BC technologies will provide several advantages at different spheres of the 5G ecosystem. Networks equipped with BC are modified based on the location and needs of subscribers and dynamically adapted to satisfy supply and demand. A taxonomy of BC applications in 5G networks is shown in Table 8.2 based on an overview of the results published in research papers [19–29].

• **Network security management**: The authentication of the access control plane is very important. Next, the risk of having a single point of failure and attack (DDoS) is minimized by decentralizing the SDN control. However, between the SDN controller and the switch, there is a vulnerability with regards to the information. The network can be compromised by an attacker which pretends to be an SDN controller. Security vulnerabilities can also emerge due to the absence of software development standards and guidelines. Third-party providers can, for example, pose a risk of data leakage by accessing the network without the permission of the SDN controller and modify control rules. There is a possibility that VNFs work on equipment that do not belong to network operators and represent a security flaw. To operate in an environment devoid of trust, it is important to ensure that VNF chains are correct. A software router in a virtual machine (VM) that has common physical resources with another network function can still affect each other, even in the case of centralized operation of one network operator. The complexity of VNF integration of different vendors has the potential of causing security liabilities. For security and audit purposes, it is also important that proper validation, approval, and recording are done along with the creation and management of any network slice (NS). It is required to check the whole set of virtual

Table 8.2   Taxonomy of BC application in 5G mobile networks

Network management	Computing management	Communication management	Application and services	Security and privacy
SDN	MEC	Spectrum sharing	Billing and payment	Authentication
VNF	Content caching	Infrastructure sharing	Roaming	Identity service
NS	Data storage	Resource allocation	Content distribution	Fraud management
	Distributed computing	Interference management	Digital rights	Data privacy
	Cloud computing			Access control

functions constituting the NS instance (end-to-end) and verify their integrity and correct VNF deployment.

- **Computing security management:** In 5G networks, security is the principal challenge while moving to the cloud. The core network is deployed across different local and national call management data centers in a hierarchical model. Serious challenges to privacy, integrity, and data ownership are posed since data are exchanged between dynamic cloud networks. In a trusted environment it is very challenging to perform authentication across several domains, stakeholders, and devices (virtual or real). Moreover, the immunity of the data to modifications is significant not only from attackers, but also from unintentional activity. It is essential that a generic C-RAN guarantees service security and device credibility. In mobile edge computing (MEC), decentralized participants collaborate in resource management at the edge of the network, which requires authentication, authorization and accounting (AAA) platforms from several parties as well as trust coordinators that can be scaled while decreasing management intricacy. MEC improves throughput and minimizes latency by distributing the content to be cached across the network. Improved confidentiality and authentication becomes mandatory with distributed and pervasive deployment.

- **Communication security management**: When multiple parties participate in the infrastructure management chain, several challenges, such as trust building, authentication, identity management, and confidentiality, have to be addressed. Next, dynamic spectrum access by auction or sharing requires seamless transaction and fulfillment of service level agreements (SLAs). The high flexibility of 5G RAN is essential to enable operators to manage a diverse set of access technologies and to enhance access based on service requirements. A significant challenge is cooperative and collaborative communication within 5G networks, management of heterogeneous networks, and resource provisioning to satisfy different QoS levels.

- **Application and services**: It is essential that the network operators and content provider work in close collaboration for efficient optimized content delivery. However, due to the lack of a secure and efficient platform, there is a restriction on the collaboration between content creators. Furthermore, the actual techniques employed by operators for roaming user authentication are not efficient in the 5G network due to authentication delays, costs, and security concerns. For invoicing, billing, and other transactions, BC allows network operators to resolve financial issues and provide better management of contracts. An alternative way for establishing intermediaries for monetary transactions is through the use of mobile money and BC-based micro-payments. By implementing a smart contract-based policy and charging control framework in the 5GC network, it is possible to address the roaming issue.

- **Security and privacy**: A fundamental security need for any network is preventing unauthorized access to information and data privacy. Data provision and origin are also equally important in a distributed and decentralized network. The sharing of data sharing, establishment of data communications among distinct network components, centralization of data and the participation of any external party, require ensuring the confidentiality of data. Efficient management of data flow and storage in a complex network with multiple end users and multiple operators is essential. To guarantee that only recognized and trustworthy devices are admitted to the network, authentication of each network participant is necessary. The growing number of devices in the network is causing centralized authentication to cause downtime and increased latency. A possible solution is to delegate (or rent) authentication and access control to a third party. Ensuring point-to-point integrity, dependability, accuracy, consistency, and trustworthiness of information throughout the life cycle is a challenge in a complex network such as 5G. The risks associated with security and that of having a single point of failure are increased when data validation is performed by encryption algorithms or by a reliable party. BC enables secure network management, authentication, trust, and automation.

However, the following issues of BC integration in 5G networks need to be analyzed:

- **Standardization requirement**: Joint cooperation of network operators on standardization of BC integration in 5G network and beyond is necessary. To address the issue of interconnectivity and interoperability, a Consortia has been created.
- **Scalability and performance**: The performance of most existing BC solutions is low transaction rates and is inappropriate for 5G networks. The transactions processing rate in the BC is quantified in terms of transactions per second (TPS) and is primarily determined by the efficiency of the consensus algorithm and the way the BC is designed (private, public, consortium). The performance of a private or consortium BC is higher in a controlled environment of a limited number of users participating in the transaction in contrast with a public BC.
- **Resource constraints and allocation**: It is not possible for all network nodes to be involved in the transaction validation as BC consensus algorithms have high are computational complexity and this will lead to a degradation of network performance. An optimization framework that adaptively chooses the mining node in a secured network is required because of constrained resources. It is necessary to investigate the provision of computer resources to support BC in the 5G network.
- **Energy efficiency**: 5G networks significantly increase the consumption of energy because of the specificity of the network design and greater number of network components. BC consensus algorithms are computer-intensive and energy efficient algorithms are needed, which is a major research issue to be addressed for BC integration into 5G networks.
- **Security**: BC is also a source of its own security problems. For example, consensus protocols can become the target of an attacker. Extensive testing of security algorithms is necessary. Also, a digital agreement that is key to BC's realization can compromise the security due to poor coding. The main research target is to merge solutions to improve BC resistance to combined attacks in the 5G network.

A high degree of coordination will be required across several stakeholders in 5G networks. All these constraints pose challenges to security and privacy, manageability, SLA, and interoperability. It is possible that the complexity of 5G will make it impossible for only single operator to control the whole network. Sharing of resources between many stakeholders will be required in order to provide end-user services in the wider region in several vertical sectors such as massive IoT, vehicle-to-vehicle communication, augmented reality (AR)/virtual reality (VR) interactive communication, and UltraHD video streaming. The requirements are quite different in terms of speed, latency, and capacity, so fast resource allocation and network orchestration are necessary.

8.3   Social network multimedia platforms

5G is a key network technology that responds to challenges and enables the realization of a hyper-connected society in which billions of users exchange data and offer/receive services through their devices. Today, social media is a platform for establishing connections, sharing content, and social interaction of a huge number of users. Digital media has changed the way we connect and share our experiences. The decentralized integration of BC technology into the digital social network ensures privacy and enables e-commerce, crowdfunding transactions, as well as smart applications and contracts. Multimedia content is a key ingredient of social media, and BC integration optimizes content management and improves security. Significant progress has been made in multimedia communication and in defining approaches, architectures, standards, and solutions. From the user's perspective, 5G multimedia communication enables faster connection, zero latency, and infinite capacity. 5G mobile networks support ultra-high quality multimedia content and impressive real-time communication, providing social network users with a new level of experience [30–33].

8.3.1   High-quality multimedia content

Today, consumers expect more from conventional voice and video services and are increasingly interested in experiencing digital interactive and multisensory experiences. In this context, multimedia communication is becoming increasingly impressive with the use of new formats UltraHD video, 360° panorama, AR/VR, and other emerging 3D technologies [34,35].

However, it is necessary to check the integrity of multimedia content. The integrity of the video is confirmed by checking the hash values against the hash values of the videos stored via the BC. In traditional methods of active video integrity, previous data such as signatures or hash values are needed as evidence. The methods include digital signatures and digital watermark schemes. The easiest method is to use BC on each video frame, that is, to store each frame on BC. However, the process is too complex and requires a long processing time, so it causes an increase in processing and archiving costs. An alternative means is to place distinct video segments over the BC network, and this can decreasing computational and storage overhead.

On-demand video systems that support BC also reduce late payments to various parties and automate the system based on smart contracts. BC-supported video content systems also address privacy issues. Each generated video can be recorded on the BC network, so that false ownership rights on the video content can be checked.

8.3.2   AR immersive communication

5G network architecture and advanced multimedia technologies enable new elements of AR, VR, and mixed reality (MR), together known as augmented reality (XR). Augmented reality introduces physical objects into the digital environment and digital objects into physical reality. XR technology is evolving rapidly and is increasingly becoming ubiquitous in a variety of applications. As 5G mobile networks combine high transfer speeds, low latency, and high energy efficiency, various options have emerged that include AR technology [36].

The evolution of 3D immersive media supports applications and services based on ultra-high video resolutions, a new type of device, and immersive perception. Immersive technologies face new issues in terms of interaction, perception of distance, coexistence, and presence. Immersion is used in the AR context as a sense of being surrounded by virtual content, as well as a presence with a sense of physical and spatial location in a virtual environment. Virtual content is made up of images or videos and is extendable to several sensory modalities (visual, auditory, haptic). One of the basic AR advantages is the unchanged perception of the actual environment, only overlapping data with the environment and integrating immersive sensory stimuli that are seen as a real component of the environment. Our senses create minimal performance requirements for technologies such as tracking, latency, persistency, and video resolution.

The basic QoS parameters for the XR interactive service are defined by 3GPP Release-17. In the 5G-Advanced Release-18 phase, interactive communication also requires the following key technical support:

- **Distributed convergent media**: A unified convergent media level is being established as an upgrade of basic audio/video services and support for new media services of collaborative AR/VR activities. Distributed scheduling allows the nearest available media resources to be allocated to services that require the lowest possible latency and largest uplink bandwidth.
- **Enhanced QoS**: Multi-flow services are coded and transmitted on different QoS layers based on a specific QoS identifier as a pointer to a set of features such as priority level, packet delay, or packet error rate. QoS characteristics are standardized or non-standardized. Moreover, QoS control is implemented by fine granularity for different data packets, such as delay or reliability-based control. In addition, new QoS parameters (delay, reliability, bandwidth) have been introduced for efficient transmission of all data types, including those from tactile sensors.
- **Collaboration of multi-media communication data flows**: Uninterrupted coordination and central planning of different service flows is based on the

collection of all data characteristics of services. Synchronous arrival of data packets on servers or terminals is provided.

- **Enhanced network capability exposure mechanism**: The 5G system directly supports a better user experience and more efficient use of network resources for intensive interactive business scenarios such as AR/VR sue, by exposing more and more real-time information.

AR communication is more natural, unobtrusive, and easily accessible on most electronic devices. Flawlessly integrated AR is already part of many online social media experiences. There is also no doubt that in the coming period, AR will continue to reshape the way it communicates and interacts.

8.4   Concluding remarks

Currently, the integration of BC and 5G networks has attracted broad research interests of academia and industry. However, addressing the issue of trust in integrated networks is far from a solution. We have found that BC supports 5G technology mainly from three main dimensions of security, system performance, and resource management. BC is especially useful for creating a secure environment for radio spectrum sharing or data transmission in 5G mobile networks. In addition, the BC simplifies the virtualization of 5G networks with a strong security level and allows limitations of prior centralized virtual network configuration settings, to be overcome.

BC has been explored and incorporated into several major 5G applications. BC integration with 5G technologies improves existing systems and enables enhanced decentralization, security, privacy, service efficiency, and simplified system operation with lower costs. More interestingly, BC helps establish secure multimedia communication among users and potentially reduces communication delays, transaction costs, and provides global availability for every user, which altogether improves the general system performance. Also, it should be recognized that BC based methods have normal limitations in 5G services. The complexity of BC operations, including block generation, reduces the efficiency of services. It is necessary to consider further research of BC integration with 5G systems and services.

Key challenges requiring thorough investigations as well as future research direction towards 5G beyond networks are highlighted and discussed in detail in this chapter. The new BC technology has the potential to modify the existing infrastructure and transform the network architecture. However, BC and 5G integration are for the time being facing some crucial obstacles that have to be overcome and then implemented. The current infrastructure is not fully adequate for integration 5G-BC systems. Then, the unavailability of sufficient standardization and regulation is also a critical challenge for integration. Current BC operations are non-standardized and deregulated due to lack of cooperation. High security and versatility applications for the 2030 smart data society set strict specialized requirements. The Federal Communications Commission (FCC) is also proposing

BC as a key innovation for 6G administration. BC is expected to retain a significant role in 5G and beyond systems.

References

[1] Bojkovic Z, Milovanovic D, and Fowdur TP (eds.). *5G Multimedia Communication: Technology, Multiservices, and Deployment.* CRC Press, 2020.

[2] Cao B, Zhang L, Peng M, and Imran MA. *Wireless Blockchain: Principles, Technologies and Applications.* Wiley, 2021.

[3] Nguyen DC, Pathirana PN, Ding M, and Seneviratne A. Blockchain for 5G and beyond networks: a state of the art survey. *Journal Network and Computer Applications*, vol. 166, 2020, p. 1–84.

[4] Wang J, Ling X, Le Y, Huang Y, and You X. Blockchain-enabled wireless communications: a new paradigm towards 6G. *National Science Review*, vol. 8, 2021, p. 1–25.

[5] Poongodi T, Sujatha R, Sumathi D, Suresh P, and Balamurugan B. Blockchain in social networking. In: *Cryptocurrencies and Blockchain Technology Applications* (eds. G. Shrivastava, D-N. Le, K. Sharma), Scrivener Publishing, 2020 (Chapter 4).

[6] Belotti M, Bozic N, Pujolle G, and Secci S. A vademecum on blockchain technologies: when, which, and how. *IEEE Communications Surveys & Tutorials*, vol. 21, no. 4, 2019, p. 3796–3838.

[7] Sankar LS, Sindhu M, and Sethumadhavan M. Survey of consensus protocols on blockchain applications. In: *4th IEEE International Conference on Advanced Computing and Communication Systems (ICACCS)*, 2017, p. 1–5.

[8] Khan SN, Loukil F, Guegan CG, Benkhelifa E, and Bani-Hani A. Blockchain smart contracts: applications, challenges, and future trends. *Journal Peer-to-Peer Networking and Applications*, vol. 5, no. 8663, 2021, p. 1–25.

[9] Monrat AF, Schelén O, Andersson K. A survey of blockchain from the perspectives of applications, challenges, and opportunities. *IEEE Access*, vol. 7, 2019, p. 117134–117151.

[10] Casino F, Dasaklis TK, Patsakisa C. A systematic literature review of blockchain-based applications: current status, classification and open issues. *Telematics and Informatics*, vol. 36, 2019, p. 55–81.

[11] Bhutta MNM, Khwaja A, Nadeem A, *et al.* A survey on blockchain technology: evolution, architecture and security. *IEEE Access*, vol. 9, 2021, p. 61048–61073.

[12] Liu Y, Yu FR, Li X, Ji H, and Leung VCM. Blockchain and machine learning for communications and networking systems. *IEEE Communications Surveys & Tutorials*, vol. 22, no. 2, 2020, p. 1392–1431.

[13] Tahir M, Habaebi MH, Dabbagh M, and Mughees A. A review on application of blockchain in 5G and beyond networks: taxonomy, field-trials, challenges and opportunities. *IEEE Access*, vol. 8, 2020, p. 15876–115904.

[14]   Benzaïd C, Taleb T, and Farooqi MZ. Trust in 5G and beyond networks. *IEEE Network*, vol. 35, no. 3, 2021, p. 219–222.

[15]   Hojjati M, Shafieinejad A, and Yanikomeroglu H. A blockchain-based Authentication and Key Agreement (AKA) protocol for 5G networks. *IEEE Access*, vol. 8, 2020, p. 216461–216476.

[16]   Okon A, Jagannath N, Elgendi I, Elmirghani JMH, Jamalipour A, and Munasinghe K. Blockchain-enabled multi-operator small cell network for beyond 5G systems. *IEEE Network*, vol. 34, no. 5, 2020, p. 171–177.

[17]   Ling X, Wang J, Le Y, Ding Z, and Gao X. Blockchain radio access network beyond 5G. *IEEE Wireless Communications*, vol. 27, no. 6, 2020. p. 160–168.

[18]   Huang T, Yang W, Wu J, Ma J, Zhang X, and Zhang D. A survey on Green 6G network: architecture and technologies. *IEEE Access*, vol. 7, 2019, p. 175758–175768.

[19]   Zhang Z, Song X, Liu L, Yin J, Wang Y, and Lan D. Recent advances in Blockchain and Artificial Intelligence integration: feasibility analysis, research issues, applications, challenges, and future work. In *Security and Communication Networks*, vol. 2021 Hindawi, p. 1–15.

[20]   Uddin MA, Stranieri A, Gondal I, and Balasubramanian V. A survey on the adoption of blockchain in IoT: challenges and solutions. *Journal of Blockchain: Research and Applications*, vol. 2, 2021. p. 1–81.

[21]   Ali MS, Vecchio M, Pincheira M, Dolui K, Antonelli F, and Rehmani MH. Applications of blockchains in the Internet of Things: a comprehensive survey. *IEEE Communications Surveys and Tutorials,* vol. 21, no. 2, 2019, p. 1676–1717.

[22]   Zhang K, Zhu Y, Maharjan S, Zhang Y. Edge intelligence and blockchain empowered 5G beyond for the Industrial Internet of Things. *IEEE Network*, vol. 33, no. 5, 2019. p. 12–19.

[23]   Kumar R, Sharma R, and Pattnaik PK. *Multimedia Technologies in the Internet of Things Environment*. Springer, 2021.

[24]   Fan C, Ghaemi S, Khazaei H, and Musilek P. Performance evaluation of blockchain systems: a systematic survey. *IEEE Access*, vol. 8, 2020. p. 126927–126950.

[25]   Amjad M, Musavian L, and Rehmani MH. Effective capacity in wireless networks: a comprehensive survey. *IEEE Communications Surveys & Tutorials*, vol. 21, no. 4, 2019. p. 3007–3038.

[26]   Gorla P, Chamola V, Hassija V, and Niyato D. Network slicing for 5G with UE state based allocation and blockchain approach. *IEEE Network*, vol. 35, no. 3, 2021, p. 184–190.

[27]   Salleras X and Daza V. SANS: self-sovereign authentication for Network Slices. *Journal of Security and Communication Networks*, Special issue: *Trustworthy networking for Beyond 5G networks*, vol. 2020, Hindawi, p. 1–8.

[28]   Amjad M, Rehmani MH, and Mao S. Wireless multimedia cognitive radio networks: a comprehensive survey. *IEEE Communications Surveys & Tutorials*, vol. 20, no. 2, 2018. p. 1056–1103.

[29]   Maksymyuk T, Gazda J, Volosin M, *et al.* Blockchain-empowered frame-work for decentralized network management in 6G. *IEEE Communications Magazine*, vol. 58, no. 9, 2020. p. 86–92.

[30]   Dashtipour K, Taylor W, Ansari S, *et al.* Public perception of the Fifth Generation of cellular networks (5G) on social media. *Frontiers in Big Data*, vol. 4, 2021, p. 1–10.

[31]   Fu D and Liri F. Blockchain-based trusted computing in social network. In: *2nd IEEE International Conference on Computer and Communications, ICCC*, 2016, p. 19–22.

[32]   Chakravorty A and Rong C. User controlled social media based on block-chain. In: *11th International Conference on Ubiquitous Information Management and Communication, IMCOM*, 2017, p. 1–6.

[33]   Yue L, Junqin H, Shengzhi Q, and Ruijin W. Big data model of security sharing. In: *3rd International Conference BigCom*, 2017, pp. 117–121.

[34]   Barman N, Deepak GC, and Martini MG. Blockchain for video streaming: opportunities, challenges, and open issues. *Computer*, vol. 53, no. 7, 2020. p. 45–56.

[35]   Ghimire S, Choi JY, and Lee B. Using blockchain for improved video integrity verification. *IEEE Transactions on Multimedia*, vol. 22, no. 1, 2020, p. 108–121.

[36]   Bojkovic Z, Milovanovic D, Fowdur TP, and Indoonundon M. 6G ultra-low latency communication in future mobile XR applications. In: *SIRS (Advances in Signal Processing and Intelligent Recognition System).* Springer, 2020, p. 302–312.

Chapter 9

IoT-based system for intellectual property protection in social media using blockchain

Mona Kumari[1] and Ajitesh kumar[1]

Abstract

Since the creation and analysis of such data are essential to the functioning of the IoT, they must be safeguarded throughout the extended device life span. Due to the fact that cryptocurrency mining introduced blockchain technology, which is its primary technology, to the world. But it now heavily involves the Internet of Things (IoT). Scalability, privacy, and confidence in IoT security are issues that blockchain technology is the ideal ally to address.

The purpose of this chapter is to investigate trends in the adoption of blockchain-related approaches and advancements in an IoT environment. The curiosities that go along with this chapter are as follows, as for related work: a brief introduction of blockchain is given, followed by a description of its benefits. Additionally, we look into the underlying concerns that the examination network has with the seamless integration of BC and IoT and highlight the key unresolved problems and directions for future research. In the final section of this chapter, we also provide a prospective use case for blockchain and IoT.

Keywords: Blockchain; Cloud; Edge computing; IoT; Gateway

9.1 Introduction

Blockchain is a term used to describe a distributed, decentralized, encrypted computer filing system intended to make it easier to create real-time, tamper-proof documents. IoT is a term used to describe how computing devices integrated into ordinary objects are connected over the Internet so they may transmit and receive data [1,2].

Combining these two technologies results in a prototype for a dependable, secure, and long-lasting method of storing data processed by intelligent, or more precisely "smart," devices. The scope only seems to be expanding, as experts predicted.

[1]CEA Department, GLA University, India

Blockchain technology has a lot of promise and provides a tonne of alternatives for all kinds of infrastructure thanks to its wide variety of uses. Secure communication and effective resource management are supported by the technology [3–5]. Because blockchain reduces the likelihood of fraud and automatically keeps track of activities, confidence is increased when parties conduct financial transactions using it. Any system user's background can be examined automatically. Because of its decentralized properties, blockchain is dependable and reduces the danger of engaging in a business transaction with an unknown party. Modern technology is used by everyone to converse online today. You can use the Internet to send messages, photos, voice calls, and video calls. The sender and the receiver in this transaction must continue to be separated by a trustworthy third party. People need to rely on a third party in the traditional system in order to make financial transactions. Blockchain will, nevertheless, offer the best transaction security in this instance. A block, which works like a record book, should be used to store all transactions [6]. The blockchain, which acts as a permanent database, receives a block after a transaction is complete. When a block is complete, a new block is generated or inserted along with it. A hash of the block before it can be found in every block. Centralization differs greatly from decentralization. Instead of using a centralized application, this one offers more security and flexibility. Decentralization was chosen by many organizations due to the need for quick decision-making [7].

Figure 9.1 shows how the data are pressed in IoT-based systems. Everything is done in one spot when the environment is centralized. In Blockchain technology, each block contains information about the previous block. It will provide an authentication mechanism during the transaction [8,9].

9.1.1   Blockchain technology's importance for IoT

The function of BC in the IoT is to offer a process for processing secured records of data through IoT nodes. BC is a safe technique that can be utilized in a public setting. In order to provide secure communication across IoT nodes in a diverse environment, this kind of technology is required. A further degree of security would be added by using blockchain to store IoT data, making it more difficult for hackers to access the network. It is almost difficult to erase existing data records because to the far more powerful encryption offered by blockchain. Blockchain makes it easier to verify and track multistep transactions that call for verification and traceability. It can assure secure transactions, cut costs associated with compliance, and quicken the processing of data transfers [10].

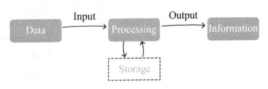

Figure 9.1   Data processing in IoT system

A big question arrived here *"How Blockchain can be used to identification and authentication in IoT?"*

Blockchain is distributed ledger that a combine IoT make possible M2M (Machine-to-Machine) transaction. It is an application which is used to store information with data integrity [11,12].

- Data chunks are encrypted in blockchain, integrity protected, digitally authorized and authenticated.
- Even in case where the owner key is leaked. Blocks cannot be modified because is imputable (except current block) blockchain.
- Integration of IoT with blockchain to improve with can help the security of IoT system with the help of automatically updating.

An IoT device may have its complete "identity" or just some alterable properties stored on the blockchain. This has not been possible without blockchains, as blockchains have certain properties that classic databases do not have. The information stored on a blockchain is absolutely unique, immutable, and has a chronology. This way you can link a state of a device with a state on the blockchain. Let me give you a few examples:

Smart door lock: The key to open the door lock is stored on the blockchain. The key is now transferable, in a way that the sender is losing access. In contrast to a simple password solution, where the sender is keeping access for the lifetime of the password.

Self-driving taxi: Someone can hail a ride by sending money on the blockchain to an address that belongs to a self-driving taxi. The taxi will run as long as there is enough credit on that address.

Supply chain tracking: Whenever a good with an RFID tag containing a unique ID is passing a sensor in the supply chain, the sensor is registering the ID in the blockchain, signed with its own private key. Now it is recorded on the blockchain, when the good passed this specific sensor.

Today's IoT already includes more than a billion intelligent, linked gadgets. We are on the verge of a revolution that will affect a wide range of industries, including the electronics sector, with the predicted proliferation of hundreds of billions more. Industries may now collect data, get insight from the data, and make decisions based on the data thanks to the development of IoT. As a result, there is a great deal of "confidence" in the knowledge acquired. The fundamental question, however, is whether we truly understand where these data originated from and whether we should be making judgments and conducting business based on information that we cannot verify. IoT makes it possible for Internet-connected devices to transmit data to private blockchain networks in order to build impenetrable records of shared transactions. Your company partners may exchange and access IoT data with you using IBM blockchain, but without the requirement for centralized management and control. To prevent disputes and foster confidence among all users of a permissioned network, each transaction can be independently validated [13–15].

9.1.2   Examples of how they can be combined are:

9.1.2.1   The logistics and supply chain

Thanks to IoT-enabled equipment, businesses will be able to track shipments at every stage, and blockchain will make the entire transaction transparent. IoT sensors (such as temperature sensors, motion sensors, GPS, and others) can offer details on the position of consignments. This evidence is subsequently stowed on the Block chain network for increased transparency. All supply chain parties identified in the Smart Contracts will then have immediate access to the data. The supply chain network's traceability and dependability can be improved by combining blockchain and IoT [16].

9.1.2.2   Automotive industry

IoT-enabled sensors are being used by automotive businesses today to create fully automated vehicles. The automobile sector is more eager to link IoT-enabled cars with blockchain technology so that many users may rapidly and easily exchange vital information. Additionally, the sector is already taking advantage of blockchain IoT use cases that have the potential to improve automated traffic control, smart parking, and autonomous vehicles [17,18].

9.1.2.3   Smart homes industry

IoT device-generated data exchange under the traditional centralized model lacks security standards and data ownership. However, thanks to blockchain IoT, homeowners are now able to remotely control their home security system from a smartphone. Blockchain could improve the security of Smart Homes by getting rid of the restrictions imposed by centralized infrastructure.

9.2   Key aspects of blockchain security

A blockchain is a continuously expanding ledger that maintains a secure, chronological, and immutable record of every transaction that has ever occurred. Because of the things listed below, blockchain technology has gained popularity.

1. **Shorter settlement times**: Blockchain can speed up transaction settlement in the banking sector. Verification, settlement, and clearance do not require a drawn-out procedure. It is as a result of all stakeholders having access to the same single version of agreed-upon data.
2. **Unchangeable transactions**: Blockchain records transactions in a chronological order, ensuring that no operation can be changed or removed after it has been added to the chain of ledgers.
3. **Dependability**: Blockchain authenticates and confirms the identity of all parties involved. This eliminates duplicate records, lowers rates, and speeds up transactions.

4. **Security**: To ensure that the information is locked inside the blockchain, blockchain technology makes use of highly sophisticated cryptography. With the help of distributed ledger technology, which allows each party to hold a copy of the initial chain, the system can continue to function even when many other nodes are lost.
5. **Collaboration**: It enables all parties to conduct business directly with one another without the need for a middleman.
6. **Decentralized**: There is no centralized authority in charge of overseeing anything, hence it is decentralized. Every node must abide by certain standards when exchanging blockchain data. This procedure makes sure that each transaction is examined for validity before adding each one at a time.

Keep the question in the mind "*How can blockchain solve IoT security and scalability challenges?*" The IoT has been one of the fastest developing technology trends in recent years. And it is predicted that till 2025 more than 27 billion devices will connected. But security concerns like software vulnerabilities and cyberattacks can stop customers to use IoT devices. Such IoT security challenges are dangerous for organizations like healthcare, finance, manufacturing, logistics, retail and other industries that started using IoT devices [19,20].

Software vulnerabilities:

1. Lack of computational capacity for built in security.
2. Poor control over IoT components.
3. Low budget for testing and improve security.
4. With time, security updates might be unable.

Scalability, which refers to a system's ability to handle a growing amount of work by adding more resources, continues to be a problem for many developers because of problems with IoT technology.

Scalability challenges:

1. Lack of planning phase
2. Compatibility with future devices
3. Budgetary constraints

Blockchain to solve the challenges over IoT:

1. It is public, so those who participate can see the block, not the actual content of the transaction.
2. It is decentralized and there is enough trust.
3. Network participants reach a consensus to approve transactions.
4. The database expands, although records are kept, but if anybody tries to modify then it will pay very high price.
5. It will allow you to share multiple files.
6. It guarantees robustness and scalability of resources, eliminating the flow of traffic to one, and lowering the delay.
7. The network is secure; the user's identity will be private.

9.3 Design of an IoT and blockchain-based framework to secure intellectual property

A blockchain-based methodology [16] and framework for China's intellectual property protection for microfilms, particularly for the cursives and terms of microfilms. Both names and scripts, which can be kept in databases and blockchains, can be used to distinguish one microfilm from others.

A lightweight binary watermark is employed in their methodology to safeguard the scripts on microfilms (including plot summaries, outlines, scene-by-scene summaries, etc.) [16].

Blockchain aims to allow for the distribution or recording of digital information. The term was first used in 1991 by Stuart Haber and W. Scott Strorntta to describe this technology. It gathers data in a collective manner. Every blockchain has a certain amount of space. The intangible works of individual humans or collective human understanding, such as imperceptible information, notions, or crafts, are included in the category of property known as intellectual property (IP). First off, the digitalization of information or creativity makes it easier for works to be copied or plagiarized, and it becomes much more difficult and expensive to determine which works are truly original. Additionally, we are living in a time of big data and data detonation. System for enhancing intellectual property defense with blockchain and IoT. The suggested method can assist individuals in setting up a reliable, self-organized, open, and biological logical property protection system using the blockchain peer-to-peer system and IoT strategies [21,22].

Our daily lives are affected by the IoT and blockchain technology's rapid advancement. According to a Gartner report, blockchain will increase company value by $3.1 trillion by 2030, while according to another analysis, the worldwide IoT industry will increase from $157 billion in 2016 to $457 billion in 2020 [23].

In Figure 9.2, with blockchain and IoT, we are set to experience greater change than we could have ever imagined. The processes currently used in a variety of industries, including manufacturing, trading, shipping, the financial sector, and healthcare,

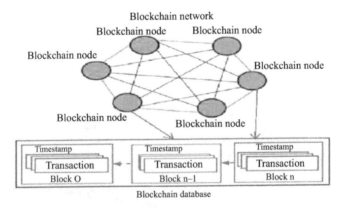

Figure 9.2 Blockchain-based secure architecture for IoT-based system [24]

will be disrupted by these applications. Security remains a primary worry for the IoT ecosystem despite these developments since it exposes numerous devices, enormous volumes of data, supply chain partners, and the community at large to security breaches. For instance, in the healthcare industry, data access control and privacy integrity are of utmost importance. There are more access points for hackers since there are more links between different IoT devices that track a patient's real-time medical data.

One particular piece of technology, blockchain, has made it possible for the third generation of the Internet to emerge. This distributed, data-first, authoritative internet revolves around a blockchain. Why is blockchain technology such a key component of this revolution?

The following characteristics of blockchain will make this shift possible: In Figure 9.1, a distributed ledger is a form of ownership. The ownership of the data on a blockchain is not centralized. A blockchain is accessible to everyone and anyone can read from it. A blockchain's distribution is open to everyone. Data saved in a blockchain is valid and authoritative since it is immutable, irrevocable, and cryptographically signed. All data can be verified as to its source and veracity, and everyone knows who is its owner and creator.

This raises confidence in the accuracy of the data. The data in a blockchain cannot be curated, moderated, prioritized, or filtered by a single company. No one can control how the data is used by users because there is no single owner of the data. The information that is exchanged is not controlled or managed by data power brokers, such as social media firms. In other words, by making all transactions visible and data verifiable, blockchain promotes trust in data and its source. As there is no single owner of the Internet's communications backbone, blockchain is akin to the IP transportation infrastructure of the internet. The backbone is supported by organizations including AT&T, Verizon, Deutsche Telekom, and NTT Communications. However, no single owner is able to entirely isolate, filter, or prevent internet traffic. Even strong nations like China and Russia, which seek to keep certain areas of the Internet off-limits to their population, find the task to be an ongoing fight. All filtering is useless since all it takes to establish a new communications line is a new, unfiltered provider [25,26].

What the Internet backbone has done for information dissemination, block-chain will do for Internet data. It will produce a reliable, censorable, and accessible global data and information repository. This quality will guide the development of the third generation of the Internet.

IoT systems have adopted blockchain as a developing deep protocol in large numbers. Blockchain technology offers valuable qualities like logical, homogeneous reliability, and traceability as an IoT data sharing platform. However, when division of information from a significant quantity of IoT sensors, such a combination results in considerable cryptographic overhead and consensus latency. We suggest a unique blockchain-based architecture for IoT data sharing platforms to overcome these problems. In this architecture, data packets are bundled into information chunks and sent to the blockchain grid after being digitally signed by IoT sensors. To secure data integrity from malware or hostile sink nodes and lower the communication, storage, and processing costs associated with signatures, we suggest a data block structure with an identity-based entire signature. IoT systems have adopted blockchain as a developing deep protocol in large numbers. Blockchain technology offers valuable qualities like logical, homogeneous reliability, and traceability as an IoT data sharing platform. Separating data from a large number of IoT sensors, however, leads in a significant amount of cryptographic overhead and consensus latency. Many researchers suggested a unique blockchain-based architecture for IoT data sharing platforms to overcome these problems [27].

In Figure 9.3, IoT systems have adopted blockchain as a developing deep protocol in large numbers. Blockchain technology offers valuable qualities like logical, homogeneous reliability, and traceability as an IoT data sharing platform. However, when allocation of information from an important quantity of IoT sensors, such a combination results in considerable cryptographic overhead and consensus latency. We suggest a unique blockchain-based architecture for IoT data sharing platforms to overcome these problems. In this architecture, data packets are bundled into data blocks and sent to the blockchain network after being digitally signed by IoT sensors. To secure data integrity from malware or hostile sink nodes and lower the communication, storage, and processing costs associated with signatures, we suggest a data block structure with an identity-based entire signature. IoT systems have adopted blockchain as a developing deep protocol in large numbers. Blockchain technology offers valuable qualities like logical, homogeneous reliability, and traceability as an IoT data sharing platform. However, when sharing data from a significant number of IoT sensors, such a combination results in considerable cryptographic overhead and consensus latency. Many researchers suggest a unique blockchain-based architecture for IoT data sharing platforms to overcome these problems [29].

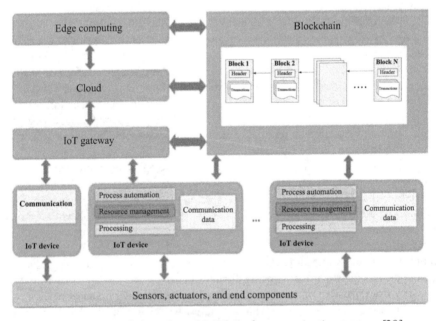

Figure 9.3   Blockchain-based IoT-based communication system [28]

The IoT is becoming more widely used. The use of IoT by businesses increased from 13% to 25% between 2014 and 2019, according to consultancy company McKinsey & Company. The IoT is predicted to connect 45 billion devices by 2023, laying the groundwork for the growth of smart cities. Security concerns still prevent the widespread development and integration of IoT, despite the popularity of linked devices. But this issue can be rectified with blockchain technology. Data is stored in a form that guards against hacking and data manipulation via a decentralized digital ledger of transactions called a "blockchain." This is accomplished by replicating communications and spreading them over extra network "nodes." Blockchain and IoT have the potential to fundamentally alter the creation in a quantity of traditions, including:

1. *Protected smart cities*: Blockchain distributes data throughout the network, rather than keeping it centralized. This implies that can be very difficult, if not dreadful, to hack the infrastructure of smart cities.
2. *Safe, pay-as-you-go conveyance*: The decentralized network made possible by blockchain has the potential to revolutionize transportation by offering secure, pay-as-you-go IoT-based mobility solutions for vehicle sharing customers.
3. *Better manufacturing*: Manufacturing companies are using IoT sensors more regularly to check their equipment and in-flight operations. This makes it possible for producers to spot issues before they arise. Blockchain technology is being incorporated by manufacturers into their systems in an effort to boost security and guarantee correct information within the classification.
4. *Translucent supply chains*: Companies not just in the manufacturing industry but also in other sectors using the system based on IoT, that will try to locate the correct positions and circumstances. Assimilating blockchain and IoT enables secure data sharing throughout the whole supply chain. As a result, a more rapid and efficient system is made possible. Additionally, it can assist companies in raising the caliber of their goods and services, which might increase client loyalty.
5. *Customer transparency*: Many clients are currently unaware of the methods used to transport, store, or control their data. Since blockchain records and retains all communications that take place within IoT devices, it would give consumers access to this data.
6. *More effective regulations*: Regulators would profit from having access to a system that is more secure, transparent, uniform, and centralized in order to handle IoT data on individuals, organizations, assets, and activities.
7. *Additional inexpensive auto protection*: The IoT can assist in lowering the cost of auto insurance, which is now based on average estimations, by deploying wireless devices that can connect to diagnostic ports on cars (which track per-mile usage). Financial data will become secure, stable, and auditable by incorporating block chain into this system. Regulators will be able to track driving records, vehicle histories, and technological checks more effectively thanks to blockchain. It may also aid in reducing fraud.

9.4   Future of blockchain in IoT ecosystem

IoT devices will be able to connect in a reliable manner on secure mesh networks, thanks to blockchain technology, avoiding hazards like device spoofing and impersonation. A number of companies are already utilizing blockchain technology to power IoT networks. As an example, consider the company Filament, which sells IoT hardware and software for industrial, oil and gas, and commercial agricultural applications. Business organizations can monitor real mining activities or water flows over agricultural areas with the Taps wireless sensors from Filament without relying on centralized cloud solutions. Low-power autonomous mesh networks are built via taps. Using machine-to-machine (M2M) connectivity as the foundation for a shared economy, blockchain has the potential to succeed in this scenario. The first initiatives in this field are already beginning to take shape. It can use smart contracts to negotiate for the best price depending on the preferences of its owner is one of the situations in which the platform has been tested [30,31].

Blockchain can create a trusted, self-organized, open, and ecological IP protection system with the aid of blockchain and IoT technology, even though the parties involved may not be completely trustworthy of one another. How can the physical world's objects and the digital world's data be connected. The usage of IoT technology is only a very early effort to address this issue, as more real-world data enters the system [32].

9.5   Conclusions

The usage of blockchain technology in the IoT environment is examined in this chapter. In line with this goal, answers have been sought to questions such "Why is block chain technology significant for IoT?" "What is the direction of blockchain in IoT technologies?" "What are the obstacles in its use?" and "What are the difficulties of implementing blockchain in current IoT technologies?" The application of IoT-blockchain, which has been growing since 2015, is seen in the existing literature. There are many instances of structures from the literature.

In the coming years, there is an expectation for the development of compromise solution procedures that will improve the functionality of IoT systems within the blockchain infrastructure. This anticipation is driven by the increasing growth of IoT-blockchain applications. Furthermore, there are intriguing challenges that need to be addressed, such as ensuring sustainability, optimizing processing capabilities, and overcoming storage limitations associated with IoT devices in the blockchain system.

References

[1]   Andoni, M., Robu, V., David Flynn, S., *et al.* (2019), "Blockchain technology in the energy sector: a systematic review of challenges and opportunities", *Renewable and Sustainable Energy Reviews*, vol. 100, pp. 143–174, doi: 10.1016/j.rser.2018.10.014.

[2] Casino, F., Dasaklis, T.K., and Patsakis, C. (2019), "A systematic literature review of blockchain-based applications: current status, classification and open issues", *Telematics and Informatics*, vol. 36, pp. 55–81, doi: 10.1016/j. tele.2018.11.006, ISSN 0736-5853.

[3] Lin, J., Long, W., Zhang, A., and Chai, Y. (2020), "Blockchain and IoT-based architecture design for intellectual property protection," *International Journal of Crowd Science*, vol. 4, pp. 283–293.

[4] Duy, P.T., Hien, D.T.T., Hien, D.H., and Pham, V.H. (2018), "A survey on opportunities and challenges of blockchain technology adoption for revolutionary innovation", In *Proceedings of the Ninth International Symposium on Information and Communication Technology (SoICT 2018)*. ACM, New York, NY, pp. 200–207, doi: 10.1145/3287921.3287978.

[5] Gurkaynak, G., Yılmaz, İ., Yeşilaltay, B., and Bengi, B. (2018), "Intellectual property law and practice in the blockchain realm", *Computer Law and Security Review*, vol. 34, no. 4, pp. 847–862, doi: 10.1016/j.clsr.2018.05.027.

[6] Holland, M., Nigischer, C., and Stjepandić, J. (2017), "Copyright protection in additive manufacturing with blockchain approach", *Transdisciplinary Engineering: A Paradigm Shift*, vol. 5, pp. 914–921, 10.3233/978-1-61499-779-5-914.

[7] Holland, M., Stjepandić, J., and Nigischer C. (2018), "Intellectual property protection of 3D print supply chain with blockchain technology", In *Proceedings of 2018 IEEE International Conference on Engineering, Technology and Innovation (ICE/ITMC)*. IEEE, Stuttgart, 10.1109/ ice.2018.8436315.

[8] Huckle, S., Bhattacharya, R., White, M., and Beloff, N. (2016), "Internet of Things, blockchain and shared economy applications", *Procedia Computer Science*, vol. 98, pp. 461–466, doi: 10.1016/j.procs.2016.09.074.

[9] Joshi, A., Han, M., and Wang, Y. (2018), "A survey on security and privacy issues of blockchain technology", *Mathematical Foundations of Computing*, vol. 1, no. 2, pp. 121–147, doi: 10.3934/mfc.2018007.

[10] Lin, J., Shen, Z., and Miao, C. (2017), "Using blockchain technology to build trust in sharing LoRaWAN IoT", In *Proceeding of the 2nd International Conference on Crowd Science and Engineering (ICCSE'17)*. ACM, New York, NY, pp. 38–43, doi: 10.1145/3126973.3126980.

[11] Lin, J., Shen, Z., Miao, C., and Liu, S. (2017), "Using blockchain to build trusted LoRaWAN sharing server", *International Journal of Crowd Science*, vol. 1, no. 3, pp. 270–280, doi: 10.1108/IJCS-08-2017-0010.

[12] Lin, J., Shen, Z., Zhang, A., and Chai, Y. (2018), "Blockchain and IoT based food traceability for smart agriculture", In *Proceedings of the 3rd International Conference on Crowd Science and Engineering (ICCSE'18)*. ACM, New York, NY, Article 3, pp. 1–6, doi: 10.1145/3265689.3265692.

[13] Reyna, A., Martín, C., Chen, J., Soler, E., and Díaz, M. (2018), "On blockchain and its integration with IoT. Challenges and opportunities", *Future Generation Computer Systems*, vol. 88, pp. 173–190, doi: 10.1016/j. future.2018.05.046.

[14]   Savelyev, A. and Ivanovitch. (2017), "Copyright in the blockchain era: promises and challenges (November 21, 2017)", Higher School of Economics Research Paper. No. WP BRP 77/LAW/2017, Available at SSRN: https://ssrn.com/abstract=3075246, doi: 10.2139/ssrn.3075246.

[15]   Schönhals, A., Hepp, T., and Gipp, B. (2018), "Design thinking using the blockchain: enable traceability of intellectual property in problem-solving processes for open innovation", In *Proceedings of the 1st Workshop on Cryptocurrencies and Blockchains for Distributed Systems (CryBlock'18)*. ACM, New York, NY, pp. 105–110, doi: 10.1145/3211933.3211952.

[16]   Tsai, W.-T., Feng, L., Zhang, H., You, Y., Wang, L., and Zhong, Y. (2017), "Intellectual-property blockchain-based protection model for microfilms", In *Proceedings of 2017 IEEE Symposium on Service-Oriented System Engineering (SOSE)*. IEEE, San Francisco, CA, April 6–9, doi: 10.1109/SOSE.2017.35.

[17]   Swan, M. (2015), *Blockchain Blueprint for a New Economy*. O'Reilly Media.

[18]   Mahdavinejad, M.S., Rezvan, M., Barekatain, M., Adibi, P., Barnaghi, P., and Sheth, A. P. (2018, August), Machine learning for internet of things data analysis: a survey. *Digital Communications and Networks*, vol. 4, pp. 161–175, https://doi.org/10.1016/j.dcan.2017.10.002.

[19]   Ahmet Ali Süzen. (2020), "A risk-assessment of cyber attacks and defense strategies in industry 4.0 ecosystem", *International Journal of Computer Network and Information Security (IJCNIS)*, vol. 12, no. 1, pp. 1–12, doi:10.5815/ijcnis.2020.01.01.

[20]   Charmonman, S., Mongkhonvanit, P., Ngoc Dieu, V., and van der Linden, N. (n.d.). Applications of Internet of Things in E-Learning. *International Journal of the Computer, the Internet and Management*, vol. 23. Retrieved from www.charm.SiamTechU.net.

[21]   Mouri, N.J. (2019), *IOT Protocols and Security Faculty of Computing and Electrical Engineering*. Tampere University.

[22]   Banerjee, M., Lee, J., and Choo, K.K.R. (2018), "A blockchain future for Internet of Things security: a position paper," *Digital Communications and Networks*, vol. 4, no. 3, pp. 149–160, https://doi.org/10.1016/j.dcan.2017.10.006.

[23]   Wang, X., Zha, X., Ni, W., *et al.* (2019), "Survey on blockchain for Internet of Things," *Computer Communications*, vol. 136(August 2018), pp. 10–29, https://doi.org/10.1016/j.comcom.2019.01.006.

[24]   Shaik, K. (2018), Why blockchain and IoT are best friends – Blockchain Pulse: IBM Blockchain Blog. Retrieved April 25, 2020, from IBM website: https://www.ibm.com/blogs/blockchain/2018/01/whyblockchain-and-iot-are-best-friends/.

[25]   Ferrag, M.A., Derdour, M., Mukherjee, M., Derhab, A., Maglaras, L., and Janicke, H. (2019), "Blockchain technologies for the Internet of Things: research issues and challenges," *IEEE Internet of Things Journal*, vol. 6, no. 2, pp. 2188–2204, https://doi.org/10.1109/JIOT.2018.2882794.

[26] Lao, L., Li, Z., Hou, S., Xiao, B., Guo, S., and Yang, Y. (2020), "A survey of IoT applications in blockchain systems: architecture, consensus, and traffic modeling," *ACM Computing Surveys*, vol. 53, no. 1, pp. 1–32, https://doi.org/10.1145/3372136.

[27] Wang, H., Zheng, Z., Xie, S., Dai, H.N., and Chen, X. (2018), "Blockchain challenges and opportunities: a survey," *International Journal of Web and Grid Services*, vol. 14, no. 4, pp. 352, https://doi.org/10.1504/ijwgs.2018.10016848.

[28] Pavithran, D., Shaalan, K., Al-Karaki, J.N., and Gawanmeh, A. (2020), "Towards building a blockchain framework for IoT," *Cluster Computing*, vol. 23, no. 3, pp. 2089–2103.

[29] Li, Z., Kang, J., Yu, R., Ye, D., Deng, Q., and Zhang, Y. (2018), "Consortium blockchain for secure energy trading in industrial Internet of Things," *IEEE Transactions on Industrial Informatics*, vol. 14, no. 8, pp. 3690–3700, https://doi.org/10.1109/TII.2017.2786307.

[30] Khan, M.A. and Salah, K. (2018), "IoT security: review, blockchain solutions, and open challenges," *Future Generation Computer Systems*, vol. 82, pp. 395–411, https://doi.org/10.1016/j.future.2017.11.022.

[31] Novo, O. (2018), "Blockchain meets IoT: an architecture for scalable access management in IoT," *IEEE Internet of Things Journal*, vol. 5, no. 2, pp. 1184–1195, https://doi.org/10.1109/JIOT.2018.2812239.

[32] Seok, B., Park, J., and Park, J.H. (2019), "A lightweight hash-based blockchain architecture for industrial IoT," *Applied Sciences (Switzerland)*, vol. 9, no. 18, p. 3740, https://doi.org/10.3390/app9183740.

Chapter 10

Blockchain architecture for social opinion vote-cast system

Yadunath Pathak[1], P.V.N. Prashanth[1], Jasminder Kaur Sandhu[2] and Varun Mishra[3]

Abstract

Elections play a crucial role for a democratic country. However, there is wariness among the people of these democratic countries over their electronic voting systems which further is a major issue for these citizens. Rigging votes, EVM hacking, vote manipulation are some of the major concerns among the people with the electronic voting systems. These shortcomings need to be addressed in order to achieve widespread adoption. Blockchain technology can be used to address these problems. Blockchain offers decentralized nodes that can be used for electronic voting and hence provide a complete framework for voting because of its end on verification benefits. With the blockchain technology, voting solutions can be created which are distributed, non-repudiated, and security protected. This chapter gives an insight to the existing vote-cast system using blockchain technology. The current state-of-the-art of blockchain architecture for voting-cast systems are presented. The blockchain architecture fundamental concepts and its characteristics are discussed with respect to the social opinion vote-cast system.

Keywords: e-Voting; Blockchain; Voting security; Privacy; Electronic voting machine (EVM); Democracy

10.1 Introduction

Voting is defined as the process of making a collective decision as majority of electorates have a common opinion [1]. A democracy uses a voting system to elect representatives to run a government by casting a vote. A vote has become a primary

[1]Department of Computer Science and Engineering, Visvesvaraya National Institute of Technology (VNIT), India
[2]Department of Computer Science and Engineering, Chandigarh University, India
[3]Department of Computer Science and Engineering, ASET, Amity University, India

indicator of the opinion of the citizens to make a choice by selecting a capable leader. This makes it essential to be assured that confidence in voting does not diminish.

Most democracies use a paper-based polling method to cast votes but that poses several questions regarding fairness and equality of the vote [2]. Electronic voting methods on the other hand have some benefits over the paper-based ballot system:

- Increased reliability compared to manual polling
- Enhanced the efficiency and integrity of the process
- Flexibility
- Easier to set up
- Cost-effective

Social opinion-based vote-cast system is more efficient and resilient. There has been a great progress in this area by using computers for counting and tallying the votes. Earlier computing systems permitted voters to cast their votes on a paper, then that paper went through the scanning, tallying process which was later replaced by the direct recording electronic (DRE) voting systems. It is somewhat similar to the EVMs used where the voter goes to the polling booth and gets a token which he uses at the voting terminal to vote, after selecting a candidate DRE asks for confirmation and then the final selection is done and the vote is cast [3].

While e-voting methods take several precautions against vote tampering, encryption alone cannot guarantee the anonymity needed by e-voting, a vote must not be traceable back to the voter otherwise any party can threaten the voters in order to vote for them or they would find out otherwise [4]. It uses a centralized system, which means it is licensed by a central authority (election commission). It is controlled and monitored by them and this practice poses a threat to transparent voting it can lead to erroneous selections due to a corrupt central authority which is difficult to rectify with these practices in place [5].

A decentralized voting system can be used to circumvent this issue of having a central authority. Blockchain offers decentralization, non-repudiation, and security protection which ensures anonymity, security, and concreteness of the votes.

10.2   Background

Cryptocurrencies are the most popular applications of blockchain in the modern world, Bitcoin was the first cryptocurrency solution to use a blockchain data structure and Ethereum introduced smart contracts. These contracts are set of promises prepared in the digital format and include the set of protocols within which political parties must perform their actions. Blockchain is now referred to as a collection of technologies that combine the data structure blockchain as well as a distributed consensus algorithm, smart contracts, and public-key cryptography [6].

Figure 10.1 illustrates the blockchain structure, it is basically chain of blocks that is united with some cryptography-based connection. The components are a

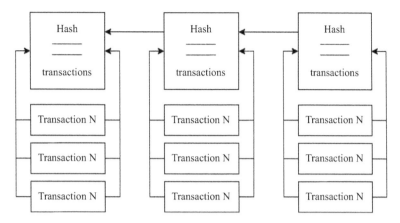

Figure 10.1   Structure of blockchain

block are: hash, transaction data of previous block, and the timestamp. Blockchain is designed to exhibit the immutable property which means that it is very difficult to change any value once it is written to the blockchain which is very much required for an e-voting system to avoid vote tampering. It generates a series of blocks that are replicated on a P2P network. Each block adds a hash with timestamp to the preceding block and contains several transactions. It transmitted the data with security across an unreliable network.

The aim of using blockchain is to achieve data immutability. If a change happens in the data, the block that is containing that data needs to recalculate its hash as well as the hash of all the subsequent blocks. Validated transactions are used to store data in these blocks that ensure that no one unauthorized can insert, delete, or change any data present without being noticed. Blockchain solutions are based on distributed ledger technology (DLT) [7]. It synchronizes the ledgers replicated among multiple nodes by using community validation [8].

10.2.1   Characteristics of blockchain architecture

The architecture can be roughly sketched as consisting of a bottom sensor layer, a middle network layer, and a top application layer. As one of the primary information-acquiring means at the bottom layer of the tags has found increasingly widespread applications in various business areas, with the expectation that the use of RFID tags will eventually replace the existing bar codes in all business areas.

10.2.1.1   Immutability

Blockchain documents cannot be changed once written to, or it is very difficult to do so since each new block that is added in the ledger need reference to the prior version of blockchain in the form of a hash. This makes the blockchain immutable and very hard to tamper with.

10.2.1.2   Decentralized

The framework does not operate based on a single governing authority or a single individual. The group of nodes maintain the system as a decentralized system.

10.2.1.3   Security

Modification in any characteristics of the network is not allowed for any kind of benefit. Encryption adds another security layer to the system.

10.2.1.4   Verifiability

Blockchain is a decentralized technology. All the peers available on the network, have a copy of the blockchain hence, there are very low chances of failure since no single point of failure exists.

10.2.1.5   Consensus

It represents the decision-making method for the nodes that are active on the network. The consensus determines whether the network is trust-worthy or not. It is not obligatory for the nodes in the network to trust each other individually, but the algorithms that run at the core of the system can be trusted [9] since any changes made to the network must have require Proof of Work (PoW).

10.2.2   Essential components of the blockchain architecture

10.2.2.1   Node

Users or computers in the blockchain network are referred to as nodes. Each of the nodes in the network has a different copy of the complete ledger obtained from the blockchain.

10.2.2.2   Transaction

The minutest building block (records and details) of a blockchain.

10.2.2.3   Block

A block comprises of data structures for processing transactions over the network and are distributed to all nodes.

10.2.2.4   Chain

The series of blocks placed in a specific order.

10.2.2.5   Miners

Communicator nodes to authenticate the transaction and hence add that block into the blockchain system.

10.2.2.6   Consensus

An assortment of instructions and organizations to carry out blockchain processes.

10.2.2.7   Proof of Work

A PoW should be easy to validate but it needs to be hard to produce [10].

10.3 Literature survey

10.3.1 Dalia et al. [11]

The authors suggest multiple round systems like setup round, voting round, recovery round, commitment round which helps in announcing election results if voters abort with complete fairness and ballot security.

10.3.2 Shahandashti and Hao

Shahandashti and Hao [12] proposed an upgraded version of the centralized remote voting method-based DRE-i system named the DRE-ip system which is based on the centralized polling station voting method. In this system, the encryption on the vote is done during the voting process; it is an E2E verifiable system without any Tallying Authorities (TAs) and provides stronger privacy. A touch-screen based polling station voting system using DRE-ip was trialed in Gateshead, United Kingdom, on May 2, 2019, during the UK local elections with encouraging elector feedback.

10.3.3 Kiayias and Yung

Kiayias and Yung [13] proposed a self-tallying voting system that will not need an authenticated third-party or any private channel for totaling votes and voter privacy.

10.3.4 Chaum et al.

Chaum *et al.* [14] explain a centralized polling station voting method-based Scantegrity system that has a very low impact on the election process and is an independent E2E verification system which conserves optical scan as a basic voting system.

10.3.5 McCorry et al.

McCorry *et al.* [15] presented different solutions for all three different settings of elections: decentralized voting setting, a smart-contract enactment of OV-net over Ethereum's blockchain and the centralized remote/onsite voting settings: blockchain for "preventive" measure and mirrored websites for "detective" measure.

10.3.6 Bell et al.

Bell *et al.* [16] discuss a centralized polling station voting method created on the STAR-vote design. It while having capabilities of making comparisons between individual cast vote and paper ballot level vote extremely easy, also has some known drawbacks such as Straight Party Voting (SPV). But since with additional research it can also be resolved, STAR-vote may preferably be the next-gen e-voting system for democratic countries.

10.4 Analyzing existing blockchain implementation

In the predictable future, for any sector that require strict security, reliability and transparency requirements such as cloud storage [17], transportation systems [18], cybersecurity and identity management in general [19], real-estate and agriculture traceability [20] can benefit with the help of integration of blockchain technology. E-voting systems are the most prominent areas which benefit a lot from the integration of the blockchain technology [21].

There are a number of blockchain implementations that can be used to make a decentralized storage system. Some of them are the following.

10.4.1   Exonum

The Exonum blockchain is robust end-to-end. It uses Rust programming language for its implementation. It is built for private blockchains. Consensus is achieved through a customized Byzantine algorithm. It can support up to 5,000 transactions per second.

10.4.2   Quorum

It is an Ethereum-based distributed ledger protocol with transaction/contract privacy and new consensus mechanisms. It is based on Geth. Quorum is aimed more toward consortium chain based consensus algorithms which allow it to support hundreds of transactions per second.

10.4.3   Geth

Go-Ethereum or Geth is one of three original implementations of the Ethereum protocol. It runs smart contract applications exactly as programmed without the possibility of downtime, censorship, fraud or third-party interference. The transaction rate is dependent on whether the blockchain is implemented as a public or private network.

10.5   Analyses of existing voting systems and requirements

10.5.1   Shortcoming of existing voting systems

10.5.1.1   Non-anonymous vote casting

A vote cast needs to be anonymous to everyone including the system administrators after vote submission. Current e-Voting solutions do not provide that.

10.5.1.2   Casting verifiability by the voter

After casting their votes, voters cannot verify when their vote was cast or if it was registered at all. Verifiability is important for assurance to the voter that no malicious actions have been performed on their vote [22].

10.5.1.3   Setup costs

Even though sustaining and managing an e-Voting system is quite cheap, initial setup costs can be a bit high and that can drive away nations or organizations that do not have enough budget to dish out or have more important issues to spend money on.

10.5.1.4 Security problems

Cyber-attacks prove to be a threat to general public polls if an e-Voting system is run only through a simple cloud database, external authorities can easily manipulate election results so they work in their favor. Unpredictable attacks (TLS attacks and/or man in the middle attack [23]) can occur due to undetected vulnerabilities of software and hardware.

10.5.1.5 Lack of evidence

Even though electoral fraud can be prevented by privacy and anonymity. There is no way to ensure that the votes that are being cast are not because of a threat or any monetary benefit [24].

As a real-life example, the Virginia Information Technologies Agency (VITA) applied security tests to various parts of their e-Voting system like the network, OS and vote tally after the election in 2015. They found out that unsafe security protocols and weak passwords were used in the system and it was recognized that a malicious attacker can easily endanger the confidentiality and integrity of the voting data. This is why it is advised to endanger discontinue the use of Advanced Voting Systems [25].

10.5.2 Requirement for the proposed voting system

- The election system must ensure verifiability and transparency.
- The election system must ensure the concreteness of the vote cast, once recorded, it should not be possible to alter it in any way.
- Only eligible voters must be allowed to cast their votes.
- The system should be tamper-proof.
- Manipulation of the voting system should not be possible at any stage.
- The voting process should be private, i.e. no one but the voter should know how they have voted.
- Only one vote must be allowed per voter.
- The voting process should be easy to use and typical for any person with any proficiency in technology.
- The voting system must be scalable in order to serve any scale of the population.
- The voting system must be fast in terms of recording votes and declaring results.
- The voting system should be low-cost, it should be efficient in terms of energy consumption and resources used in order to promote adoption among developing countries.

10.6 Analysis of existing voting solutions

10.6.1 FollowMyVote

It is a web-based decentralized application that runs its backend code on a decentralized network, blockchain is used for data storage and smart contracts are used for app logic. This can be used for e-Voting if a registration process can be set up.

10.6.2 Estonian e-Voting system

Estonia has adopted e-Voting through the Internet for a while now. It is based on the Estonian ID card which is a regular and mandatory account national identity document and can be used to digitally sign their vote and authenticate the voters at the same time. Voters are able to change their electronic votes any number of times. Multiple ballots can be cast by the voters but only one vote counts in the end. It is also possible to vote at the polling stations and if anyone voting at the polling stations has already voted through the Internet, their Internet vote is overridden [26].

10.6.3 Civitas

It is a voting system that is coercion-resistant, universally and voter-verifiable, and suitable for remote voting. Assurance is established through security proofs, information flow, and security analysis. It is fully decentralized software-based and authentication is postal based [27].

10.7 Proposed system

10.7.1 Defining blocks in voting system

The blockchain is a list of voting blocks (as shown in Figure 10.2) chained to each other in a sequential manner. Each block (as shown in Figure 10.3) would contain the following.

10.7.1.1 Voter ID

A randomly assigned ID for each eligible voter.

10.7.1.2 Vote

A token depicting which candidate the voter has voted for.

10.7.1.3 Voter signature

The vote is signed by the voter's private key for authentication.

10.7.1.4 Timestamp

Used to record the submission time of the vote.

10.7.1.5 Hash

Hash for the previous block.

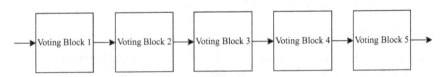

Figure 10.2   Structure of e-Voting blockchain

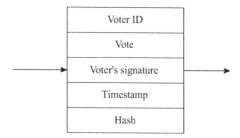

Figure 10.3   Structure of vote block

10.7.2   System structure

The designed voting system would consist of the following.

10.7.2.1   Voting blockchain

A list of voting blocks and a genesis block consisting of the information of eligible voters and candidates.

10.7.2.2   Voters

The person who casts the vote.

10.7.2.3   Election Commission

The organization for voting. They can query the voter's public key, and verify and query the votes.

10.7.2.4   Database

There will be two types of databases in this system. One would be the blockchain database containing a blockchain of actual votes and another would be the election commission's database containing the information about voter registration, candidate registration, and other election-related information.

10.7.2.5   Miners

The miners are the ones responsible for the voting blocks generated and adding them to the blockchain they are randomly selected by means of a miner selection algorithm.

10.7.2.6   Public key infrastructure

A set of procedures that handle public-key encryption.

10.7.3   Smart contract

For vote casting, a smart contract will be used, the roles for which are described in the following section.

10.7.3.1   Voter verification

The voter will need to log into the system using their private key. The blockchain checks the list of registered and authorized voters in the genesis block and if the voter information matches, then the voter is shown the list of candidates available for voting.

10.7.3.2 Block creation

Once the voter chooses one of the candidates and casts their vote, the vote is signed with a digital signature and sent to the smart contract. The vote count for the chosen candidate is incremented and a new block with the voter's ID, vote, timestamp, and other information is generated.

10.7.3.3 Selection of a miner

First, a minor is selected using miner selection algorithm. The target hash of specific block is generated by the minor.

10.7.3.4 Hash generation

The block is updated by the nominated miner using hash of preceding block. This hash is added to the current block and updates the nonce. Figure 10.4 shows the process of hash generation and its transmission towards blockchain.

10.7.3.5 Block verification

Every node of the blockchain is verified before adding to the blockchain. After successfully adding the block to the blockchain, the smart contract removes the hash of the voter from the genesis block. Another list called already voted voters is maintained to which this hash is added to so that double voting can be avoided. The voter ID is then returned which can be used to verify that the voter has voted.

10.7.4 Voting registration

The voting registration process goes as in the following section.

10.7.4.1 Step 1

For a voter to be legitimate, they have to register with their election commission as a voter with appropriate details. We propose using biometrics for the generation of a pair of keys, a public and a private key. The public key is used to identify the voter in the blockchain network. The private key is used to actually cast their vote and must be kept private. To generate the key pair, a unique hash is generated from fingerprints algorithm.

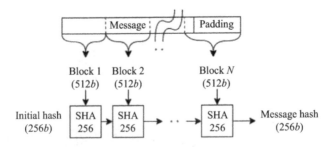

Figure 10.4 SHA-256 Hash generation

Figure 10.5 shows in detail how voter fingerprints can be used to generate a unique hash. It can also be combined with hashes from other unique information about the user as well. For example, their identity cards can be used as well. The final generated hash is then stored in the genesis block of the blockchain which is equal to the voter's list as illustrated in Figure 10.6.

10.7.4.2   Step 2

Candidates also need to register beforehand in order to be a part of the election. Their registration procedure is similar to the voter's. The party symbol, party ID, the public key is then warehoused in the genesis block.

10.7.5   *Tallying votes*

Tallying is the most important part of a voting system and it must be done accurately and transparently. Since the vote is counted as soon as the vote is cast, so vote tampering and fraud voting are not possible.

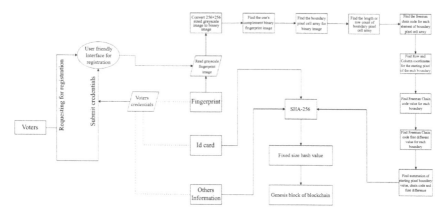

Figure 10.5   Hash generation using biometrics and unique identity car

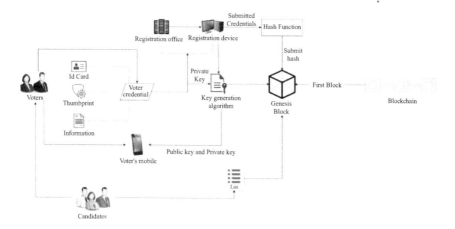

Figure 10.6   Structure of blockchain-based E-Voting system

10.8   Conclusion

In this chapter, the shortcomings of the traditional voting systems and how they can pose a source of distrust amongst the people and malpractices in terms of choosing candidates are discussed. Blockchain technology and what advantages it has over traditional data storage methods are presented. Because of these advantages, blockchain proves to be a useful tool that can be used to overcome few security threats of the existing voting systems.

Further, how an e-Voting system can be designed using a blockchain system and how it can be easier to set up and be convenient to use for the voters at the same time as it being secure is discussed.

Acknowledgement

We thank anonymous reviewers for their useful and constructive comments.

References

[1]   Y. Xie, Who overreports voting? *J. Am. Polit. Sci. Rev.* 80, 613–624 (2017).

[2]   N. Weaver, Secure the vote today. *Lawfare* (2016). https://www.law-fareblog.com/secure-vote-today.

[3]   A.A. Lahane, J. Patel, T. Pathan, and P. Potdar, Blockchain technology based e-voting system. In *ITM Web of Conferences*, vol. 32, p. 03001 (2020).

[4]   A. Kiayias, T. Zacharias, and B. Zhang, An efficient E2E verifiable E-voting system without setup assumptions. *IEEE Secur. Priv.*, 15(3), 14–23 (2017).

[5]   B. Wang, J. Sun, Y. He, D. Pang, and N. Lu, Large-scale election based on blockchain. *Procedia Comput. Sci.*, 129, 234–237 (2018).

[6]   G. Wood, Ethereum: a secure decentralised generalised transaction ledger. *Ethereum Proj. Yellow Pap.*, 151, 1–32 (2014).

[7]   A. Dorri, M. Steger, S. Kanhere, *et al.*, Blockchain: a distributed solution to automotive security and privacy. *IEEE Commun. Mag.*, 55(12), 119–125 (2017).

[8]   M. Li, J. Weng, A. Yang, *et al.*, CrowdBC: a blockchain-based decentralized framework for crowdsourcing. *IEEE Trans. Parallel Distrib. Syst.*, 99, 1 (2018).

[9]   D. Kraft, Difficulty control for blockchain-based consensus systems. *Peer-to-Peer Netw. Appl.*, 9(2), 397–413 (2016).

[10]   A. Judmayer, N. Stifter, K. Krombholz, and E. Weippl, Blocks and chains: introduction to bitcoin, cryptocurrencies, and their consensus mechanisms. *Synth. Lect. Inform. Secur. Privacy Trust*, 9, 1–123 (2017).

[11]   K. Dalia, R. Ben, P.Y.A. Ryan, and H. Feng, A fair and robust voting system by broadcast. *Electronic Voting*, 285–299 (2012).

[12]   S.F. Shahandashti and F. Hao, DRE-ip: a verifiable E-voting scheme without tallying authorities. In *ESORICS 2016: Computer Security – ESORICS 2016. European Symposium on Research in Computer Security*, 26–30 September 2016, GRC, pp. 223–240.

[13]   A. Kiayias and M. Yung, Self-tallying elections and perfect ballot secrecy. In *Part of the Lecture Notes in Computer Science Book Series* (LNCS, vol. 2274), 2002.

[14]   D. Chaum, A. Essex, R. Carback, *et al.*, Scantegrity: end-to-end voter-verifiable optical-scan voting. *IEEE Secur. Priv.*, 6(3), 40–46 (2008).

[15]   P. McCorry, S.F. Shahandashti, and F. Hao, A smart contract for board-room voting with maximum voter privacy. In *International Conference on Financial Cryptography and Data Security*. Springer, Cham, 2017, pp. 357–375.

[16]   S. Bell, J. Benaloh, M.D. Byrne, *et al.*, {STAR-Vote}: a secure, transparent, auditable, and reliable voting system. In *2013 Electronic Voting Technology Workshop/Workshop on Trustworthy Elections (EVT/WOTE 13)*, 2013.

[17]   J. Li, Z. Liu, L. Chen, P. Chen, and J. Wu, Blockchain-based security architecture for distributed cloud storage. In *Proceedings of the 2017 IEEE International Symposium on Parallel and Distributed Processing with Applications and 2017 IEEE International Conference on Ubiquitous Computing and Communications (ISPA/IUCC)*, Guangzhou, China, 12–15 December 2017, pp. 408–411.

[18]   Y. Yuan and F.-Y. Wang, Towards blockchain-based intelligent transporta-tion systems. In *Proceedings of the 2016 IEEE 19th International Conference on Intelligent Transportation Systems (ITSC)*, Rio de Janeiro, Brazil, 1–4 November 2016, pp. 2663–2668.

[19]   C. DeCusatis, M. Zimmermann, and A. Sager, Identity-based network security for commercial blockchain services. In *Proceedings of the 2018 IEEE 8th Annual Computing and Communication Workshop and Conference (CCWC)*, Las Vegas, NV, 8–10 January 2018, pp. 474–477.

[20]   K. Demestichas, N. Peppes, T. Alexakis and E. Adamopoulou, Blockchain in agriculture traceability systems: a review. *Appl. Sci.*, 10, 4113 (2020).

[21]   Z. Zhao and T.-H.H. Chan, How to vote privately using Bitcoin. In Qing, S., Okamoto, E., Kim, K., and Liu, D. (eds.), *Information and Communications Security, Lecture Notes in Computer Science*. Springer: Cham, Switzerland, 2016, vol. 9543, pp. 82–96, ISBN 978-3-319-29813-9.

[22]   D. Chaum, Secret-ballot receipts: true voter-verifiable elections. *IEEE Secur. Priv.*, 2(1), 38–47, (2004).

[23]   A. Cardillo and A. Essex, The threat of SSL/TLS stripping to online voting. In Krimmer, R., Volkamer, M., Braun, *et al.* (eds.), *E-Vote-ID 2018: Electronic Voting*, Lecture Notes in Computer Science. Springer: Cham, Switzerland, 2018, vol. 11143, pp. 35–50, ISBN 978-3-030-00419-4.

[24]   National Academies of Sciences, Engineering, and Medicine. 2018. Securing the Vote: Protecting American Democracy. Washington, DC: The National Academies Press. https://doi.org/10.17226/25120.

[25] Security Assessment of WINvote Voting Equipment for Department of Elections. www.wired.com/wp-content/uploads/2015/08/WINVote-final.pdf

[26] Estonian e-Governance Website. https://e-estonia.com/solutions/e-governance/e-democracy/

[27] R.C. Michael, S. Chong, and M.C. Andrew, Toward a secure voting system. In *IEEE Symposium on Security and Privacy*, 2008, pp. 354–368.

Chapter 11

Blockchain technology for next-generation society: current trends and future opportunities for smart era

Meghna Manoj Nair[1] and Amit Kumar Tyagi[2]

Abstract

Blockchain, a relatively novel technology, is often termed as the internet of value. Even though there are predictions that indicate that the future of blockchain is likely to be perilous, it has contributed remarkably and has already brought about revolutionary changes in terms of transactions and digital currencies. This paper is a survey and analysis of one of the fast-evolving technologies called Blockchain. It covers all essential information required for a beginner to venture into this complicated field while also covering necessary concepts that can be useful for experts; the first provides a general introduction and discusses the disruptive changes initiated by blockchain, the second discusses the unique value of blockchain and its general characteristics, the third presents an overview of industries with the greatest potential for disruptive changes, the fourth describes the four major blockchain applications with the highest prospective advantages, and the fifth part of the paper ends with a discussion on the most notable subset of innovative blockchain applications—Smart Contracts, Decentralized Autonomous Organizations (DAOs), and super safe networks—and their future implications. There is also a concluding section, which summarizes the chapter, describes the future of blockchain, and mentions the challenges to be overcome.

Keywords: Blockchain technology; Internet of Things; Smart applications; Smart contracts

11.1 Introduction to blockchain

Blockchain, as the word suggests, is a distributed ledger (refer Figure 11.1) storage technique wherein each block (except for the first block) has a pointer that points to the immediately previous block through a reference mechanism which focuses on the

[1]School of Computer Science and Engineering, Vellore Institute of Technology, Chennai, India
[2]Department of Fashion Technology, National Institute of Fashion Technology, New Delhi, India

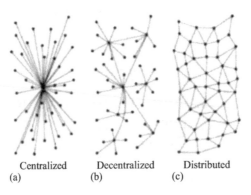

Centralized   Decentralized   Distributed
(a)   (b)   (c)

Figure 11.1   Structures in general

hash values. The very first block in the chain is called the genesis block and it ideally does not have any parent block. The data is stored in each of the block and every block has certain information which includes the block version, the hash value of its parent block, timestamp which records the input entries into the block, nonce (number used only once) value, the number of transactions recorded in the block and the Merkle root pointer [1]. The recent surge in the use of blockchain technology has been in the field of cryptocurrency systems such as bitcoins because of its security features and decentralized nature of transactions. The main highlight of blockchain is its guarantee of reliable services and safekeeping of data which ultimately generates trust and loyalty by eliminating the requirement of a third-party mediator. One of the major strategies followed is that a given transaction can be successfully recorded within a block only when the involved miners adopt the Proof of Work (PoF) technique so as to acquire bitcoins in the form of rewards. The incentive-based system works by ensuring that the miner who stimulates and broadcasts the block first is the one who will be rewarded. It is also important to note that work done by the miners of finding suitable hash values for the block is excessively time consuming and difficult which is made in such a manner so that a maximum of six blocks can be generated at a steady rate. Once the blocks are generated, they are then chained and linked together in a chronological order. Now Figure 11.1 shows the difference between centralized, decentralized, and distributed structure with respect to blockchain.

The diagram shown in Figure 11.2 elaborates on the work flow of blockchain and procedures involved Consider the case wherein Bob transfers some bitcoins to Alice. This leads to the creation of a new transaction which is stored in a block. Following this, the nascent block is broadcasted to the network and all corresponding nodes. The nodes validate the authenticity and verify the block. If the block is considered to be valid, it is then added to the blockchain and the same process continues each time a new transaction occurs [2].

When considering blockchain, it is extremely important to understand the structure of the blockchain which is a peer-to-peer distributed ledger system. From a common man's view, the platform put forth by this technical concept is where people are able to perform and record transactions of various types without a third-party

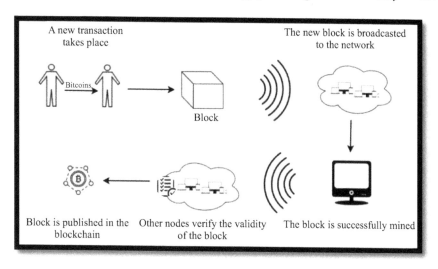

A new transaction takes place

The new block is broadcasted to the network

Bitcoins

Block

Block is published in the blockchain

Other nodes verify the validity of the block

The block is successfully mined

Figure 11.2   Workflow of blockchain

arbitrator [3]. This database of transaction records is then shared and distributed among the participants of the network through transparent and flexible means which is accessible to all. In terms of managing the database, it is taken care by peer-based networks with a time-stamped server recording every action. Furthermore, the blocks in the chain are organized in such a way that it mainly refers to the contents of the previous block. The architecture of blockchain mainly includes the nodes within a peer-to-peer network, the genesis block, transactions within the block, process of validation and verification through mining, and PoW. The framework of blockchain can be seamlessly comprehended by considering the example of Google documents. Just like how one can open up a Google doc, add editors and track the real-time edits through which people from different parts of the world can work simultaneously on the same document, blockchain system also follows a similar technique that enables the distribution of digital data by adhering to trust, transparency, and data security. The structure and architectural aspect of blockchain is not the same as that of any other conventional database. Here, each participant in the network is capable of maintaining, approving, and updating novel transaction entries and the power, hence, is not vested in the hands of a single node/individual [4]. The blockchain structures mainly fall into one of the three categories—public, private, and consortium block-chain architecture. The public architecture is the one that involves data accessibility to anyone willing to join the network such as Bitcoin, Ethereum, and Litecoin. The private architecture, on the other hand, is completely controlled by users from a certain organization or group who can participate only on invitation.

The last type of architecture, the consortium architecture, is the one owned by a group of organizations wherein, the procedures and rules are set up by the assigned users at the rudimentary level. Figure 11.3 shows an elaborate view of the

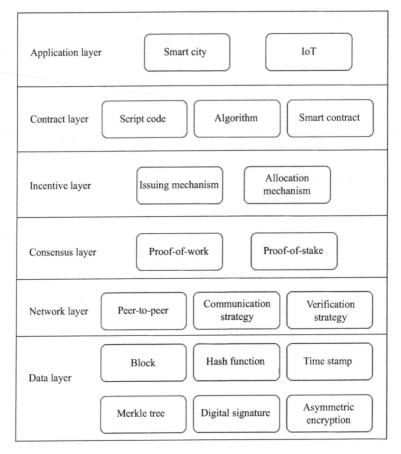

Figure 11.3   Architecture of blockchain

various layers involved in a blockchain architecture including layers like application, contract, incentive, consensus, network, and data layers.

Figure 11.4 elucidates the structure of blockchain. Each block has a set of information which consists of the hash value of previous node, hash value of current node, nonce (number used only once) value, the timestamp at which it was processed, and the Merkle root pointer. Each Merkle root pointer points to a tree-like structure where the transaction details are essentially stored. Also, Figure 11.5 shows the creation of new block in a blockchain network.

The architecture of the can be roughly sketched as consisting of a bottom sensor layer, a middle network layer, and a top application layer. As one of the primary information-acquiring means at the bottom layer of the tags have found increasingly widespread applications in various business areas, with the expectation that the use of RFID tags will eventually replace the existing bar codes in all business areas.

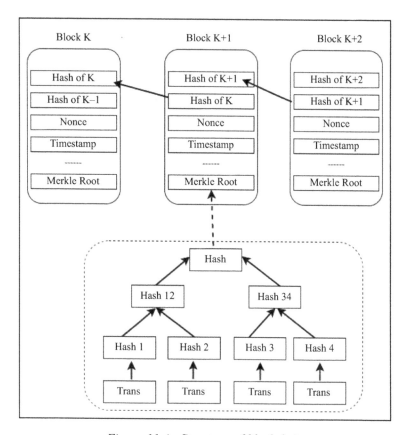

Figure 11.4   *Structure of blockchain*

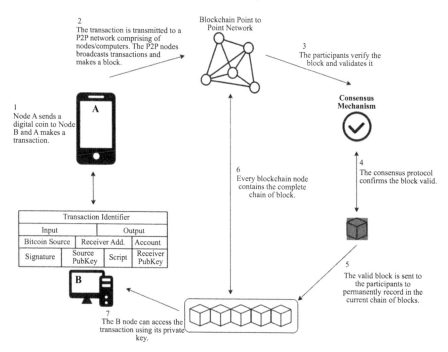

Figure 11.5   *Creation of new block in a blockchain network*

11.2   Related work

There are quite a few similar technologies and concepts of blockchain in use today. Many of the financial transaction records and tracks are maintained through a central controlling authority and a ledger concept is utilized for this purpose. This is because only a ledger can reliably ensure the integrity and safety of highly confidential financial details of customers. In the very first stages, blockchain was majorly known for its core use in cryptocurrency wherein transactions and transmission of amounts from one person to the other did not require the mediation of a third-party central control [5]. In the case of cryptocurrency, the ledgers and storage details of all participating individuals are shared among each other so as to maintain transparency and a sense of loyalty. The possibility of attacks and data breaches by malicious users and crackers is almost impossible because of the decentralized and distributed nature of the blockchain technology and also because of the consent-oriented mechanism followed before recording transactions. In other words, there is no single individual in whose hands the power is vested. This additionally provides a benefit of easing out the process of updating or modifying the blockchain system [6]. The works of authors in [7] focused on the systematic review of blockchain and further initiatives taken up in the same area. They have reviewed and analyzed more than a hundred blockchain research works through which they have curated an opinion that surveys the relevance of blockchain for energy applications. In [8], the research conducted by the authors highlights the societal impacts, possible opportunities and bottlenecks, along with some of the major trends observed in blockchain. Similarly, the work put forth in [9] describes and clarifies the holistic aspect of blockchain technology from the view-point of energy usage of bitcoins. It also elaborates on the various types of blockchain consensus and draws conclusive elucidations. In [10], the basics of blockchain along with a detailed explanation of the various types of blockchain technology are described. It also highlights some of the major attacks and issues that blockchain technology may be exposed to. Note that many useful works related to blockchain can be found in [11–13].

11.3   Evolution and timeline of blockchain

The very first phase of blockchain sparked off with the out surge of transactions. There were many technologies, right from the start, which were based on the logical concept of bitcoins and blockchain long before it actually began. Merkle tree is one among these which is named after the infamous scientist Ralph Merkle which is ideally a data structure that stores and verifies the individual records [7]. However, this was not the only setup stage for blockchain. The very early years of blockchain technology in the 1990s were the contributions of Stuart Haber and W. Scott Stornetta which mainly revolved around the fields of cryptographic implementations to secure a chain of data blocks such that no external attacker would be able to tamper with the data and timestamps. By 1992, this system was further upgraded to integrate the use of Merkle trees so as to increase the efficiency and allow a greater number of data to be stored within each block. Up until 2008, blockchain did not gain much significance or relevance. However, in 2008, blockchain history comes into spotlight and its beneficial aspect is noticed at large capacities. This was because of the works put forth by the individual/group Satoshi Nakamoto who was the first one to work on bitcoins which is the very first and rudimentary application of the digital ledge technology. In the current world, the application of blockchain has definitely evolved and is being used in several applications apart from cryptocurrencies. After putting forth the ideology and concept of using blockchain technology for bitcoins, Satoshi Nakamoto exited the scene and from then on it was taken up by various core developers across the globe leading to exciting and innovative evolutions [8].

11.3.1   Phase 1 of blockchain evolution

During the years of 2008–2013, which is ideally the first phase of development in the field of blockchain technology. The paper published by Satoshi Nakamoto contained details and information pertaining to an electronic peer-based system. He had curated the very first genesis block on the basis of which further blocks were mined and incorporated leading to one of the longest chains of data-carrying blocks. Ever since this incident, a variety of use-cases have emerged that leverage and utilize the working principle and abilities of the distributed ledger technology [9]. Figure 11.6 shows all of its evolution since 1.0–4.0 in detail.

11.3.2   Phase 2 of blockchain evolution

The years 2013–2015 mark the second phase of evolution in the blockchain history. Among the various developers that were extracting and experimenting with blockchain, Vitalik Buterin was one of the developers who believed that bitcoin

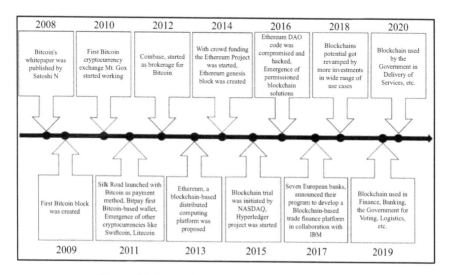

Figure 11.6   Evolution of blockchain since 2008

had not reached its full potential level. He opined that bitcoin still had many limitations and disadvantages and initiated his work on a form of blockchain that was malleable and could perform additional functions apart from a peer-to-peer network. This led to the birth of Ethereum in 2013 which was initiated out of a novel public blockchain technology. Ethereum had nascent capabilities in comparison to bitcoin. This truly was pivotal moment in the evolving history of blockchain [10].

The main difference between Ethereum and bitcoin was that Ethereum has a particular functionality that permits people to record and track information such as slogans and contracts and not just mere transactions. Ethereum was officially launched in the year 2015 and is definitely one of the biggest applications of blockchain considering its capacity to aid smart digital contracts and other functions.

11.3.3   Phase 3 of blockchain evolution

Following the year 2018, a plethora of projects and initiatives that revolve around the advantages of blockchain have emerged and many of the researchers have also highlighted some of the possible deficiencies in the use of bitcoin and Ethereum which are further being worked upon. The rise of many applications such as China's first blockchain platform NEO, integration of blockchain with Internet of Things (IoT), development of other blockchain platforms such as Monero Zcash and Dash have taken the world by a storm [14]. In 2015, the Linux group initiated one of its side projects that focuses on an open-source blockchain system called Hyperledger and to date, it continues to act as a combined emergence of numerous ledgers. The main aim of Hyperledger is to encourage the advanced utilization of blockchain to enhance the efficiency and reliability of the system for global transactions. In 2017, the birth of EOS took place which is the child of a private firm "blocl.one." Their proposal was a novel blockchain protocol which was fueled by EOS as the original cryptocurrency. The future of blockchain is definitely bright and shiny with an increasing number of applications across the globe in various disciplines and aspects be it finance, supply chains, transportation, etc. [15].

11.4   Blockchain in IoT and other computing platforms

IoT is a broad and rising concept in the modern era which refers to the interconnection and integration of smart gadgets and devices to gather data and information and make suitable decisions. The use of IoT in various aspects of life has been on a rampant increase over the last few years making it ubiquitous and empowering the connection and interconnection of devices. Cloud computation, Machine Learning (ML), information modeling, etc. are some of the technologies that have made use of the IoT fabric for further advancements. Amidst these growing opportunities, one of the dark sides of IOT is in terms of its security and privacy concern. There are more than a 100 "things" or nodes getting connected to the web with every passing second and each of these nodes are involved in exchanging some form of data or information within and outside the network. Blockchain technology is capable of fully addressing these raised issues (mentioned above). Also, with integration of IoT, blockchain can efficiently resolve the security concerns. This combination is often termed as BIoT [16]. One of the main reasons why blockchain can provide a secure and stable platform for IoT devices is its need to validate all transactions before confirming and recording the transactions to the ledger. The execution of this approach ensures that there is no single authority or power responsible for making decisions and, therefore, offers a massive amount of trust and reliability to the followers of this network. On the other hand, if the conventional IoT approach is being used, then a centralized system comes into action and the transactions that are published into the ledger are verified by a third-party organization leading to increased expenditure and a single power making decisions. This often results in lack of transparency and high possibility of fraudulent activities.

In terms of publicity, the IoT devices mainly consist of a dynamic and galvanic system, all of which are configured in a way to exchange information and data with the privacy of users remaining protected. When blockchain comes into play, the situation becomes such that the participants can get insights on the transaction details being recorded and each participant will have its own ledger. The fact that each of the nodes in a blockchain have its own ledger and storage facility is what makes the system of BIoT resilient and strong enough to withstand any sort of attack. In case of a node being maliciously captured or compromised, the overall performance would still not be affected as the data stored in the captured node is also available individually to all other nodes. Security is one of the other features that integration of blockchain guaranteed and is a foundational aspect for IoT considering the large number of devices that are linked together over the web [17]. It is also a cost-effective solution in comparison to the alternative solutions which often call for extremely high main-tenance costs and infrastructural developments with a centralized framework. Furthermore, the fact that blockchain technology uses a ledger which is decentralized and distributed ensures that it is immutable in nature and this further warrants for an enhanced privacy and security preserved environment for IoT.

In the case of transactions being processed by blockchain, the anonymity of both the sender and the receiver with respect to their address is maintained with the help of distinctive addresses which are masked to preserve the actual identity. Though this has been exposed to criticism in cryptocurrencies, it has been advan-tageous for applications such as digital voting and healthcare records. Also, the fact that each node in IoT can be validated easily though BIoT via accessible identity management and its commitment toward accountability and data traceability is what makes it unique [18].

11.5 Characteristics of blockchain over other technologies

The main factor that contributes to blockchain having an upper-hand over other technologies is the following characteristics:

- *Decentralization*: In a conventional system for managing and controlling transactions, the verification process usually takes place through a third-party agency that is reliable like a bank or government. However, this often adds up the cost and leads to bottlenecks or catastrophic conditions in case of single-point failures. In contrast to this, if blockchain is used, then the transactions are verified between peers without the need for an additional authentication or intervention by a third-party agent or mediator. This helps reduce the cost drastically and mitigate any problems that are likely to arise [19].

- *Immutability*: Blockchain mainly contains a sequential collection of blocks of data which are linked to each other through hash pointers and values. A slight change or modification in the previous block would break the chain and all subsequent blocks would be invalidated. From the point of view of a Merkle tree, the root hash of the tree acts as the hash value of all confirmed transactions such that a change in any of these leads to the generation of a new root. This is what guaranteed the integrity of sustenance of data [20].
- *Non-repudiation*: In blockchain, a private key is notably used to attest or sign a transaction which can further be verified by all other participants using the corresponding public key that is accessible to all [21].
- *Transparency*: Majority of the blockchain frameworks ensure that each of its participants can access and engage with the network on equal grounds. Each of the new transactions is not only validated and recorded in blockchain but is also made available to each of the users in the network [22].
- *Pseudonymity*: Another feature of blockchain to be highlighted is its ability to maintain a certain level of anonymity while also ensuring transparency. This can-not just help in fraud detection but also help in identifying illicit transactions.
- *Traceability*: One of the unique and useful features of blockchain is the easy traceability factor with the help of a timestamp attached to the block in the chain. This comes in handy to validate and trace the origins of past data.

11.6 Types of blockchain and comparisons

Blockchain is generally classified into three main types: public, private, and consortium blockchain.

- *Public blockchain*: It is the type that allows all the stored transactions to be openly and publicly available to the public. The nodes or participants also have the liberty to join or leave the network as per their convenience and each individual can validate and cross-verify the transactions before it gets published. Examples of public blockchain include Bitcoin and Ethereum [6].
- *Private blockchain*: This type of blockchain is completely owned and regulated by a private organization and they provide limited or restricted access only to particular participants. Not every node can actively contribute to the blockchain network. They have stringent management techniques and methods for access to data and regulation policies. Enterprise Ethereum, Tezos, etc. are examples [5].
- *Consortium blockchain*: This type of blockchain is mixture of both public and private consisting of certain nodes that require permission to engage in the

Table 11.1   Types of blockchain

Feature	Private blockchain	Consortium blockchain	Public blockchain
Determining consensus	One organization	Selected number of nodes	All miners
Read permission	Restricted or public	Restricted or public	Public
Immutability	Can be tempered	Can be tempered	Nearly impossible to tamper
Efficiency	High	High	Low
Centralization	Yes	Partial	No
Consensus technique	Permissioned	Permissioned	Permission-less

consortium chain process and other nodes which have the freedom to take part in transactions. This is in fact, a partially decentralized framework. R3CEV and Hyperledger fabric are examples of the consortium blockchain [5].

Table 11.1 shows the differentiation of each type of blockchain based on the major characteristic features as described in the previous section.

11.7   Types of consensus algorithms

Consensus algorithms are crucial in the case of blockchain networks and it is a field that has been researched and worked upon extensively to ensure a robust and reliable architecture. When it comes to blockchain, the consensus algorithms mainly need to deal with malicious, selfish, or faulty nodes such that they do not affect the global state of the chain of nodes. Majority of the consensus algorithms tend to address the three major characteristics through which the efficiency and impact can be determined.

- *Safety*: This property ensures that there is never a possibility of leakage or misuse of data and other confidential information. In general terms, a consensus mechanism is considered to be secure and safe it there is at least one node that generates an authentic output such that every other node receives the same. This leads to the consistency of data and information across the network making it safe and atomic [7,9].
- *Liveness*: The feature of liveness is to guarantee the best possible option to happen with due time and is often termed as a termination of conventional consensus in decentralized and distributed systems. This points to the fact that each genuine process would gradually decide on the same correct value. The consensus algorithm guarantees the feature of liveness and does not contain any tie bound restrictions to decide on a certain value [14,15].
- *Fault tolerance*: Consensus algorithms need to provide a hefty fault tolerance feature to ensure that the system is free from failures and is resilient to external

attacks. There are two possibilities in terms of node failures. One being fail stop category that leads to nodes being disabled from processing for temporary/permanent periods of time. The other failure possibility is a Byzantine failure where the malicious nodes are specifically curated to overcome the features of a consensus protocol [4,23].

11.7.1 Types

The literal meaning of consensus translates to an agreement or mutual understanding between participating nodes. It is essential in analyzing and comprehending the process of authentication of blocks when being added to the chain of blocks. Figure 11.4 elaborates on the various types of consensus techniques. There are two main types of consensus algorithms. The first type is the proof-based algorithm while the second type is the vote-based algorithm. Some very commonly used consensus mechanisms are as follows:

- *Proof-of-Work (PoW)*: This type of consensus resembles a puzzle which is to be solved and figured out by the various participant nodes so as to mine and add a new block to the existing chain. The principle of this algorithm resonates to the node which has computed the maximum amount of work is the one that receives maximum reward or return of interest. This is the consensus used in bitcoin system. Some of the algorithms that make use of this consensus mechanism include Cuckoo hash function, finding prime numbers, ghost protocol, etc. [24].
- *Proof-of-Stake (PoS)*: The PoS mechanism requires far less amount of processing and compute power in contrast to PoW and is utilized in scenarios which necessitate an energy efficient technique. The nodes participating in a system using the PoS consensus is least involved in attacking/hacking it and hence, they only need to showcase their engagement gradually through currency [25].
- *Delegated PoS (DPoS)*: The DPoS is different from the conventional PoS mechanism with regards to the number of participants and only certain selected participants can develop, validate, or adjust the size of the blocks [20].
- *Proof-of-Activity (PoA)*: This algorithm motivates every involved node and stakeholders in participation leading to the passive and silent nodes also earning rewards [20].
- *Proof-of-Burn (PoB)*: The PoB consensus mechanism calls for the dedications of node miners with the proof of work in the form of digital currencies. It correlates to the fact that rather than wasting energy, compute power, etc., the currencies need to be burnt [21].
- *Practical Byzantine Fault Tolerance (PBFT)*: This is one unique consensus mechanism for commercial organizations wherein the participants are partially trusted. The bottleneck of this strategy is the possibility of exponentially rising message counts each time they're added to the set [18].

Apart from the above-mentioned types of consensus algorithms, one of the popular techniques is the distributed consensus algorithm. Coming to a conclusion and mutual understanding of the blocks of data that need to be accepted and added

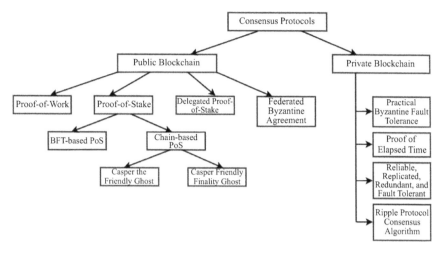

Figure 11.7   Types of consensus mechanisms in blockchain

can be quite challenging and tedious. However, in order to reach an agreement efficiently in a distributed framework, a few conditions are to be met. Termination, agreement, validity, and integrity are the major pillars that contribute to a safe and secure distributed consensus mechanism. The application of this distributed strategy spans along the lines of electing leader nodes in a fault tolerant space to kickstart a global uniform action, maintaining a level of consistency and atomicity in a distributed framework, etc. [22]. Figure 11.7 shows several types of consensus mechanisms in blockchain in detail.

11.8   Applications and use cases of blockchain

The growth of blockchain across the world has led to its implementation in numerous arenas of life and it has given rise to a plethora of use cases, some of which are discussed below.

- *Supply chain*: Integrating blockchain along with supply chains can aid the participants to easily track and keep records of price, location, quantity, quality, etc. which would in turn positively affect the efficacy of the supply chain system. It could not only help reduce the bureaucratic hurdles but also improve the operations in general. This would further prove beneficial as the costs get reduced dramatically. The decentralized structure of blockchain is a guarantee to the fact that it provides space for storage which is permanent and unalterable. Large tech corporations like IBM have invested on and developed blockchain frameworks to complement them in terms of integrating data between the various people and groups involved logistically [1].
- *Agriculture*: The discipline of agriculture and farming surely is a potent area for blockchain technology to dwell on as it helps in securing the possibility of

tracing information and details pertaining to the supply chain in the food avenue. This is further used to innovate and generate ideas for smart farming and index-based insurances for agricultural development. Not only does this technique help in decreasing the environmental footprints, but it also guarantees to cater to the growing demands of increasing population while maintaining transparency throughout [2]. The fact that blockchain technology can be succinctly used for handling forecasted dangers and issues so as to maintain uniformity and consistency throughout the systems is an added advantage. Ranging from initiating a sustainable business and decreasing waste, all the way to ensuring informed customer decisions and smooth transaction processes, all of it can be taken care of with incorporating blockchain in the agricultural sector.

- *Healthcare*: The health industry is yet another field that undergoes evolutionary changes, especially with the incorporation of technology. Incorporating a blockchain network in this field can support the easy ways to preserve and interchange health records of patients and can also contribute towards recognizing risky and dangerous flaws in the medical sector. The main advantage is its ability to revolutionize the process of analyzing health and medical records for the better [5]. Not only does blockchain integrated healthcare facilities ensure a safe way of transmitting medical and health records of patients, but it is also very useful to deal with the healthcare supply chains and aids medical researchers as well. Akiri, a company in California, utilizes a network-based blockchain service to protect and preserve the privacy of patients with respect to their health records and information. Similarly, MedicalChain is one of the other companies in England that helps in maintaining the cohesive and integrated nature to protect the identity of its patients.

- *Governance*: Blockchain can be effectively used to provide and substantiate a massive framework for public management and this technology can be utilized at the micro, meso, and macro tiers. This distributed ledger technology has the power and resources to make government operations smooth and seamless. Be it in terms of enhancing the execution and delivery of public services or to establish a higher level of trust, blockchain sure does work for the best. The features of data protection and security, reduced manpower needs, high levels of transparency, and improved robustness are what makes it a great platform to intersect with public governance. In 2020, China had initiated the blockchain-based service network (BSN) to support public blockchain and in 2017, the USA signed a contract with IBM Watson Health to collaborate on blockchain systems to transmit health data safely [8].

- *Transportation*: The sector of transportation and automobiles can derive quite a few benefits from blockchain. Be it for smart delivery tracking, scalable and immediate solutions for validating orders, and what not; blockchain has the potential to resolve these problems with utmost efficiency. It can help as a trustworthy data verification tool in transport and logistics, aid in tracking and monitoring fleets of trucks, accidents, routes, etc. The fact that it helps reduce time and involves a faster and straightforward execution process is what adheres to the successful integration of blockchain with the transportation sector [9]. It can be clearly observed that blockchain is truly contributing towards the evolution of transportation industries by accelerating its efficiency and customer experience while diminishing costs. It improves the efficiency by enhancing delivery processes and by initiating steps to advance productivity levels, which in turn also strengthens the supply chain process. Therefore, transportation is definitely the perfect solution for the sophisticated and decentralized transportation services in the urban areas today.

- *Smart contracts*: In simple terms, smart contract are programs that are stored and leveraged on a blockchain system which are executed whenever certain conditions are met. They are ideally meant to automate the process of executing agreements such that each node miner can acquire the outcome at the earliest. Using smart contracts ensures that transactions are traceable, irreversible, and transparent. Ethereum-based smart contracts can be used to generate digitized token to carry out transactions [15]. The biggest highlight of smart contracts developed on blockchain is its feature to enable loyal transactions and agreement processes to be conducted between anonymous parties and groups without the requirements of a central legal authority or power.

- *Artificial Intelligence (AI)*: The combination of blockchain and AI is extremely powerful and has the capacity to upgrade the status quo of anything its being applied to. An integration of these two means that while AI can take care of processing and mining large datasets and discover patterns from experience, blockchain can contribute towards removing bugs and detecting fraudulent or malicious data. On the whole, the outcome would have improved business models, globalized and distributed validating systems, intelligent financing, and creative compliance systems when AI meets blockchain [16]. Companies like CertiK, located in New York, offer tools that are fueled by AI to safeguard blockchain-related applications by detecting any sort of security breaches, supervise data insights, and analyze the movement of crypto-based funds. This insinuating combination of strong technologies offers massive benefits including those of advanced security features, accessing and handling the data market, and optimized use of consuming energy.

- *Cyber security*: The discipline of cyber security is highly relevant in the 21st century world where we tend to thrive on social media and virtual platforms which have access to our personal information and details. In such circumstances, there are high chances of cyberattacks and crimes that can prove to be deleterious. The integration of blockchain technology with that of cyber security would lead to the development of integrity for software download, protection and safeguarded data transmission, decentralized technique of storing critical data, and mitigating denial of services attacks. It would conclusively cover the triad that consists of confidentiality, availability, and integrity [5,17].

- *Cloud/edge computation*: The relationship between blockchain and clod/edge computing is mutual and symbiotic. Edge computing, with its distributed

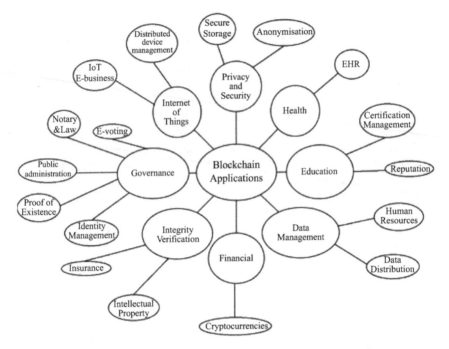

Figure 11.8   Blockchain uses in finance and non-finance applications

framework, can provide the framework for the nodes in blockchain to store the data while blockchain could derive the benefits of using a completely open cloud platform. This combo packed combination can lead to a platform that is perfect for a secure, scalable, and distributed avenue for IoT as well [24]. The balanced mix of blockchain and edge computation can be effectively utilized for various cryptocurrency-based applications, IoT in the industrial sector, healthcare, smart cities, and smart homes for automation purposed. Here too, the major highlighted feature is the safety and integrity of data being utilized across the various edge and cloud-based platforms through a distributed framework.

Figure 11.8 shows several types of applications which are relied on blockchain now a days.

11.9   Attacks and threats

Though blockchain is known for its security features, these systems are also prone to various security and integrity attacks externally. It could be in terms of the PoW (proof-of-work) consensus-based attacks like the 51% majority manipulation, delay or latency in consensus due to a distributed denial of service, pollution log, etc. [25]. One of the attacks is the selfish mining attack which is performed by the selfish miners to acquire rewards and returns or to waste the compute powers of the genuine participants and miners. In this case, the attacker would hold back some of the privately discovered blocks and would fork the chain on which they build further. They try to get the private chain to be longer than the actual one and the honest miners would unknowingly mine on the public chain. After the private chain becomes long enough, it gets published by the attacker and the efforts of the genuine miner are at waste. This consolidation and cumulation of power into the favor of the attacker is what undermines the decentralized nature of blockchain at large [26].

One of the other attacks is the DAO attack. DAO is simply a smart contract which is deployed on Ethereum and it basically executes a crowd funding platform. Though it seemed to be a promising and reliant application, one of the hackers brought to light the major flaw of DAO which was able to drain out millions of Ether into a specific private account leading to a massive panic. This was one of its kind and highlighted the grey areas that surround the world of cryptocurrency and blockchain systems [27].

The Border Gateway Protocol (BGP) Hijacking attack is one other malicious attack. BGP is a de-facto routing protocol that focuses on maintaining and regulating the transmission of IP packets to their respective sources. In order to interject the traffic in the network, hijackers often manipulate the routing of this protocol and gains control over the network operators. The fact that blockchain is a decentralized system which indicates that the entire system would be adversely affected in case of a BGP hijack event. Furthermore, even if the attack is detected or recognized, it costs a lot of money and computations to restore the system back to its altering configuration and calls for large amounts of manpower [28].

The type of attack that facilitates its attackers and hackers to grab away all of the incoming and outgoing connections of the victim, desolating the attacked from the peer network, is called the Eclipse attack. On successfully attacking, the attacker is capable of filtering and parsing through the victim's view of blockchain or cost up the compute power of the victim unnecessarily. The power extracted during the attack can also be used by the attacker to perform his/her own malicious activities. The botnet and infrastructural attacks come under the umbrella of the Eclipse attack [29].

Last but not the least is the liveness attack that has the potential to delay and interject latency pertaining to the confirmation time for as long as possible during the transaction period. This attack is carried out in three phases—preparation phase, transaction denial phase, and blockchain retarder phase. Ultimately, the attacker tends to build on the private chain so as to gain an undue advantage over the public chain. Following this, the attacker would publish the private chain of theirs to retard the growth of the original public chain [30,31].

11.10   Challenges and future trends

Blockchain, a revolutionary technology, is sure to exist and contribute to some of the major fields in the long run. Considered as the heart and soul of Web 3.0, the advancement in this technology seems to be approaching ahead of its time. Even though blockchain is often associated with cryptocurrencies, it no longer is the only field of relevance. Health sector, supply chain, transportation, finance, etc. are some of the many aspects in which blockchain has made ground breaking progress [32–34]. The blockchain market is growing at a rampant pace with the financial and insurance sectors leading the way. If you take a look at the current and possible future trends, it is very evident that blockchain technology is modifying the conventional financial system with around 90 countries already investing in central bank digital currencies. Furthermore, non-fungible tokens (NFT) have also been gaining increasing momentum over the last year or so and are sure to remain efficiently prevalent in the coming years [35,36]. NFT's have proven to be a great means of income generation for artists across the world through their virtual and digital art forms. One of the other leading trends which is likely to take a massive leap in the future is the Blockchain-as-a-Service (BaaS) concept with tech giants like Amazon and Microsoft already implementing the same. BaaS will not only act as a cloud service but will also provide the added benefits of blockchain in terms of scalability and efficiency. Furthermore, blockchain is likely to grow a fanbase for enhancing social networking and e-commerce in the coming years [37].

Blockchain, without doubt, is one of the most significant technical developments that has impacted the society at a positive level over the last few years with an exponential growth in its adaptation [33]. However, this revolutionary industry also poses challenges and hurdles. Large level scalability continues to be a challenge for blockchain as it does offer difficulty in managing many users at a time which severely affects the processing power and speed of transactions [34,38]. Blockchain also tends to lack a collection of regulations to be followed globally leading to a volatile base and higher chances of manipulation [39]. Lack of awareness in technology is also one of the major challenges that often tends to leave blockchain as a distant dream [40].

11.11 Conclusion

Blockchain is a novel technology that definitely has a massive scope in the present and future generations but also has quite a number of challenges to overcome and hustle through. This decentralized, transactional ledger storage base has enhanced and led to developments across the globe. It supports users to validate, preserve/store, and synchronize the contents of a data sheet which is mined and worked upon by various users. Due to the vast and enormous possibilities of applications, it is expected that blockchain will complement in trusted transactions. The emergence of Bitcoins is what gained maximum attention for blockchain and its framework. This chapter provides a detailed analysis and survey of what is blockchain, its architecture and framework, the history and evolution of blockchain, its types, its applications, and possible attacks.

References

[1] F. Casino, T. K. Dasaklis, and C. Patsakis, "A systematic literature review of blockchain-based applications: current status classification and open issues," *Telematics Informat.*, vol. 36, pp. 55–81, 2019.

[2] J.A. Jaoude and R. George Saade, "Blockchain applications–usage in different domains," *IEEE Access*, vol. 7, pp. 45360–45381, 2019.

[3] V. Chang, P. Baudier, H. Zhang, *et al.*, "How blockchain can impact financial services – the overview, challenges and recommendations from expert interviewees," *Technol. Forecast. Soc. Change*, vol. 158, 2020, Article 120166.

[4] C.S. Tang and L.P. Veelenturf, "The strategic role of logistics in the industry 4.0 era," *Transport. Res. E Logist. Transport. Rev.*, vol. 129, pp. 1–11, 2019.

[5] C.M.S. Ferreira, R.A.R. Oliveira, J.S. Silva, *et al.*, "Blockchain for machine-to-machine interaction in Industry 4.0," in *Blockchain Technology for Industry 4.0*, Springer, Singapore, 2020, pp. 99–116.

[6] P. Sandner, A. Lange, and P. Schulden, "The role of the CFO of an industrial company: an analysis of the impact of blockchain technology," *Future Internet*, vol. 12, no. 8, p. 128, 2020.

[7] M. Andoni, V. Robu, D. Flynn, *et al.*, "Blockchain technology in the energy sector: a systematic review of challenges and opportunities," *Renew. Sustain. Energy Rev.*, vol. 100, pp. 143–174, 2019.

[8] P. Dutta, T.M. Choi, S. Somani, and R. Butala, "Blockchain technology in supply chain operations: applications, challenges and research opportunities," *Transp. Res. Part E: Log. Transp. Rev.*, vol. 142, p. 102067, 2020.

[9] B. Esmaeilian, J. Sarkis, K. Lewis, *et al.*, "Blockchain for the future of sustainable supply chain management in Industry 4.0," *Resour. Conserv. Recycl.*, vol. 163, 2020, Article 105064.

[10] Golosova, J. and Romanovs, A., "The advantages and disadvantages of the blockchain technology," in *2018 IEEE 6th Workshop on Advances in Information, Electronic and Electrical Engineering (AIEEE)*. IEEE, 2018, pp. 1–6.

[11] A.K. Tyagi, S. Chandrasekaran, and N. Sreenath, "Blockchain technology: a new technology for creating distributed and trusted computing environment," in *2022 International Conference on Applied Artificial Intelligence and Computing (ICAAIC)*, 2022, pp. 1348–1354, doi:10.1109/ICAAIC53929.2022.9792702.

[12] A.K. Tyagi and A. Abraham (eds.), *Recent Trends in Blockchain for Information Systems Security and Privacy,* 1st ed., CRC Press, 2021. https://doi.org/10.1201/9781003139737

[13] A.K. Tyagi, G. Rekha, and N. Sreenath (eds.), *Opportunities and Challenges for Blockchain Technology in Autonomous Vehicles*. IGI Global, 2021. 10.4018/978-1-7998-3295-9

[14] J.W. Leng, G. Ruan, P. Jiang, *et al.*, "Blockchain-empowered sustainable manufacturing and product lifecycle management in industry 4.0: a survey," *Renew. Sustain. Energy Rev.*, vol. 132, 2020, Article 110112.

[15]   G. Zyskind, O. Nathan, and A.S. Pentland, "Decentralizing privacy: using blockchain to protect personal data," in *Proceedings of the IEEE Security and Privacy Workshops*, pp. 180–184, May 2015.

[16]   J.J. Xu, "Are blockchains immune to all malicious attacks?", *Financial Innov.*, vol. 2, no. 1, pp. 1–9, 2016.

[17]   Y. Guo and C. Liang, "Blockchain application and outlook in the banking industry," *Financial Innov.*, vol. 2, p. 24, 2016.

[18]   A. Alketbi, Q. Nasir, and M. A. Talib, "Blockchain for government, services—use cases, security benefits and challenges," in *Proceedings of the 15th Learning and Technology Conference (LT)*, Feb. 2018, pp. 112–119.

[19]   S. Seebacher and R. Schüritz, "Blockchain technology as an enabler of service systems: a structured literature review," in *Proceedings of the 8th International Conference on Exploring Service Science*, 2017, pp. 12–23.

[20]   R. Hull, V.S. Batra, Y.M. Chen, A. Deutsch, F.F.T. Heath, and V. Vianu, "Towards a shared ledger business collaboration language based on data-aware processes," in Q. Z. Sheng, E. Stroulia, S. Tata, and S. Bhiri, (eds.), *Service-Oriented Computing (Lecture Notes in Computer Science)*, vol. 9936, Cham, Switzerland: Springer, 2016, pp. 18–36, doi: 10.1007/978-3-319-46295-0_2.

[21]   A. Kosba, A. Miller, E. Shi, Z. Wen, and C. Papamanthou, "Hawk: the blockchain model of cryptography and privacy-preserving smart contracts," in *Proceedings of the IEEE Symposium on Security and Privacy (SP)*, May 2016, pp. 839–858.

[22]   G. Zyskind, O. Nathan, and A.S. Pentland, "Decentralizing privacy: using blockchain to protect personal data," in *Proceedings of the IEEE Security and Privacy Workshops*, May 2015, pp. 180–184.

[23]   J.J. Xu, "Are blockchains immune to all malicious attacks?" *Financial Innov.*, vol. 2, no. 1, pp. 1–9, 2016, doi: 10.1186/s40854-016-0046-5.

[24]   M.M. Crossan and M. Apaydin, "A multi-dimensional framework of organizational innovation: a systematic review of the literature," *J. Manage. Stud.*, vol. 47, no. 6, pp. 1154–1191, 2010.

[25]   D. Tapscott and A. Tapscott, "The impact of blockchain goes beyond financial services," *Harvard Business Review*, 2016. https://hbr.org/2016/05/the-impact-of-the-blockchain-goesbeyond-financial-services

[26]   C. Wood, B. Winton, K. Carter, S. Benkert, D. Lisa, and B. Joseph, "How blockchain technology can enhance EHR operability," in *Proc. Ark Invest Gem*, 2016, pp. 1–13.

[27]   N. Kshetri, "Blockchain's roles in strengthening cybersecurity and protecting privacy," *Telecommun. Policy*, vol. 41, no. 10, pp. 1027–1038, 2017.

[28]   R. Cole, M. Stevenson, and J. Aitken, "Blockchain technology: implications for operations and supply chain management," *Supply Chain Manage, Int. J.*, vol. 24, no. 4, pp. 469–483, 2019.

[29]   N. Kshetri and E. Loukoianova, "Blockchain adoption in supply chain networks in Asia," *IT Prof.*, vol. 21, no. 1, pp. 11–15, 2019.

[30]   H. Kakavand, N.K. De Sevres, and B. Chilton, "The blockchain revolution: an analysis of regulation and technology related to distributed ledger technologies," *Social Sci. Res. Netw. (SSRN)*, New York, NY, Tech. Rep. 2849251, 2017, pp. 1–27, doi: 10.2139/ssrn.2849251.

[31]   T. Ahram, A. Sargolzaei, S. Sargolzaei, J. Daniels, and B. Amaba, "Blockchain technology innovations," in *Proceedings of the IEEE Technology, Engineering, Management Conference (TEMSCON)*, Jun. 2017, pp. 137–141.

[32]   S. Mondal, K. P. Wijewardena, S. Karuppuswami, N. Kriti, D. Kumar, and P. Chahal, "Blockchain inspired RFID-based information architecture for food supply chain," *IEEE Internet Things J.*, vol. 6, no. 3, pp. 5803–5813, 2019.

[33]   J. Mendling, I. Weber, W.V. Aalst, *et al.*, "Blockchains for business process management–challenges and opportunities," *ACM Trans. Manage. Inf. Syst.*, vol. 9, no. 1, pp. 1–16, 2018, doi: 10.1145/3183367.

[34]   J. Poon and T. Dryja, "The bitcoin lightning network: Scalable off-chain instant payments," in *Proc. Coin Rivet*, 2016, pp. 1–59. [Online]. Available: https://coinrivet.com/research/papers/the-bitcoinlightningnetwork-scalable-off-chain-instant-payments/

[35]   M. Pilkington, "Blockchain technology: principles and applications," in F. Xavier Olleros and M. Zhegu (eds.), *Research Handbook on Digital Transformations*. Edward Elgar, 2016.

[36]   A. Lazarovich, "Invisible ink: Blockchain for data privacy," *Massachusetts Inst. Technol.*, Cambridge, MA, *Tech. Rep.*, 2015, pp. 81–85.

[37]   R. Kestenbaum, "Why bitcoin is important for your business." *Forbes*, 2017. https://www.forbes.com/sites/richardkestenbaum/2017/03/14/why-bitcoinis-important-for-yourbusiness/3/#2da6d4c72b3b

[38]   E. Munsing, J. Mather, and S. Moura, "Blockchains for decentralized optimization of energy resources in microgrid networks," in *Proceeding of the IEEE Conference on Control Technology and Applications* (CCTA), Aug. 2017, pp. 2164–2171.

[39]   R. Ali, J. Barrdear, R. Clews, and J. Southgate, "Innovations in payment technologies and the emergence of digital currencies," *Quart. Bull.*, vol. 53, no. 4, pp. 262–275, 2014.

[40]   Y. Li, B. Wang, and D. Yang, "Research on supply chain coordination based on block chain technology and customer random demand," *Discrete Dyn. Nature Soc.*, vol. 2019, pp. 1–10, 2019, doi: 10.1155/2019/4769870.

Chapter 12

Blockchain technologies in healthcare social media computing: trends and opportunities

Surendra Kumar Shukla¹, Devesh Pratap Singh² and Bhasker Pant²

Abstract

Social media has influenced almost all computing domains including information communication. The most benefited areas are entrepreneurs, startups, and other business domains. Social media has not only transformed the Business, rather, sectors such as healthcare are equally benefited to a large extent. The "idea generation" by intellectuals (active in social sites) is a fundamental source of social media to address enormous issues of the society. Nevertheless, having a tremendous potential for social media this field is not harnessed up to the maximum extent due to the limitations imposed in terms of identity fraud, misinformation, and fake news. To address the above breaches, blockchain technology which is well established in the computing domain would be beneficial to a large extent. Blockchain technology which is known for transparency, ensuring confidentiality, and security have scope to alleviate the capabilities of social media computing.

Keywords: Social media; Blockchain; Healthcare; Disease; Security

12.1 Introduction

Blockchain technology has enormous applications in distinct fields including healthcare, business, agriculture, and so on [1,2]. These fields are benefiting and are growing exponentially. Another research area which is trending is social computing. Social media enables finding the vital opinions related to the novel diseases like COVID. Interestingly, knowing the people's sentiments, tracing the liking, and dislikings of individuals could be helpful to get the knowledge of related fields [3]. These aspects further help to motivate the people to participate in preparing health policies, awareness, clinical trials, etc. Social media enables distinct individuals of

¹Department of Computer Engineering, SVKM'S NMIMS MPSTME Shirpur Campus, India
²Department of CSE, Graphic Era Deemed to be University, India

diverse fields to interact and generate new ideas. In the healthcare sector, such virtual groups exchange their novel thoughts to cope up with life-threatening diseases by exploiting conventional, historical and novel approaches [4]. Conversely, in some social sites, fraudulent people spread fake news related to health using personal, political, or unethical business tactics. Keys findings indicate that the fake news disseminate faster in social sites than the factual contents, which is a serious concern to be addressed under the blockchain technology. One of the key challenges is to identify the source of fake news, and the concerned person. To address such challenges, analysis of text further labeling under machine learning approaches looks prominent to mark such fake news. In its initial phase, blockchain technology has been extensively used in the area of bitcoin cryptocurrency. And it has got recognition in society by Bitcoin and all other cryptocurrencies [5,6].

In this chapter, an in-depth analysis has been performed related to the challenges of applying blockchain technology to harness the true potential of social media under the healthcare sector. Now the notable question would be how social computing and healthcare are related to each other, and how they could help to grow in the presence of blockchain technology. It could be viewed as: the information of a patient could be gathered from various sources employing IoT especially from wearable devices. The patient associates itself with various apps to make itself fit. The positive information (weight loss/gain) and negative information (high level of blood pressure) automatically kept stored to the said wearable devices [7]. Therefore, data is available through social computing IOT devices, only needs to be added in the blockchain architecture. The data stored in the blockchain would be analyzed to find the general and specific trends of the patients health [8].

Moving to healthcare, blockchain ensures that the patients records should not be tempered in case the history of the patient is developed. The said data could not be modified further by anyone in the system [9]. The blockchain infrastructure is supported by the commodity hardware available at the hospitals. The researchers could easily access the saved records for suggesting various therapies, medicines, and new disorders discovered in the process of diagnosis and treatments. Blockchain saves the patients and service provider's resources and time for providing the quality treatment and medicines. In the similar context, blockchain has been extensively employed for clinical trials. Clinical trial is a method of knowing the effectiveness of a particular medicine for the contemporary novel disease. In the clinical trial process, scientists have to collect the data on varying parameters such as test results, total number of persons involved in the test, patient previous medical history, and other relevant information [10]. The authenticity of the data recorded by the scientists decides the effectiveness of the invented medicine for a particular disease. In the said whole process, blockchain could play a vital role in providing transparency and accuracy.

Social computing should bridge the gap between healthcare and the blockchain. On the one side, the healthcare aspects are discovered through the social groups and on the other side the collected knowledge should be applied to the blockchain [11]. There should be a filter which could clean the unwanted data collected from the social cities and applied to the blockchain. Healthcare providers, practitioners, and drug manufacturers are also part of social computing, who would certainly play a vital role for harnessing the potential of blockchain to move the healthcare facilities to the next level [12,13]. Furthermore, social computing would lead to addressing the challenges: awareness to be part of the clinical trials, traceability of the prescriptions/medications, and keeping the individual records safely.

The blockchain seemingly carries the opportunities in the healthcare sector in terms of tracing the fraud cases for getting the insurance claims/medical benefits, mitigating the record-keeping expenses, and reliably creating the jobs. Blockchain would especially be highly beneficial on tracing the medicines (provided during the medical emergencies), therapies, health equipment service charges, in the process of inhouse treatments of the patients [14,15]. Recording the Doctors medication history provided to the patient would be helpful to verify and trace the authenticity and ethical practices followed during the treatments. Consequently, the patients would have power in terms of better voice to tackle the fraudulent cases.

There are various domains where blockchain technology has been adopted. Some of the contemporary areas where the blockchain has got the maturity is illustrated in Figure 12.1.

This chapter communicates the following research information:

RI1: To explore the blockchain technology and its importance in healthcare considering social aspects.

RI2: To identify the potential of blockchain technology to explore the social computing in broader scope.

RI3: Exploring the trends of social media to leverage the blockchain computing.

RI4: To identify the opportunities of blockchain in the perspective of social computing applications.

RI5: To develop the blockchain-oriented social computing architecture in the presence of healthcare aspects.

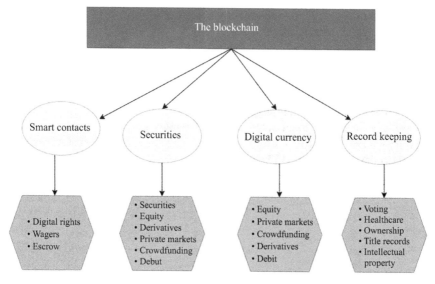

Figure 12.1   Benefits of blockchain: in a general perspective

12.2   Contemporary aspects of blockchain technology

The "cryptocurrency" which is also known as Bitcoin came into existence in 2008, since then numerous researchers have started exploring the Blockchain technology to a large extent [16]. Furthermore, over $8 trillion money was put into the blockchain technology by various companies related to finance, energy, healthcare, etc. [17]. Investors are not only interested in knowing the benefits of blockchain, rather various studies show researchers are also actively working on this technology to harness its true potential. Web of science data shows that more than 7,000 research articles are indexed in only a few years of time span.

Blockchain technology is essentially a decentralized connection of systems (peer-to-peer) that helps to maintain the ledger [18]. It means that data in the blockchain is not stored in a central database but maintained across the network/ nodes in the system [19]. Transactions performed under the blockchain technology are transparent in nature and are further verifiable. Third party intervention is not allowed in the blockchain approach. The key feature of blockchain technology is decentralization, where all the information is stored in a non-centralized manner with no centralized authority to control the said transactions. In blockchain, records are added for one time and cannot be edited without modifying the previous block. This could be done by taking the consent of all the blocks in the chain. This feature makes the blockchain a safe place to carry out business transactions.

Blocks of blockchains are linked (to one another) and secured through the cryptography techniques [20]. Blockchain technology was initially employed for the cryptocurrencies, contact of digital in nature, securing the financial records, and putting the ownership on the properties. Nevertheless, blockchain techniques have started expanding for the medical records, education, and medicine supply chain management. Blockchain technology could also be helpful for the area of the food supply chain as it provides the traceability further creating the trust among the food producers and the consumers.

The scope of blockchain in the medical field is broad, which is exponentially growing towards saving health records digitally, exploiting the health insurance domain and research in the field of biomedical and so on. Bitcoin is an example of a public blockchain, where the intervention of third parties is minimal [21]. Nevertheless, other blockchain might be more beneficial for the healthcare sector.

Melanie Swan has proposed three adoption phases of the blockchain. According to Swan, we are in the first phase, witnessing the transactions of cryptocurrency in our day-to-day life. The next phase Blockchain 2.0 would be realized in terms of digital contracts, records related to finance of common people, and ownership of the property. It is estimated that the Blockchain 3.0 will help in leveraging the medical field, education, and supply chain management domains. Blockchain has moved healthcare and social computing to a higher acceptance rate in society. Thus, the medical sector is highly dependent on blockchain technology. Furthermore, the data storage ability of blockchain eases the process of recording the patient's medical history such as diagnosis reports, pre-existing disease information, and measurements performed through the handheld sensors and IOT devices. A doctor when moving to

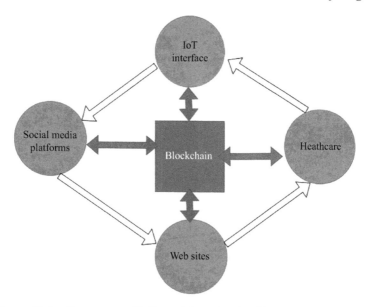

Figure 12.2   Ecosystem of IoT, social media, healthcare, and blockchain

practice for patients disease identification gets all medical data availed in prior that helps the diagnosis be accurate in less time consuming [22].

In its contemporary form, the blockchain is illustrated in Figure 12.2. It could be noted that blockchain applications are not only limited to the cryptocurrencies. Rather, it has been adopted as a tool to study various research fields such as IoT, Social media computing, online websites security, and so on. In view of security, to manipulate the data in the blockchain, the consent from all the blocks are necessary which makes it tamperproof. The transactions carried out in the blockchain are traceable easily.

12.3   Need of blockchain in social sectors

Past two decades social media has witnessed the single source of making the connections, information sharing, by the number of users. These users are also essentially the customers whose general information such as their liking, habits, daily routines, location visits, and connections would be prevalent for social computing which further benefits healthcare. The health service providers exploit social media to create their target audience for the clinical trials by putting their attractive advertisements related to health awareness and routine checkups in cost effective packages [23]. Nevertheless, privacy of the social media users is a prime concern to incorporate it with other computing domains. In such instances, blockchain could play a vital role by providing its decentralized security aspects which further help to protect the content and identity of its users. Although social computing platforms have the provision of end-to-end encryption to achieve the security goals.

However, when users bring and transfer its meta data along with the actual contents, the third party takes it as an opportunity to steal the personal information of the individuals. Thus, blockchains which have added security features could be used for purchasing and payment of contents in social media. Blockchain could address the key issues of social networks such as trolling, fake news detection, and further authentication.

Social networking involves a massive amount of computing resources where distinct peoples and related/unrelated organizations collaborate with each other of having the same or distinct interest/fields. The role of social networking is not limited to only liking or disliking, rather people provide their valuable reviews on a particular trending topic, citations to the posts, and invitations to particular groups for the information and knowledge sharing. The data collected and analyzed from these cites helps to find the in depth opinions of different groups about some topics especially to health and fitness. The content generated through social networking is tremendous which has to be transformed into knowledge by social computing and secured employing the blockchain technology [24].

Authentic monitoring of the trends in social networking sites could be resulted into the important highlights which might help to come to some fruitful conclusion like spread of a particular disease or the rumors about the medication in the market. This process would also help to find out mischievous entities to help the society to save from false disease information in the social healthcare system.

The power of social networking has been visualized in Figure 12.3. It could be noted in Figure 12.3 that thousands of millions of peoples are connected to each other for exchanging their thoughts, contents, and the metadata.

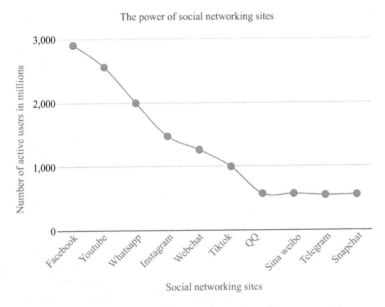

Figure 12.3   Trends of social networking sites. Source: *statista.com.*

There are various computing domains (sectors) where blockchain would play a vital role. All the areas where there is a need for an intermediary or central authority to keep track (and provide the ownership) the transactions/changes in the data, blockchain would be beneficial. Some of the areas where social elements involves/computing incur are: in money transfer, stocks, banks, insurance companies, elections, and for the implementation of government policies. These sectors are highly dependent on the central authority which leads to the chances of corruption, delay in transactions, risk of data security, and consistency. Therefore, a need for social computing, aware ownership, mathematically cross-verified transactions, and transparency further consistency to manage the social issues in a more effective manner.

The role of intermediary becomes ineffective when applying blockchain approaches in social media computing. The benefit of applying the blockchain is enormous. It helps in creating the cheaper systems as they do not involve elements who have to be paid for the services continuously [25].

Once the system is established considering the blockchain, it works autonomously further any intervention. In general, blockchain databases work in online mode, secured through cryptography, any organization/user could associate itself to the blockchain systems without incurring additional resources.

12.3.1   *Blockchain impact on social computing*

Invention of blockchain technology has created a curiosity whether the technology would make a revolution in the society or not. In various surveys, it is identified that the awareness about the blockchain in the society is not up to the matured level. Google search is also witnessed as it is found that they search the term bitcoin and blockchain; but knowing about these terms is not easy as the results found are very abstract. Although users are active on social media and share vital knowledge to each other. Therefore, a gap is identified where intellectuals are working towards the solutions of the social problems but are unaware how to harness the generated knowledge into the implementation. Here, the role of blockchain becomes vital to record the facts found in social media to further utilize for the growth of the society. There are various offerings from social media, such as verification of all the individuals registered online. Further, exploring the opportunities of finding new marketplaces [26]. The blockchain smart contracts could help to block the dissimilar content found in the social networking sites.

(i) Verifying online identities. (ii) Verification of marketplaces. (iii) Combining cryptocurrencies and blockchain technology. (iv) Cryptocurrency collectibles. (v) Blockchain smart contract blocks fake content.

12.4   Blockchain technology in the healthcare industry

Blockchain technology has improved the transparency and communication among the stakeholders (patients and healthcare service providers) [27]. There are some added advantages/scope of incorporating the blockchain technology in healthcare sectors. The well-known benefit is in managing the patient's medical records which are scattered in various medical sources such as at laboratories, hospitals, and at private clinics. The gap here identified is that the record is not placed in a common place. Therefore, availing the health records to the blockchain would help the researchers. It means, to provide quality health services, further transforming the traditional healthcare in structure blockchain is essential. Furthermore, the healthcare system is becoming patient centric which enables health services to be availed as needed at any time at any place with high patient care.

And, the patient could also provide the permissions to access the said records. This would also relieve the patients to carry the set of paper-based records (with dates) such as diagnosis results, prescriptions, medical advice, each time moving towards the consultations at various healthcare service providers. This would also ease the service providers to have a full medical history of the patent to provide better medical treatments. All the mentioned parameters would help to automate the process of providing the health insurances to the patents by just writing the smart contracts in blockchain. In Figure 12.4, it is witnessed that blockchain technology has impacted the healthcare industry by 11%. The most repetitive process of healthcare is "health information exchange" that wastes expensive health resources, consumes valuable time, and involves paperwork. This could be sorted out by blockchain that increases a patient's active involvement in health-related aspects.

The traditional healthcare system suffers in terms of data protection, patient information exchange, and paper centric insurance policies. These issues are addressed and eases through the blockchain.

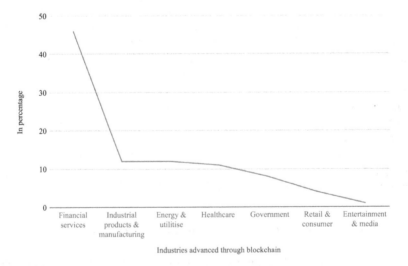

Figure 12.4   Industries that global executives think are most advanced in blockchain technology

12.4.1   Capabilities of blockchain technology in healthcare

Healthcare involves a range of services to be achieved through the blockchain. The blockchain technology enables the healthcare professionals to transfer the patient's medical records securely, ensuring and keeping the drug supply chain [28].

Figure 12.5 illustrates the number of research articles published in different research areas. It is witnessed that the healthcare research field is dominating other research areas. Thus, working towards healthcare would be beneficial to the social growth applying the blockchain technology.

There are various applications of blockchain technology in healthcare starting from the patient monitoring to drug discovery, clinical trials, supply chain management, insurance authentication etc. [29,30]. The first and foremost use of the blockchain is in storing the patient's information. Before starting any clinical trials, the information of the patient is recorded. The critical attributes/parameters of the information is their age, blood group, prior disease history, etc.

Furthermore, researchers could thoroughly examine and analyze the specific procedure performed to a number of patients. These patients are identified and selected from valid sources like from the nodes of the blockchain. The results of the analysis would be utilized by the drug manufacturers and they could address the medical issues of the said patent groups. As the data was found in real time, the effect of the medication could be monitored and specific instructions could be issued to the concerned individuals.

12.4.2   Healthcare security through blockchain

Healthcare security is one of the prominent concerns which deals with data security and prevents fraud activities. Furthermore, healthcare security has become

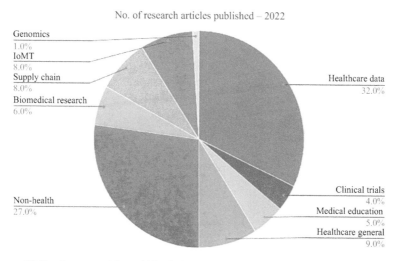

Figure 12.5   Opportunities of blockchain technology in the future of healthcare.
Source: *BMC Medicine.*

important to keep data secure and prevent criminal activities. Failure on keeping the healthcare records confidential would lead to various adverse consequences such as identity theft and disclosing of personal information.

In blockchain, security is a major concern, as attackers try to reverse the transactions, reflecting double-spend coins, and trying to absolute the transactions. Considering the security of blockchain, there are two ways where the healthcare sector might be inclined. Public blockchain and private blockchain. Public blockchain (where bitcoin is an obvious example) is an option for security; however, selecting the private blockchain has some added advantages. Therefore, moving towards the fully private blockchain might be a best alternative as here members of the blockchain are given the write permission, but others are restricted to the read permission only.

Thus, the private blockchain would successfully attain its objectives of – Keeping the patents medical record safe, updating the balances, updating the blockchain rules, etc. Since the validating process of blockchain is done by the known individuals there is no risk from the estimated 51% attackers.

12.5 Healthcare social media computing architecture

The literature studied in previous sections resulted in healthcare social computing architecture which is illustrated in Figure 12.6. It is found that individuals are connected through software (Healthcare apps) and Hardware (Wearable devices like watches). These interfaces lead the users to exchange the content (health and other data) to the social networking sites. These sites further generate numerous data in the form of comments, discussions resulting in the information. The information generated by the social networking sites are further used by the healthcare providers, hospitals, and clinical trial scientists. The data is secured through the

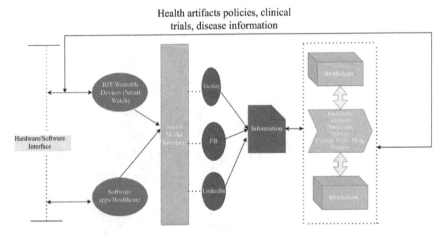

Figure 12.6 Proposed healthcare social media computing architecture

blockchain technology and further fed back to the IoT devices and software platforms. Proposed healthcare social architecture gets refined over time and more fruitful information is generated for the users. The proposed feedback loop provides the opportunities of providing better health services to the patients. The information is also useful in general to society for taking precautions in case of the spread of a particular disease.

Together, IoT, social computing, blockchain strengthens the healthcare sector. Persons are getting the authenticated information. People are exchanging the content in a highly confidential environment. Healthcare professionals have all the history of patients to provide the better treatments.

12.6   Discussion

The literature detailed above have resulted in the interested findings: together, social media (by proving the tremendous amount of content), healthcare (individuals with various health concerns), and blockchain (providing the security and authenticity to the content and personal records of the individuals) have the capability to emerge as a new era to transform society. It is noted from various research findings that cryptocurrency is going to affect the social media environment and further user experiences in the coming future. Additionally, crowdfunding for the benefits of needy patients are going to be transformed and conventional sites are going to be obsolete in coming years. The blockchain would maximize the peer-to-peer (P2P) sales to a next level.

It is identified that the social networks which are in existence and are coming in the society have a decentralized view. It means, each social site has their own target audience. These audiences are connected to the social sites with their own objectives. However, their goals intersect at some points. A person attached to a social site which deals with searching or changing jobs also creates posts related to happiness and health issues. On the other hand, a dedicated social site related to the personal and political aspects also provides the trends related to the health issues. Therefore, there is a scope of having social computing to collect the relevant information from the various social sites and add them to the relevant blockchain. That blockchain would dedicatedly provide the fruitful information relevant to a social issue, at the same time fulfilling the authenticity and hiding the personal identity of the individuals.

12.7   Conclusion

Although blockchain technology is in a semi-mature stage, still we are witnessing its benefits in day-to-day life, especially in banking and the medical field. The blockchain disruptions lead to the access of huge amounts of medical data (anonymous individuals) further helps in creating the drugs, Furthermore, creating health insurance trustworthiness in terms of incurred cost, and development/revision of health policies. Similarly, the health information is provided to the patient's hand further allowing them to provide it to needy institutions with certain conditions like finding a vaccine for a particular disease, simultaneously in a limited time frame. The patients could exploit the medical records by sharing to the trustworthy social groups and use it for getting the general trend about a particular disease. Together, patients, social groups, computing, healthcare providers and blockchain could move healthcare to an advanced level finally to the new era.

References

[1] Hisseine, M.A., Chen, D., and Yang, X. The application of blockchain in social media: a systematic literature review. *Applied Science*, 2022, 12, 6567. https://doi.org/10.3390/app12136567.

[2] Hussien, H.M., Yasin, S.M.D., Udzir, N.I., Hafez Ninggal, M.I., and Salman, S. Blockchain technology in the healthcare industry: trends and opportunities. *Journal of Industrial Information Integration*, 22, 2021, 100217, https://doi.org/10.1016/j.jii.2021.100217, ISSN 2452-414X.

[3] Radanović, I. and Likić, R. Opportunities for use of blockchain technology in medicine. *Applied Health Economics and Health Policy*, 16, 2018, 583–590. https://doi.org/10.1007/s40258-018-0412-8

[4] Dobson D. The 4 Types of Blockchain Networks Explained: ILTA. https://www.iltanet.org/blogs/deborah-dobson/2018/02/13/the-4-types-of-blockchain-networks-explained?ssopc=1. Accessed 19 Apr 2018.

[5] Haleem, A., Javaid, M., Singh, R.P., Suman, R., and Rab, S. Blockchain technology applications in healthcare: an overview. *International Journal of Intelligent Networks*, 2, 2021, 130–139, https://doi.org/10.1016/j.ijin.2021.09.005, ISSN 2666-6030.

[6] Faisal, M., Sadia, H., Ahmed, T., and Javed, N. Blockchain technology for healthcare record management. In: *Pervasive Healthcare*. Hershey, PA: IGI Global, 2022, pp. 255–286.

[7] Vyas, S., Shukla K., Vinod, S.G., and Prasad, A. (eds.), *Blockchain Technology: Exploring Opportunities, Challenges, and Applications [online]*. Boca Raton: CRC Press, 2022. ISBN 9780367685584. Available from: doi:https://doi.org/10.1201/9781003138082

[8] Vivekanadam, B. Analysis of recent trend and applications in block chain technology. *Journal of ISMAC*, 2(04), 2020, 200–206.

[9] Poongodi, T., Sujatha, R., Sumathi, D., Suresh, P., and Balamurugan, B. Blockchain in social networking. In: *Cryptocurrencies and Blockchain Technology Applications*. Hoboken, NJ: John Wiley & Sons, Ltd., 2020, pp. 55–76, Chapter 4.

[10] Abad-Segura, E., Infante-Moro, A., González-Zamar, M.D., and López-Meneses, E. Blockchain technology for secure accounting management: research trends analysis. *Mathematics*, 9(7), 2021, 1631, https://doi.org/10.3390/math9141631.

[11] Xiong, H., Dalhaus, T., Wang, P., and Huang, J. Blockchain technology for agriculture: applications and rationale. *Frontiers in Blockchain*, 3, 2020, 7, doi: 10.3389/fbloc.2020.00007

[12] Gad, A.G., Mosa, D.T., Abualigah, L., and Abohany, A.A. Emerging trends in blockchain technology and applications: a review and outlook. *Journal of King Saud University – Computer and Information Sciences*, 34(9), 2022, 6719–6742, https://doi.org/10.1016/j.jksuci.2022.03.007, ISSN 1319-1578.

[13] Javaid, M., Haleem, A., Singh, R.P., Khan, S., and Suman, R. Blockchain technology applications for Industry 4.0: a literature-based review. *Blockchain: Research and Applications*, 2(4), 2021, 100027, https://doi.org/10.1016/j.bcra.2021.100027, ISSN 2096-7209.

[14] Giungato, P., Rana, R., Tarabella, A., and Tricase, C. Current trends in sustainability of bitcoins and related blockchain technology. *Sustainability*, 9, 2017, 2214, https://doi.org/10.3390/su9122214

[15] Elbashbishy, T.S., Ali, G.G., and El-adaway, I.H. Blockchain technology in the construction industry: mapping current research trends using social network analysis and clustering, *Construction Management and Economics*, 40 (5), 2022, 406–427, doi: 10.1080/01446193.2022.2056216

[16] Singh, J. Artificial intelligence and blockchain technologies for smart city. In: *Book Title: Intelligent Green Technologies for Sustainable Smart Cities*. Scrivener Publishing, Wiley.

[17] Prakash, R., Anoop, V.S., and Asharaf, S. Blockchain technology for cybersecurity: a text mining literature analysis. *International Journal of Information Management Data Insights*, 2(2), 2022, 100112, https://doi.org/10.1016/j.jjimei.2022.100112, ISSN 2667-0968.

[18] Zhang, Y. and Zhang, C. Improving the application of blockchain technology for financial security in supply chain integrated business intelligence. *Security and Communication Networks*, 2022, 2022, 8, Article ID 4980893, https://doi.org/10.1155/2022/4980893

[19] Verma, S. and Sheel, A. Blockchain for government organizations: past, present and future. *Journal of Global Operations and Strategic Sourcing*, 15 (3), 2022, 406–430, https://doi.org/10.1108/JGOSS-08-2021-0063

[20] Mareddy, S. and Gupta, D. Analysis of Twitter data for identifying trending domains in blockchain technology. In: Smys, S., Bestak, R., Palanisamy, R., Kotuliak, I. (eds.), *Computer Networks and Inventive Communication Technologies. Lecture Notes on Data Engineering and Communications Technologies*, vol. 75. Singapore: Springer, 2022, https://doi.org/10.1007/978-981-16-3728-5_49

[21] Tibrewal, I., Srivastava, M., and Tyagi, A.K. (2022). Blockchain technology for securing cyber-infrastructure and Internet of Things networks. In: Tyagi, A.K., Abraham, A., Kaklauskas, A. (eds.), *Intelligent Interactive Multimedia Systems for e-Healthcare Applications*. Singapore: Springer, 2022, https://doi.org/10.1007/978-981-16-6542-4_17

[22] Kumar, T. and Kaur, S. Blockchain technology: present and future perspectives. In: *Applications, Challenges, and Opportunities of Blockchain Technology in Banking and Insurance*. Hershey, PA: IGI Global, 2022; pp. 258–265.

[23] Saeed, H., Malik, H., Bashir, U., *et al.* Blockchain technology in healthcare: a systematic review. *PLoS One*, 17(4), 2022, e0266462.

[24] Jaya, S., and Latha, M. Applications of IoT and blockchain technologies in healthcare: detection of cervical cancer using machine learning approaches. In: *Internet of Things based sMarcht Healthcare*. New York, NY: Springer, 2022;pp. 351–377.

[25] Lohmer, J., Ribeiro da Silva, E., and Lasch, R. Blockchain technology in operations & supply chain management: a content analysis. *Logistics Research*, 14, 2021, 6192.

[26] Nehme, E., El Sibai, R., Abdo, J.B., Taylor, A.R., and Demerjian, J. Converged AI IoT and blockchain technologies: a conceptual ethics framework. *AI Ethics*, 2, 2021, 12–13.

[27] Rehman, A., Abbas, S., Khan, M.A., Ghazal, T.M., Adnan, K.M., and Mosavi, A. A secure healthcare 5.0 system based on blockchain technology entangled with federated learning technique. *Computers in Biology and Medicine*, 150, 2022, 106019.

[28] Kuzior, A. and Sira, M. A bibliometric analysis of blockchain technology research using VOSviewer. *Sustainability*, 14, 2022, 8206.

[29] Anoop, V.S. and Asharaf, S. Integrating artificial intelligence and blockchain for enabling a trusted ecosystem for healthcare sector. In: Chakraborty, C. and Khosravi, M.R., (eds.) *Intelligent Healthcare*. Singapore: Springer, https://doi.org/10.1007/978-981-16-8150-9_13

[30] Polara, V., Bhatt, P., Patel, D., and Rathod, K. Blockchain technology in application development and associated challenges. In: Pandian, A.P., Fernando, X., Haoxiang, W., (eds.) *Computer Networks, Big Data and IoT. Lecture Notes on Data Engineering and Communications Technologies*, vol. 117. Singapore: Springer, https://doi.org/10.1007/978-981-19-0898-9_2

Chapter 13

Conclusion and wrap-up

*Robin Singh Bhadoria[1], Neetesh Saxena[2] and
Bharti Nagpal[3]*

This book primarily discusses the different security framework trends and future opportunities in the social media-computing.

Chapter 1 significantly points out the issues in online social media (OSM) decentralization of social services and it could be extended with applications in intelligent systems based on IoT, cloud, and social media analytics.

Chapter 2 briefs out the importance distributed ledger-based payment infrastructure, which helps in improvement payment with business-to-business marketplace for developing trust formation. This chapter could be a role model in terms of guidelines and recommendations in developing trust-based system for replacing the third party transaction in future.

Chapter 3 describes the different types of social networks and its analysis. It also points out the factors which are affecting the design for social networks. The future scope of this chapter can be extended towards healthcare, social engineering in epidemiology, terrorism, and counterterrorism activities.

Chapter 4 points out the security issues in social networking platforms regarding different attacks to steal the users' personal information like identity and location. It provides the several security risks affecting internet users. This chapter could be extended into theoretical understanding of the work in terms of Social Networking Sites (SNS).

Chapter 5 presents with the insights for smart contracts-based high level programming like solidity. The role of Ethereum Virtual Machine (EVM) can be utilized to protect privacy in the decentralized social network. The work presented in this chapter can be extended with gaming technology to prediction and make better decisions in controlling the multimedia applications.

Chapter 6 mentions different schemes and strategies for secure computation in blockchain privacy-provisioning solutions. The application of the work presented

[1]Department of Computer Engineering & Applications, GLA University, Mathura, India
[2]School of Computer Science and Informatics, Cardiff University, UK
[3]Department of Computer Engineering, NSUT East Campus (Formerly Ambedkar Institute of Advanced Communication Technologies & Research), India

in this chapter can be found in smart social media ecosystem like know your customer (KYC) implementation model.

Chapter 7 points out different aspect of blockchain technology and its role in handling issues and challenges using semantic technology and knowledge graph. The extended work application can be seen in the area of manufacturing and unmanned aerial vehicles in industry.

Chapter 8 clearly depicts the application of 5G mobile networks as emerging area with blockchain technology. 5G applications have evolved significantly including voice, video, wireless, information access, and social interaction networks. And, blockchain helps in lowering transaction costs and communication delay while facilitating secure multimedia communication between end-users.

Chapter 9 discusses the role of IoT and blockchain-based framework to secure intellectual property (IP). The work demonstrated the different trends and approaches with the advancements in an IoT environment and platform.

Chapter 10 presents the state-of-art of blockchain architecture for voting-caste systems. Also, discusses the fundamental principles and features of the blockchain architecture are explained in the context of the social opinion vote-caste system.

Chapter 11 discusses the potential applications in the field of next-generation based computing for Industry 5.0 digital society, smart cities data implications, and intelligent transportation system.

Chapter 12 presents the aspects of social media computing with respect to healthcare sector and the work can also be extended in particular disease detection model, record system in healthcare 4.0, and related medical sectors.

Further Reading

[1] Chen, Y., Li, Q., and Wang, H., 2018. Towards trusted social networks with blockchain technology. *arXiv preprint arXiv:1801.02796.*

[2] Ciriello, R., Beck, R., and Thatcher, J., 2018. The paradoxical effects of blockchain technology on social networking practices. *Available at SSRN 3920002.*

[3] Sivasankar, G.A., 2022. Study of blockchain technology, ai and digital networking in metaverse. *IRE Journals, 5*(8), pp. 110–115.

[4] Mnif, E., Mouakhar, K., and Jarboui, A., 2021. Blockchain technology awareness on social media: Insights from twitter analytics. *The Journal of High Technology Management Research, 32*(2), p. 100416.

[5] Oguntegbe, K.F., Di Paola, N., and Vona, R., 2022. Communicating responsible management and the role of blockchain technology: social media analytics for the luxury fashion supply chain. *The TQM Journal, 35*, pp. 446–469.

[6] Paul, S., Joy, J.I., Sarker, S., Ahmed, S., and Das, A.K., 2019, June. Fake news detection in social media using blockchain. In *2019 7th International Conference on Smart Computing & Communications (ICSCC)* (pp. 1–5). IEEE.

[7] Nicoli, N., Louca, S., and Iosifidis, P., 2022. Social media, news media, and the democratic deficit. Can the blockchain make a difference? *tripleC: Communication, Capitalism and Critique, 20*(2), pp. 163–178.

[8] Ush Shahid, I., Anjum, M.T., Hossain Miah Shohan, M.S., Tasnim, R., and Al-Amin, M., 2021, December. Authentic facts: a blockchain based solution for reducing fake news in social media. In *2021 4th International Conference on Blockchain Technology and Applications* (pp. 121–127).

[9] Poongodi, T., Sujatha, R., Sumathi, D., Suresh, P., and Balamurugan, B., 2020. Blockchain in social networking. In *Cryptocurrencies and Blockchain Technology Applications* (pp. 55–76). New York, NY: Wiley.

[10] Zhu, X. and Badr, Y., 2018, July. Fog computing security architecture for the Internet of Things using blockchain-based social networks. In *2018 IEEE International Conference on Internet of Things (iThings) and IEEE Green Computing and Communications (GreenCom) and IEEE Cyber, Physical and Social Computing (CPSCom) and IEEE Smart Data (SmartData)* (pp. 1361–1366). IEEE.

[11] Ahmed, J., Yildirim, S., Nowostaki, M., Ramachandra, R., Elezaj, O., and Abomohara, M., 2020, March. GDPR compliant consent driven data protection in online social networks: a blockchain-based approach. In *2020 3rd International Conference on Information and Computer Technologies (ICICT)* (pp. 307–312). IEEE.

[12]   Hasan, H.R. and Salah, K., 2018. Proof of delivery of digital assets using blockchain and smart contracts. *IEEE Access, 6,* pp. 65439–65448.

[13]   Kripa, M., Nidhin Mahesh, A., Ramaguru, R., and Amritha, P.P., 2021. Blockchain framework for social media DRM based on secret sharing. In *Information and Communication Technology for Intelligent Systems: Proceedings of ICTIS 2020,* vol. 1 (pp. 451–458). Singapore:Springer.

[14]   Shahbazi, Z. and Byun, Y.C., 2022. NLP-based digital forensic analysis for online social network based on system security. *International Journal of Environmental Research and Public Health, 19*(12), p. 7027.

[15]   Dhall, S., Dwivedi, A.D., Pal, S.K. and Srivastava, G., 2021. Blockchain-based framework for reducing fake or vicious news spread on social media/messaging platforms. *Transactions on Asian and Low-Resource Language Information Processing, 21*(1), pp. 1–33.

[16]   Yi, H., 2021. Secure social internet of things based on post-quantum blockchain. *IEEE Transactions on Network Science and Engineering, 9*(3), pp. 950–957.

[17]   Matta, M., Lunesu, I., and Marchesi, M., 2015, June. Bitcoin spread prediction using social and web search media. In *UMAP Workshops* (pp. 1–10).

[18]   Mai, F., Bai, Q., Shan, J., Wang, X.S., and Chiang, R.H., 2015. The impacts of social media on Bitcoin performance. In *ICIS2015 Proceedings* (pp. 1–46).

[19]   Gill, S.S., Tuli, S., Xu, M., *et al.,* 2019. Transformative effects of IoT, Blockchain and Artificial Intelligence on cloud computing: evolution, vision, trends and open challenges. *Internet of Things, 8,* p. 100118.

[20]   Alfa, A.A., Alhassan, J.K., Olaniyi, O.M., and Olalere, M., 2021. Blockchain technology in IoT systems: current trends, methodology, problems, applications, and future directions. *Journal of Reliable Intelligent Environments, 7*(2), pp. 115–143.

[21]   Schinckus, C., 2020. The good, the bad and the ugly: an overview of the sustainability of blockchain technology. *Energy Research & Social Science, 69,* p. 101614.

[22]   Ba, C.T., Zignani, M., Gaito, S., and Rossi, G.P., 2021. The effect of cryptocurrency price on a blockchain-based social network. In *Complex Networks & Their Applications IX: Volume 1, Proceedings of the Ninth International Conference on Complex Networks and Their Applications COMPLEX NETWORKS 2020* (pp. 581–592). Springer International Publishing.

[23]   Agarwal, B., Harjule, P., Chouhan, L., Saraswat, U., Airan, H., and Agarwal, P., 2021. Prediction of dogecoin price using deep learning and social media trends. *EAI Endorsed Transactions on Industrial Networks and Intelligent Systems, 8*(29), pp. e2–e2.

[24]   Dubey, V., 2019. Banking with social media Facebook and Twitter. *International Journal of Recent Trends in Engineering dan Research, 5*(10), pp. 10–15.

[25]   Li, C. and Palanisamy, B., 2019, June. Incentivized blockchain-based social media platforms: a case study of Steemit. In *Proceedings of the 10th ACM Conference on Web Science* (pp. 145–154).

[26] Bahri, L., Carminati, B., and Ferrari, E., 2018. Decentralized privacy preserving services for online social networks. *Online Social Networks and Media*, 6, pp. 18–25.

[27] Ochoa, I.S., de Mello, G., Silva, L.A., Gomes, A.J., Fernandes, A.M., and Leithardt, V.R.Q., 2019. Fakechain: a blockchain architecture to ensure trust in social media networks. In *Quality of Information and Communications Technology: 12th International Conference, QUATIC 2019, Ciudad Real, Spain, September 11–13, 2019, Proceedings 12* (pp. 105–118). Springer International Publishing.

[28] Jing, T.W. and Murugesan, R.K., 2019. A theoretical framework to build trust and prevent fake news in social media using blockchain. In *Recent Trends in Data Science and Soft Computing: Proceedings of the 3rd International Conference of Reliable Information and Communication Technology (IRICT 2018)* (pp. 955–962). Springer International Publishing.

[29] Shrestha, B., Halgamuge, M.N., and Treiblmaier, H., 2020. Using blockchain for online multimedia management: characteristics of existing platforms. In *Blockchain and Distributed Ledger Technology Use Cases: Applications and Lessons Learned* (pp. 289–303). Springer.

[30] Bai, C., Zhu, Q., and Sarkis, J., 2021. Joint blockchain service vendor-platform selection using social network relationships: a multi-provider multi-user decision perspective. *International Journal of Production Economics*, 238, p. 108165.

[31] Keskin, Z. and Aste, T., 2020. Information-theoretic measures for nonlinear causality detection: application to social media sentiment and cryptocurrency prices. *Royal Society Open Science*, 7(9), p. 200863.

[32] Dhall, S., Dwivedi, A.D., Pal, S.K., and Srivastava, G., 2021. Blockchain-based framework for reducing fake or vicious news spread on social media/messaging platforms. *Transactions on Asian and Low-Resource Language Information Processing*, 21(1), pp. 1–33.

[33] Mirtaheri, M., Abu-El-Haija, S., Morstatter, F., Ver Steeg, G., and Galstyan, A., 2021. Identifying and analyzing cryptocurrency manipulations in social media. *IEEE Transactions on Computational Social Systems*, 8(3), pp. 607–617.

[34] Ba, C.T., Zignani, M., and Gaito, S., 2022. The role of cryptocurrency in the dynamics of blockchain-based social networks: the case of Steemit. *PLoS One*, 17(6), p. e0267612.

[35] Tandon, C., Revankar, S., and Parihar, S.S., 2021. How can we predict the impact of the social media messages on the value of cryptocurrency? Insights from big data analytics. *International Journal of Information Management Data Insights*, 1(2), p. 100035.

[36] Kripa, M., Nidhin Mahesh, A., Ramaguru, R., and Amritha, P.P., 2021. Blockchain framework for social media DRM based on secret sharing. In *Information and Communication Technology for Intelligent Systems: Proceedings of ICTIS 2020*, vol. 1 (pp. 451–458). Springer Singapore.

[37] Buccafurri, F., Lax, G., Nicolazzo, S., and Nocera, A., 2017. Tweetchain: an alternative to blockchain for crowd-based applications. In *Web Engineering: 17th International Conference, ICWE 2017, Rome, Italy, June 5-8, 2017, Proceedings 17* (pp. 386–393). Springer International Publishing.

[38] Murimi, R.M., 2019. A blockchain enhanced framework for social networking. *Ledger, 4*, https://doi.org/10.5195/ledger.2019.178.

[39] Lax, G., Russo, A., and Fasci, L.S., 2021. A blockchain-based approach for matching desired and real privacy settings of social network users. *Information Sciences, 557*, pp. 220–235.

[40] Fu, D. and Fang, L., 2016, October. Blockchain-based trusted computing in social network. In *2016 2nd IEEE International Conference on Computer and Communications (ICCC)* (pp. 19–22). IEEE.

[41] Henry, R., Herzberg, A., and Kate, A., 2018. Blockchain access privacy: challenges and directions. *IEEE Security & Privacy, 16*(4), pp. 38–45.

[42] Peng, L., Feng, W., Yan, Z., Li, Y., Zhou, X., and Shimizu, S., 2021. Privacy preservation in permissionless blockchain: a survey. *Digital Communications and Networks, 7*(3), pp. 295–307.

[43] Butt, T.A., Iqbal, R., Salah, K., Aloqaily, M., and Jararweh, Y., 2019. Privacy management in social internet of vehicles: review, challenges and blockchain based solutions. *IEEE Access, 7*, pp. 79694–79713.

[44] Jing, T.W. and Murugesan, R.K., 2021. Protecting data privacy and prevent fake news and deepfakes in social media via blockchain technology. In *Advances in Cyber Security: Second International Conference, ACeS 2020, Penang, Malaysia, December 8-9, 2020, Revised Selected Papers 2* (pp. 674–684). Singapore:Springer.

[45] Rajendran, S., 2021. Application of blockchain technique to reduce platelet wastage and shortage by forming hospital collaborative networks. *IISE Transactions on Healthcare Systems Engineering, 11*(2), pp. 128–144.

[46] Schaffers, H., 2018. The relevance of blockchain for collaborative networked organizations. In *Collaborative Networks of Cognitive Systems: 19th IFIP WG 5.5 Working Conference on Virtual Enterprises, PRO-VE 2018, Cardiff, UK, September 17–19, 2018, Proceedings 19* (pp. 3–17). Springer International Publishing.

[47] Meng, S., Chen, Y., Zhou, W., and Yu, D., 2021. Multidimensional development and π-type trend of the blockchain research: a collaborative network analysis. *Mathematical Problems in Engineering, 2021*, pp. 1–15.

[48] Yang, F., Xu, F., Feng, T., Qiu, C., and Zhao, C., 2022. pDPoSt+ sPBFT: a high performance blockchain-assisted parallel reinforcement learning in industrial edge-cloud collaborative network. *IEEE Transactions on Network and Service Management.*

[49] Abou El Houda, Z., Hafid, A.S., and Khoukhi, L., 2023. MiTFed: a privacy preserving collaborative network attack mitigation framework based on federated learning using SDN and blockchain. *IEEE Transactions on Network Science and Engineering.*

[50] Mrabti, N., Gargouri, M.A., Hamani, N., and Kermad, L., 2021. Towards a sustainable collaborative distribution network 4.0 with blockchain involvement. In *Smart and Sustainable Collaborative Networks 4.0: 22nd IFIP WG 5.5 Working Conference on Virtual Enterprises, PRO-VE 2021, Saint-Étienne, France, November 22–24, 2021, Proceedings 22* (pp. 41–52). Springer International Publishing.

[51] Abodei, E., Norta, A., Azogu, I., Udokwu, C., and Draheim, D., 2019. Blockchain technology for enabling transparent and traceable government collaboration in public project processes of developing economies. In *Digital Transformation for a Sustainable Society in the 21st Century: 18th IFIP WG 6.11 Conference on e-Business, e-Services, and e-Society, I3E 2019, Trondheim, Norway, September 18–20, 2019, Proceedings 18* (pp. 464–475). Springer International Publishing.

[52] Agrawal, T.K., Angelis, J., Khilji, W.A., Kalaiarasan, R., and Wiktorsson, M., 2022. Demonstration of a blockchain-based framework using smart contracts for supply chain collaboration. *International Journal of Production Research*, 61, pp. 1–20.

[53] Tao, F., Zhang, Y., Cheng, Y., *et al.*, 2022. Digital twin and blockchain enhanced smart manufacturing service collaboration and management. *Journal of Manufacturing Systems*, 62, pp. 903–914.

[54] Alexopoulos, N., Vasilomanolakis, E., Ivánkó, N.R., and Mühlhäuser, M., 2018. Towards blockchain-based collaborative intrusion detection systems. In *Critical Information Infrastructures Security: 12th International Conference, CRITIS 2017, Lucca, Italy, October 8–13, 2017, Revised Selected Papers 12* (pp. 107–118). Springer International Publishing.

[55] Tug, S., Meng, W., and Wang, Y., 2018, July. CBSigIDS: towards collaborative blockchained signature-based intrusion detection. In *2018 IEEE International Conference on Internet of Things (iThings) and IEEE Green Computing and Communications (GreenCom) and IEEE Cyber, Physical and Social Computing (CPSCom) and IEEE Smart Data (SmartData)* (pp. 1228–1235). IEEE.

[56] Gupta, R., Kumari, A., and Tanwar, S., 2021. Fusion of blockchain and artificial intelligence for secure drone networking underlying 5G communications. *Transactions on Emerging Telecommunications Technologies*, 32(1), p. e4176.

[57] Yazdinejad, A., Parizi, R.M., Dehghantanha, A. and Choo, K.K.R., 2019. Blockchain-enabled authentication handover with efficient privacy protection in SDN-based 5G networks. *IEEE Transactions on Network Science and Engineering*, 8(2), pp. 1120–1132.

[58] Bera, B., Saha, S., Das, A.K., Kumar, N., Lorenz, P., and Alazab, M., 2020. Blockchain-envisioned secure data delivery and collection scheme for 5G-based IoT-enabled internet of drones environment. *IEEE Transactions on Vehicular Technology*, 69(8), pp. 9097–9111.

[59] Fan, K., Ren, Y., Wang, Y., Li, H., and Yang, Y., 2018. Blockchain-based efficient privacy preserving and data sharing scheme of content-centric network in 5G. *IET Communications*, 12(5), pp. 527–532.

[60] Gupta, R., Tanwar, S., and Kumar, N., 2021. Blockchain and 5G integrated softwarized UAV network management: architecture, solutions, and challenges. *Physical Communication*, *47*, pp. 101355.

[61] Rahman, M.A., Hossain, M.S., Rashid, M.M., Barnes, S., and Hassanain, E., 2020. IoEV-chain: a 5G-based secure inter-connected mobility framework for the Internet of electric vehicles. *IEEE Network*, *34*(5), pp. 190–197.

[62] Rathore, S., Park, J.H., and Chang, H., 2021. Deep learning and blockchain-empowered security framework for intelligent 5G-enabled IoT. *IEEE Access*, *9*, pp. 90075–90083.

[63] Huang, H., Miao, W., Min, G., Tian, J., and Alamri, A., 2020. NFV and blockchain enabled 5G for ultra-reliable and low-latency communications in industry: architecture and performance evaluation. *IEEE Transactions on Industrial Informatics*, *17*(8), pp. 5595–5604.

[64] Samuel, O., Omojo, A.B., Mohsin, S.M., Tiwari, P., Gupta, D., and Band, S. S., 2022. An anonymous IoT-Based E-health monitoring system using blockchain technology. *IEEE Systems Journal*.

[65] Atlam, H.F. and Wills, G.B., 2019. Technical aspects of blockchain and IoT. In *Advances in Computers* (vol. 115, pp. 1–39). Elsevier.

[66] Zhang, Y. and Wen, J., 2017. The IoT electric business model: using blockchain technology for the Internet of Things. *Peer-to-Peer Networking and Applications*, *10*, pp. 983–994.

[67] Badshah, A., Waqas, M., Muhammad, F., Abbas, G., and Abbas, Z.H., 2022. A novel framework for smart systems using blockchain-enabled internet of things. *IT Professional*, *24*(3), pp. 73–80.

[68] Ali, A., Almaiah, M.A., Hajjej, F., *et al.*, 2022. An industrial IoT-based blockchain-enabled secure searchable encryption approach for healthcare systems using neural network. *Sensors*, *22*(2), pp. 572.

[69] Hassan, M.U., Rehmani, M.H., and Chen, J., 2019. Privacy preservation in blockchain based IoT systems: integration issues, prospects, challenges, and future research directions. *Future Generation Computer Systems*, *97*, pp. 512–529.

[70] Zhang, Y., Li, B., Liu, B., Hu, Y., and Zheng, H., 2021. A privacy-aware PUFs-based multiserver authentication protocol in cloud-edge IoT systems using blockchain. *IEEE Internet of Things Journal*, *8*(18), pp. 13958–13974.

[71] Qashlan, A., Nanda, P., He, X., and Mohanty, M., 2021. Privacy-preserving mechanism in smart home using blockchain. *IEEE Access*, *9*, pp. 103651–103669.

[72] Singh, A. and Chatterjee, K., 2018, September. Secevs: secure electronic voting system using blockchain technology. In *2018 International Conference on Computing, Power and Communication Technologies (GUCON)* (pp. 863–867). IEEE.

[73] Roh, C.H. and Lee, I.Y., 2020. A study on electronic voting system using private blockchain. *Journal of Information Processing Systems*, *16*(2), pp. 421–434.

[74] Khan, K.M., Arshad, J., and Khan, M.M., 2018. Secure digital voting system based on blockchain technology. *International Journal of Electronic Government Research (IJEGR)*, *14*(1), pp. 53–62.

[75] Fusco, F., Lunesu, M.I., Pani, F.E., and Pinna, A., 2018, September. Crypto-voting, a blockchain based e-Voting System. In *KMIS* (pp. 221–225).

[76] Adiputra, C.K., Hjort, R., and Sato, H., 2018, October. A proposal of blockchain-based electronic voting system. In *2018 Second World Conference on Smart Trends in Systems, Security and Sustainability (WorldS4)* (pp. 22–27). IEEE.

[77] Kumar, D.D., Chandini, D.V., Reddy, D., Bhattacharyya, D., and Kim, T.H., 2020. Secure electronic voting system using blockchain technology. *International Journal of Smart Home*, *14*(2), pp. 31–38.

[78] Jafar, U., Aziz, M.J.A., and Shukur, Z., 2021. Blockchain for electronic voting system—review and open research challenges. *Sensors*, *21*(17), pp. 5874.

[79] Alam, A., Rashid, S.Z.U., Salam, M.A., and Islam, A., 2018, October. Towards blockchain-based e-voting system. In *2018 International Conference on Innovations in Science, Engineering and Technology (ICISET)* (pp. 351–354). IEEE.

[80] Li, X., Russell, P., Mladin, C., and Wang, C., 2021. Blockchain-enabled applications in next-generation wireless systems: challenges and opportunities. *IEEE Wireless Communications*, *28*(2), pp. 86–95.

[81] Pincheira, M., Antonini, M., and Vecchio, M., 2022. Integrating the IoT and blockchain technology for the next generation of mining inspection systems. *Sensors*, *22*(3), pp. 899.

[82] Kamath, R., 2018. Blockchain for women next generation for sustainable development goal 5. *Asian Development Perspectives*, *9*(1).

[83] Vaghani, A., Sood, K., and Yu, S., 2022. Security and QoS issues in blockchain enabled next-generation smart logistic networks: a tutorial. *Blockchain: Research and Applications, 3*, p. 100082.

[84] Singh, S., Hosen, A.S., and Yoon, B., 2021. Blockchain security attacks, challenges, and solutions for the future distributed iot network. *IEEE Access*, *9*, pp. 13938–13959.

[85] Iqbal, A., Amir, M., Kumar, V., Alam, A., and Umair, M., 2020. Integration of next generation IIoT with blockchain for the development of smart industries. *Emerging Science Journal*, *4*, pp. 1–17.

[86] Mushtaq, A. and Haq, I.U., 2019, February. Implications of blockchain in industry 4. o. In *2019 International Conference on Engineering and Emerging Technologies (ICEET)* (pp. 1–5). IEEE.

[87] Alam, T., 2019. IoT-Fog: a communication framework using blockchain in the Internet of Things. arXiv preprint arXiv:1904.00226.

[88] Zaabar, B., Cheikhrouhou, O., Jamil, F., Ammi, M., and Abid, M., 2021. HealthBlock: a secure blockchain-based healthcare data management system. *Computer Networks*, *200*, pp. 108500.

[89]   Singh, A.P., Pradhan, N.R., Luhach, A.K., *et al.*, 2020. A novel patient-centric architectural framework for blockchain-enabled healthcare applications. *IEEE Transactions on Industrial Informatics*, *17*(8), pp. 5779–5789.

[90]   Satamraju, K.P., 2020. Proof of concept of scalable integration of Internet of Things and blockchain in healthcare. *Sensors*, *20*(5), pp. 1389.

[91]   Kaushik, K. and Kumar, A., 2022. Demystifying quantum blockchain for healthcare. *Security and Privacy*, p.e284.

[92]   Paranjape, K., Parker, M., Houlding, D., and Car, J., 2019. Implementation considerations for blockchain in healthcare institutions. *Blockchain in Healthcare Today*, 2, p. 13.

[93]   Gökalp, E., Gökalp, M.O., Çoban, S., and Eren, P.E., 2018. Analysing opportunities and challenges of integrated blockchain technologies in healthcare. In *Information Systems: Research, Development, Applications, Education: 11th SIGSAND/PLAIS EuroSymposium 2018, Gdansk, Poland, September 20, 2018, Proceedings 11* (pp. 174–183).

[94]   Ratta, P., Kaur, A., Sharma, S., Shabaz, M., and Dhiman, G., 2021. Application of blockchain and Internet of Things in healthcare and medical sector: applications, challenges, and future perspectives. *Journal of Food Quality*, *2021*, pp. 1–20.

[95]   Leeming, G., Ainsworth, J., and Clifton, D.A., 2019. Blockchain in health care: hype, trust, and digital health. *The Lancet*, *393*(10190), pp. 2476–2477.

[96]   Idrees, S.M., Agarwal, P., and Alam, M.A., (eds.), 2021. *Blockchain for Healthcare Systems: Challenges, Privacy, and Securing of Data*. London: CRC Press.

Index